TRAVELS THRO**A**

TRAVELS THROUGH SACRED INDIA

ROGER HOUSDEN

Thorsons
An Imprint of HarperCollins*Publishers*

Thorsons
An Imprint of HarperCollins*Publishers*
77–85 Fulham Palace Road,
Hammersmith, London W6 8JB
1160 Battery Street
San Francisco, California 94111–1213

Published by Thorsons 1996
10 9 8 7 6 5 4 3 2 1

A catalogue record for this book
is available from the British Library

ISBN 1 85538 497 3

Printed in Great Britain by
Caledonian International Book Manufacturing Ltd,
Glasgow, G64

Frontispiece: Detail of the sun god, Surya. Temple of the Sun, Konarak.
13th century. Photo: Richard Lannoy.

CONTENTS

Dedicated to
Those who remain silent

OM

The imperishable sound,
is the seed of all that exists.
The past, the present, the future
– all are but the unfolding of OM.
And whatever transcends the three realms of time,
That indeed is the flowering of OM.

THE GAYATRI MANTRA

The Mother of Mantras, The Great Mantra of Purification,
Homage to the Great Sun which lights the world and the
depths of the human heart: this, the Gayatri Mantra, is
recited daily at sunrise by more people than any other
prayer on earth.

OM
Bhur Bhuvat Svah
Tat Savitur Varenyam
Bhargo Devasya Dhimahi
Dhiyo Yo Nah Prachodayat
Rig Veda 3, 62, 10

OM
We meditate upon the glorious splendour
of the Vivifier divine
May He himself illumine our minds.
OM
Translation from The Vedic Experience by Raimundo Pannikar

ACKNOWLEDGEMENTS

Richard Lannoy, thank you for your superb book on India, *The Speaking Tree*, and for our conversations on various aspects of this present project. You were also generous enough to lend me the manuscript of your unpublished work on Banaras, which is the best book on the subject I know. Thank you John Lane and Fr Doug Conlan for being so generous with your contacts in India, and for sharing your love of the country. Professor Saraswati in Delhi, your spontaneous generosity with your time and ideas was an example I shall endeavour to extend to others. You gave invaluable support and reflections without stint, many of which are included in this book – as did Roy Horn, the wonderful yogi who lives in Hawaii, but whose heart is in Arunachala. Asimkrisna Das, thank you for researching the material on the festival of Holi at Vrindavan; likewise, Shobita Punja, for sharing your passion and scholarship for the Mahashivaratri festival at Khajuraho; and Judy Frater, for introducing me to the Rabari of Kutch. Om Prakash Sharma and Rana Singh, you opened Banaras for me as a living book. Without you, that city would have remained a foreign world. Rana Singh, your Gazetteer section adds an invaluable resource to this book, for which many travellers and pilgrims will be grateful. Chris Fuller, Professor of Anthropology at LSE, London, you did the same for me in

Madurai, as well as providing much food for thought in your book, *The Camphor Flame*, a superb account of popular Hinduism. Bettina Baumer, thank you for your inspiration for the chapter on the Sacred Word. Jacques Vigne, and also Sharda, your comments on the Gurus and Ashrams chapter shed insight and clarity on a delicate subject. Haku Shah, and your son, Parthiv Shah, your gift to me was your devotion to the cause of art and truth; Shubha Madgal, you introduced me to some of the finer musicians in India, including yourself. Nanagaru, Chandra Swami, Vijayananda, Ramana Maharshi and Ramesh Balsekar – you are the guardians of the silence which I would like to think shadows the words of this book. Vimala Thakar, your deep friendship, your unblinking eye of truth, stirs the asleep awake. David Crosweller, you are a marvellous example of love in action: your support and administrative help have been invaluable to the whole undertaking. Chloe Goodchild, your love fills me with gratitude; your song, with the spirit these pages try to convey. Warm gratitude to Liz Puttick, commissioning editor, for your interest and enthusiasm for the project, and for your keen editor's eye which helped give the book its final shape. Finally, the same to my mother, who first instilled in me the desire to know what lies beyond the known.

INTRODUCTION: SACRED INDIA

You live in time; we live in space. You're always on the move; we're always at rest. Religion is our first love; we revel in metaphysics. Science is your passion; you delight in physics. You believe in freedom of speech; you strive for articulation. We believe in freedom of silence; we lapse into meditation. Self-assertiveness is the key to your success; self-abnegation is the secret of our survival. You're urged every day to want more and more; we're taught from the cradle to want less and less. *Joie de vivre* is your ideal; conquest of desires is our goal. In the sunset years of life, you retire to enjoy the fruits of your labour; we renounce the world and prepare ourselves for the hereafter. *'Reflections on life East and West' by Hari N. Dam, Professor of Philosophy at Brigham Young University, USA.* Ensign Magazine, *1971*

Hari Dam was describing the Old India. In the New India, the computer software companies in Bangalore are making deep inroads into the Western markets; many villages have their communal satellite dish; Biotique, an ayurvedic beauty treatment franchise along the lines of The Body Shop, has branches in all the main cities; the owners of Nirula's ice-cream parlour in Delhi (21 varieties) drop in on the USA every month or so to check the latest trends; then there is Ahla Fast Foods. The truck, emblazoned with the red and blue Pepsi logo on all sides, sits by the roadside outside of Dalhousie. 'Fast, Efficient, Clean', its billboard says – everything the Old India is not. A few minutes along the road, the tea shack is empty. Flies swarm around the yoghurt pot and over the sweets. Nomads pass by on their motorbikes bringing their milk to town from the high pastures. Ahla is doing good business. Two families sit under striped parasols eating french fries and hamburgers. The children are swigging back Pepsi. Ahla's owner, an amiable young Sikh in yellow tracksuit and Reeboks, has just returned from completing his MBa in America.

'Everyone wants this kind of food and service now,' he said. 'If the concept is Western, it'll sell.'

Especially in somewhere like Dalhousie. Ten years ago this hill station was a quiet backwater in the Himachel foothills of the Himalayas. Now there is no hill station anywhere which could match that description.

In the last few years the growing middle classes have become a powerful economic force in India, which, along with China, is one of the last frontiers for galloping consumerism. In the wake of India's recent liberalisation policies, secular Western values are cutting through traditional life like a forest fire. People with money to spend do what their counterparts in the West do – they travel, eat in restaurants, buy designer goods and modern cars. In the summer, Dalhousie is teeming with Indian tourists, and Ahla Fast Foods caters to the recently acquired tastes of their palate. Much of the new wealth is 'black' money – cash that cannot be declared and has to be spent on pleasures like a hill station holiday. Corruption has long been a feature of life in India, and has not been limited to the secular world. I know of at least one of the great temples in the south in which each scale of the administrative hierarchy pays a dividend to the level above it in order to guarantee its continuing employment. At the bottom of the pile are the beggars, who pay a portion of their takings to the peon to ensure their pitch in the temple. Corruption has always existed the world over; what is more recent in India is the sheer scale and size of it, and the degree to which it has infiltrated every corner of life.

The people of Bombay and Delhi, especially, expect the visitor to acknowledge and respect the emergence of The New India. At the same time, it is difficult to ignore the insidious effect of corruption on human values there; difficult, too, to blot out the squalor, the noise, the child labour, the abuse of human rights perpetrated by the caste system. Yet this same land, in which profits are soaring and life can seem so cheap – recently, the Shatabdi Express from Chandigarh to Delhi ran over someone without even bothering to stop – is also the one that still preserves the richest spiritual culture on earth, and where the presence of the sacred remains a living fact for the great majority of its people (who, as yet, are still to hear of french fries.) India, of all lands, is the one of extremes and paradox; the recent incursion of Western consumerism has added yet another colour to what was always a tapestry of extraordinary richness and diversity. A few hundred miles to the south of Dalhousie, in Rajasthan, an Indian friend of mine recently had a guest from New York come to stay. It was his first visit to India, and he asked her if she could show him an example of the Hindu spirituality he had read so much about.

'I don't want to meet scholars or holy men,' he told her. 'I want to see what God means for the ordinary person.'

So they took the car down the road from Mount Abu to the plains below, and stopped at the first field in which there was someone working. With my friend acting as translator, the American asked the farmer, who was in his forties,

'Can you tell me what, for you, is the meaning of God?'

The man looked at my friend, and said, 'Does he know what he is asking?'

'Of course I do,' the American replied. He picked up a handful of the earth at his feet. 'This,' he said, 'is dead matter, the material world.' Then, pointing to the sky, he asked again, 'Where is God to be found? If this is earth, what is spirit?'

He was on the point of throwing the handful of earth to the ground, when the farmer grasped his hand and took the earth from him.

'You call my Mother dead?' he said. He was on the verge of tears. He kissed the earth, then knelt to return it to the ground.

The visitor was silenced. With some embarrassment, he thanked the farmer, and returned to the car, his question answered. For the time being, the majority of Indians still live in a sacred world. For every Ahla Fast Foods, there are a thousand people like the farmer in Rajasthan. They live in the 'Old India' that Hari Dam was evoking. It is Old India this book is concerned with. It does not set out to paint some romantic picture which would be contradicted by the experience of any-one with eyes to see; but its brief is specific – it introduces the living dimensions of Sacred India, and only mentions in pass-ing the struggles and labours of an ancient culture in transi-tion. It also refers only fleetingly to well-known archaological sites like the cave temples of Elephanta and Ellora, or the rock carvings of Mahabalipuram (although these are included in the Gazetteer section); neither do I attempt to discuss major tourist attractions like the Taj Mahal and the city of Jaipur. Again, this is due to the parameters I have drawn in order to write a small book on such a huge subject: my focus is the liv-ing expression of the sacred as it is known and practised in India today, rather than monuments which are glorious mem-ories of the past more than living temples of the present. While any of these sites – especially, perhaps, the Taj Mahal – may carry a sense of the living spirit for the individual visitor, their contemporary character is more that of a tourist attrac-tion than a pilgrim centre, and I have followed this general distinction in making my choice of material.

Eighty-five per cent of all Indians are Hindus, though this is not their own term for themselves or for their religion. 'Hindu' was first used by the Arabs in the 8th century to describe those people who lived beyond the Indus river. Their own term for the religious way of life is 'Sanatana Dharma', The Eternal Way, or The Way of Truth. It has indeed existed since the beginning of history. Though it is expounded in some of the greatest spiritual literature in the world, and embraces a vast array of religious ritual and custom, the Sanatana Dharma is in essence defined by no outer ritual or even religion: it repre-sents a natural way of living in harmony with life. At the very heart of its ethos is the principle of sacred relationship. Every-thing in the universe is related, and the divine, rather than being somewhere above and beyond life, is right here in the middle of it – even, somehow, in the very squalor that seems to be its antithesis. The sacred exists in the love a man and woman share with each other; in the respect shown to par-ents; in the farmer's tenderness for the earth and his animals, as much as in the mystic's adoration of the invisible. When you board an Air India flight, you are greeted by the hostess with the traditional *Namaskar* gesture, the palms together in front of the heart. It means, 'I salute the Divine that lives in you.'

It is partly because the sacred is so rooted in daily relationships, rather than just in an ideology of transcendance, that it continues to survive in India at the end of the 20th century. Of course, much of what is termed sacred, or appears so, is no more than an empty formality handed down by tradition with no meaning for the individual beyond an unthinking respect for the tradition itself. An inate intuition that life's meaning and significance lies beyond the senses and the rational mind – the cultural context of India, by natural inclination, encourages its expression. Perhaps this is why, still today – and whatever else it may be – India remains, above all countries, the land of saints and sages; and why other religions have flowered and developed unique expressions there.

The first three parts of this book aim to bring alive the many expressions of the Sanatana Dharma. Part One explores the ancient ground of the whole tradition, which has its roots in beliefs and practices which can be traced back long before the emergence of the better known brahminical religion of the Aryans. Part Two evokes some of the many facets of the classical tradition of the brahmins, while Part Three explores the 'inner traditions', represented by different esoteric and renunciate schools, as well as the teaching and lives of individual gurus. Part Four gives a glimpse of the life and practices of other spiritual traditions which have found a home in India. A book of this size could never be more than an introduction to such a vast subject, which would need a set of ten volumes to do it full justice. It does not even attempt, for example, to discuss the fundamental role of religious belief in the perpetuation of the caste system and the oppression of women. Yet, as a traveller in the sub-continent, I have found that it was just such an introduction that was lacking, and it was my own need that first prompted the idea of writing the book.

Far from being the work of an expert or scholar, the book unfolds with the support of personal encounter and experience. It is the subjective view of a foreign eye. Rather than providing a historical or socio-cultural overview, the aim is to offer a living account of the sacred as it is expressed in India today. The book's authority lies primarily in being a labour of love, the work of an *amatore*, a lover – the original meaning of the term amateur. Like most people who love India, I find the country maddening; yet I know I will always frequent its shores. The most I can wish for the reader is that they become stricken with the same malady, which will allow them to see the blemishes and love all the more.

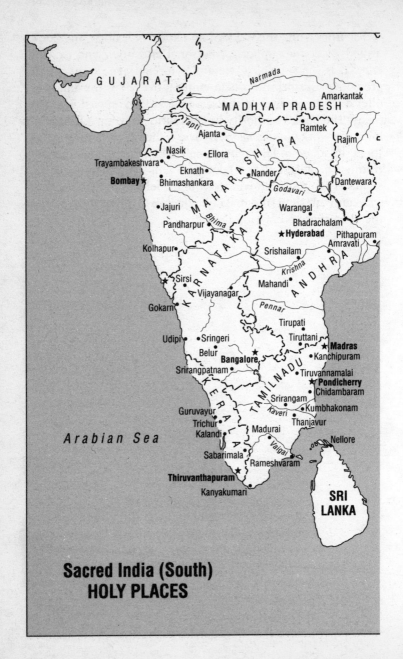

**Sacred India (South)
HOLY PLACES**

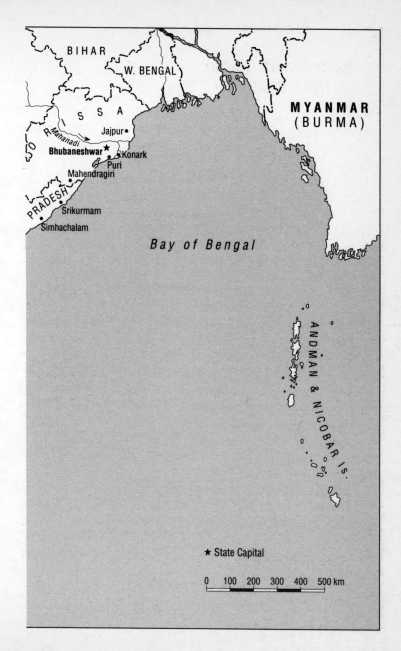

BIHAR

W. BENGAL

O   R   I   S   S   A

MYANMAR
(BURMA)

Mahanadi R.

Jajpur •

Bhubaneshwar ★   • Konark
        • Puri
Mahendragiri

PRADESH

• Srikurmam

• Simhachalam

Bay of Bengal

ANDMAN & NICOBAR IS.

★ State Capital

0   100   200   300   400   500 km

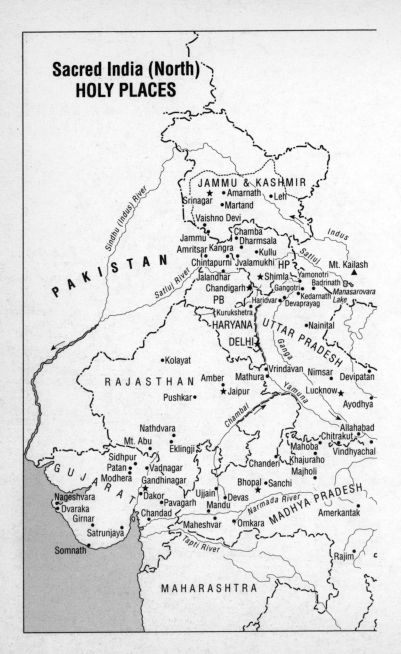

Sacred India (North)
HOLY PLACES

JAMMU & KASHMIR

★ Srinagar • Amarnath   • Leh
• Martand
• Vaishno Devi

Sindhu (Indus) River

Indus

• Chamba
• Jammu   • Dharmsala
• Amritsar • Kangra
• Chintapurni • Jvalamukhi   • Kullu   HP
Satluj
Mt. Kailash ▲

P A K I S T A N

Satluj River

• Jalandhar   ★ Shimla   Yamonotri
★ Chandigarh   Gangotri   Badrinath
PB   • Kedarnath   Manasarovara
• Haridvar   • Devaprayag   Lake
• Kurukshetra
HARYANA   U T T A R   • Nainital
DELHI   P R A D E S H
Ganga
• Kolayat   • Vrindavan   Nimsar
Amber   • Mathura   • Devipatan
R A J A S T H A N   ★ Jaipur   Yamuna   • Lucknow ★
• Pushkar   • Ayodhya

Chambal

• Nathdvara   Allahabad •
• Mt. Abu   • Chitrakut
• Eklingji   • Mahoba   • Vindhyachal
• Sidhpur   • Chanderi   • Khajuraho
• Patan • Vadnagar   • Bhopal • Sanchi   • Majholi
• Modhera • Gandhinagar
G U J A R A T   ★ Dakor   • Ujjain   • Devas
• Nageshvara   • Pavagarh   • Mandu   Narmada River   M A D H Y A   P R A D E S H
• Dvaraka   • Chandad   • Omkara   • Amerkantak
Girnar   • Maheshvar
• Satrunjaya
• Somnath   Tapti River   • Rajim

M A H A R A S H T R A

0 100 200 300 400 500 km

★ State Capital

PB PUNJAB
HP HIMACHAL PRADESH
TR TRIPURA
NL NAGALAND
MA MANIPUR
MJ MIJORAM
ML MEGHALAYA

TIBET, CHINA

Tsangpo (Brahmaputra) River

NEPAL
Muktinath
Lumbini
Gorakhpur
Pasupatinath
Kathmandu
Kushinagar
Sarnath
Varanasi
Sonepur
Patna
Nalanda
Gaya
Son River
Bodh Gaya
BIHAR
Deoghar

SIKKIM
BHUTAN
ARUNACHAL
Kamakhya
ASSAM
ML
NL
MA
BANGLADESH
Padma
TR
MJ

W. BENGAL
Navadvipa
Tarakeshvar
Calcutta
Gangasagar

ORISSA
Mahanadi

MYANMAR
(BURMA)

Bay of Bengal

PART ONE

THE POPULAR TRADITION

THE PRIMORDIAL UNITY

1

India has always had a significant urban society – before the 16th century, its cities were richer and larger than any in Europe, which is why European traders were attracted to its shores in the first place. There are dozens of cities in India today with a population of more than a million, and three with over 10 million. But with 950 million all told, there are still a lot of people to account for. The great majority of India's inhabitants live, as ever, in a rural land of thousands of villages. There are also 50 million tribal people living on the margins of orthodox Hindu society, many of them in the hills and the backwaters of central India, and all with their local shamanistic traditions whose origins are far off in remotest antiquity. Hinduism is a unique distillation of rural, classical and, to a small extent, tribal traditions which together encompass every conceivable level of relationship between the human and the divine. The popular religious traditions of rural India stretch back well beyond the time of the Vedas and the classical texts to the first agricultural communities on the subcontinent. Nowhere on earth can you find such a rich and multi-layered tradition that has remained unbroken and largely unchanged for at least three thousand years. Its early practices and beliefs were the response of a culture to a precarious existence: one in which they were at the mercy of powers which dwarfed their own – storms, flooding, drought, disease, crop failure, invasion by dangerous animals and neighbouring clans. Their only defence, it seemed to them, was to call upon powers which were a match for these adversaries, or to propitiate the malevolent forces themselves. Village India today still lives in this ancient world view. Now, as ever, it is a world in which everything, both animate and inanimate, is filled with living spirit. The spirit of a tree, a pond, a stone, an animal, a dead person, the wind, the rain, the earth itself, can be invoked to one's aid with the proper rites and rituals. Rural India is literally a magical world in which anything is possible; in which the borders between the visible and the invisible are flimsy enough to allow contracts to be made across them daily.

A French woman who has been living in the shade of Arunachala Mountain in Tamil Nadu for twenty-five years told me the following story. Since the early 1990s she has noticed a marked increase in crime and violence in the villages around her house. Two years ago she bought a dog to guard her property. Recently the dog stopped barking, and a few days later she called in the local spell maker. He told her that someone had put a spell on the dog to keep it quiet. He passed his hand along the dog's length, and dropped a stone in front of it. He did this five times, and the dog barked. That night, thieves tried to get in, but the dog raised the alarm and they were frightened away.

In the individuated adult, personal power needs are attenuated in some degree by a sense of moral and social responsibility. The realm of magic, at the primordial level we are introducing here, knows no such moral restraint.

While everything in an Indian village is unquestionably imbued with life and spirit, that spirit can be made to serve one's own purposes to the detriment of others as easily as it can be put to the common good. This is why the vast majority of rites and rituals serve the purpose of protection, either of the village or of the individual, and why the evil eye is as feared in India as in any other traditional culture. In a

3

contemporary culture whose individuals experience a degree of alienation and anxiety which is unheard of in more traditional parts of the world, it is tempting to romanticize Indian village life as a seamless unity that has yet to fall prey to the divisions and ills of contemporary urban society. Before succumbing to this idyll, we would do well to remember that this magical unity embraces as much evil as it does good.

The religious culture of rural India is often known by anthropologists as the 'little tradition' as distinct from the 'great tradition' of Vedic and Brahminical Hinduism. The actual influence of these two in the daily life of most Hindus, however, is the reverse of their titles: the 'little' is greater than the 'great', so it would seem more accurate to call them the popular and the classical traditions. Whereas the classical tradition of the great gods, Brahma, Vishnu, Shiva, and their consorts, concerns itself with cosmic affairs – with the creation, preservation and destruction of the worlds – the popular tradition is entirely absorbed in the local concerns of the immediate community or family. Each village and state has its own versions of powers and deities, which are usually propitiated with the aim of guaranteeing protection from various dangers, including the wrath of the deity itself. When no danger threatens, when there is no problem to be solved or wish to be fulfilled, the deity is given scant attention. Together, the classical and popular traditions make up the vertical and the horizontal planes of life, heaven and earth. Flowing in and out of each other, they constitute the totality of Hinduism, embracing everything from the most sublime philosophical insights to spells designed to stop a guard dog barking.

Hindus are not clearly divided in their religious beliefs and rituals along the lines of education and class; nor do urban and country dwellers differ much in their beliefs beyond a degree of emphasis. While the local gods are more directly accessible and relevant to their day to day life, villagers also worship Vishnu and Shiva, and will go to the main temples alongside their urban counterparts. On the other hand, I have watched high caste women in Banaras bow at a local shrine to the goddess Durga, take some of the sooty residue left by the flame in front of the idol, and smear it around their eyes as a protection against the evil eye.

Professor B. N. Saraswati, a Brahmin, and one of India's foremost anthropologists, is a rare combination: an urban intellectual who lives by traditional spiritual values. The professor, a tiny man with a warm and beneficent presence, still wears a dhoti to his office at The Indira Ghandi Centre for the Arts, which is in New Delhi. When I met him there, he told me of the major role the popular tradition had played in all the stages of his life. When he was born, he said, he was received into the hands of the midwife, an untouchable, who immediately made protective incantations over him. At the time of the sacred thread ceremony, when he officially entered the Brahmin community as a young adult, four hours were given over to the rituals of the classical, Vedic tradition; but the rest of the proceedings, which took four days, were filled with folk rituals of protection, presided over by the potter's wife, the local basket weaver and the washer woman. Similarly, at his marriage ceremony, which took five days, the Vedic rites took just an hour and a half to complete, while the local protective rituals took the whole night. The example of Professor Saraswati is typical: while the popular tradition is the lifeblood of the village community, it touches all Hindus, of whatever caste or degree of sophistication. For India remains a country of thousands of local communities whose immediate affairs and beliefs take precedence over any sense of national identity or religion.

Every village has its own highly complex arrangement of gods, goddesses, and protective spirits. A single community can have thirty or forty temples and shrines, most of them painted stones in the open air, some of them rough stone platforms under a tree, with stones or iron spears stuck in them to represent the deity. Norman Lewis, in his book, *The Goddess in the Stone*, mentions a meeting with a tribal whose village had recently been visited by Christian missionaries. The priests were offering free malaria tablets and all the benefits of

5

conversion if the village would only renounce its gods for Jesus. 'Most of (our gods) have always been kind and useful to us ... the missionary is asking us to exchange 23 for one, plus a month's supply of Navaquin. It seems unreasonable.'[1]

Of all their gods, the village goddess is the principal deity. In this, the Hindu village is following the ancient tradition of all agricultural communities throughout the world, who saw the earth for what She is – the fertile mother, source of all birth, nourishment, and death. The village itself is a cosmos, animated by the divine power of the local goddess, who is ritually married to the village through its headman at periodic festivals. In return for worship and sacrifice, she ensures good crops, rain, fertility, protection from demons and disease. When the villager leaves the magic circle of the village, he falls outside the protection of the goddess.

The principal goddess is often surrounded by other goddesses who take on particular functions. Many represent specific diseases, and the reason they can offer protection is that they are also the embodiment of the disease itself. As well as the common deities of cholera, and a few years ago, of smallpox, some villages in the south have shrines to Plague-Amma. When the village is threatened with an epidemic, the goddess is said to be manifesting herself. She is ambivalent: she may grace the villager by sparing him, or she may grant him the privilege of being touched by her fever. Either way, it is all the work of the same deity. The particular disease is often said to be the 'grace' of the goddess. She may strike people down, but she is said to hold her victims especially dear. Fierce and crazy, she is easily driven wild with the ecstasy of her own destructive powers. She will delight in her disease, and will kill at random with it.

Wherever there is intensity there is power, and power is what matters in a world where you want to control events that would normally be beyond you. Whether the power is good or evil is not the point; what matters is the intensity that you can have at your disposal through the appropriate rituals. So people who have met a tragic or premature death might be deified; anyone who was notorious in life, even for violent crimes, could be worshipped after their death; malevolent spirits could be turned into protective deities. The deification process is also a means of controlling the capricious power, who is liable to remain capricious, but at least its trickery may serve the community as well as trouble it.

Heroes are likely to be deified too, while perhaps one of the most poignant examples of harnessed intensity is the deified heroine known as the *sati mata*. This is the title given to the wife who ceremoniously places herself on the funeral pyre of her husband, burning herself to death in order to remain with him. Though *sati* is against the law, it is still occasionally practised, especially in Rajasthan, where there are countless *sati matas* enshrined in elaborate temples visited by huge numbers of pilgrims. The ex-human deity is thought to be especially compassionate because of its own experience of the human predicament.

In festivals, the village goddess is often portrayed as a clay figurine, or as a clay pot filled with water and decorated with flowers. The word for clay in Hindi is *mati*, which also means mother, and flesh. The pot is a symbol for the human being, and when they marry, all Hindus worship their ancestors through the symbol of two pots. The pot, then, is not just a utensil: it is a creation filled with spirit and meaning, and as such the potter has a special role to play in the life of the community. Perhaps it is for this reason that the potter is often the one called upon to officiate at the ceremonies of the gods. The *pujaris*, or priests, of village rituals and festivals are not brahmins; they are drawn from different castes in different villages, and again, the honour is an ambivalent one. While they are presiding as the representatives of the goddess, they are also obliged to oversee the act of blood sacrifice which, while integral to the religious life of the village, is a dishonourable task to be directly involved in.

Lambs, pigs, and goats are still slaughtered every day throughout India for ritual purposes. A few major temples, like the Kalighat temple in Calcutta, continue the practice, but the great majority of blood sacrifices are in village rites. Sacrifice is always made to one of the fierce or wrathful forms of the goddess, usually Kali or Durga, and the village equivalents. Originally human beings were the sacrifice, and Royina Grewal, in her recent book *Sacred Virgin*,[2] tells how occasional disappearances are still reported of young girls in the vicinity of the Narmada river. They are taken it is said, by tantric practitioners who need virgin blood to satisfy the goddess of the sacred river.

Appeasement of the goddess by the offering of the gift of life is an acknowledgement of the universal principle of mutual exchange. Everything in the universe is in an eternal process of eating and being eaten. The higher offers itself as food for the lower, and the lower in turn offers itself back to the higher. In this way, creation is sustained by an endless circle of sacrifice. The gods need the offerings of humanity to maintain themselves, and to keep the flow of life returning back to the phenomenal world, especially at the time of harvest.

An individual from contemporary society – in Delhi as much as in London or Paris – is liable to judge this ritual as primitive and even subhuman. From a contemporary perspective, of course, it is; but the same perspective would be unable to reconcile the fact that the same villager who leads his animal to sacrifice also treats it with a respect and dignity which an animal would rarely receive on a modern farm. Even in the sacrifice itself, as it is being led to the slaughter, the buffalo is worshipped as a representative of the deity. The point is, that in this ancient world view, death is not the antithesis to life; they form an eternal divine circle in which the one is as sacred as the other. I have watched men washing their buffalo in the Ganga for an hour or more with a degree of care and attention that few people in the West ever give to their children. They talk to it, stroke its ears, and smooth its flanks with a devotion that is surely fitting for such an important member of the family. The buffalo provides milk, pulls the plough, leads the cart, and offers dung for fuel. His cousin, the cow, as everyone knows, is sacred to all Hindus, and, to the amazement of many visitors, is allowed to wander undisturbed through the Delhi traffic, across the railway lines, on the station platform, and in the temple.

Sacrifice is only one way of communing with the deity. Another way is to become possessed by it. Possession is extremely common in India, and need not happen by design or even in the circumstances of religious ritual. In the early nineties, the foreman of the Arunachala Reforestation Society[3] in Tamil Nadu – to all appearances an ordinary worker like his fellows – suddenly fell on the ground and began writhing and hissing like a snake. The same performance repeated itself several times over the ensuing weeks, culminating in utterances like those of an oracle. The locals considered him to be possessed by the goddess, and he is now installed in a house where he regularly serves as the oracle for a wide community.

As I was walking along a road one day in rural Tamil Nadu, I noticed some street performers approaching from the opposite direction. A man dressed in red female robes and a high golden crown, with made-up eyes and paint on his face, was teetering along in the company of another man, also in red, though more shabby, who was banging a drum. There was a small shrine to Kali by the roadside just ahead of me, and when they reached it they turned to the goddess and began dancing drunkenly before it. This, I realized, was no performance; this was for real – they were invoking the goddess to enter them. A small crowd was already there, mostly women, and when the couple arrived, some of them began clashing hand cymbals and beating on small side drums. As the din rose to a pitch one of the women lurched out of the crowd and fell at the feet of the personifier of Kali. She writhed on the floor and then began dancing wildly round the two costumed men, her eyes somewhere up in the middle of her head. The goddess impersonator made a few feeble attempts to brush her aside, perhaps because she was beginning to steal his show. Then another woman came out from the crowd, struck a match and held the flame in the possessed woman's gaping mouth. Instantly she fell in a motionless heap. A few minutes

9

later she was helped to her feet, and was led off in a daze by her friends.

In India, rural festivals are also occasions when the whole community abandons orderly life and gives itself over to the vital, chaotic power of the goddess. Castes mix, social rules are lifted, often roles are reversed, with the rich and powerful having to accept the rebuffs and taunts of the lowest castes. Heroic acts take place – firewalking, carrying burning pots on the head, swinging while suspended from hooks in the flesh. To perform such feats you must be possessed by 'the other mind' that lies beyond the conscious self. This is the domain of the gods, and especially of the goddess. The feats express the devotee's willingness to fully encounter the dangerous power of the goddess on her own territory. In return for taking on part of her excess heat and fury, the goddess blesses them with her protection through the ordeal.

In a world where everything, suffering as well as joy, is God's will, there can be nothing which is not sacred – in the sense of being filled with spirit, but also in its being an integral part of the whole of existence. Religion, art, and the daily round are inextricably bound together in Indian life. In a world where the gods are present in everything, and express their spirit in every ordinary act, religion is not a separate activity which happens once a week. The spirit of the god or goddess is inherent in eating, in the food itself, in labour, in one's attitude to ordinary objects. If some rice falls on the floor, a Hindu will pick it up and mutter a brief prayer. My taxi driver in Delhi was just starting his day, and I was his first fare. He held out my money to the middle of the steering wheel, then put it to his forehead, then to the image of his personal deity which was fixed to the dashboard. Delhi taxi drivers can hardly be described as saintly – they will cheat you more readily than most – but they, along with most ordinary Hindus, have an innate sense of a greater power at work within the minutiae of daily life. That power does not demand that they be moral; just that they acknowledge its existence in their life and pay homage to it.

10

Art, too, is not separate from daily life. Art for a rural Hindu is never for its own sake; it is always related to function. Haku Shah is one of India's better known contemporary artists, and the curator of The Tribal Museum in Ahmedebad. He told me of a tribal couple he met in Ahmedebad who had come to the town because there was a drought in the village. The man and his wife were the village singers, as his father had been before him. Their job was to wake the village up in the morning and to sing it to sleep at night. Hakubai, as he is known, had the intuition to ask the man if he would draw him a picture. The man didn't understand at first what drawing meant, but when Hakubai explained, he asked, 'Why should I do this?' It was inconceivable to him that anyone should paint or draw or sing without a practical reason. 'For me,' Hakubai replied. This made sense to the man. Over the next few days – for a tribal, time is not measured in minutes – he began to draw the songs that he sang, lying full length on the floor, sleeping intermittently, with loud snoring, as he drew. The sleeping, Hakubai realized, was part of the drawing process. The man's drawings took time because to draw a river was only conceivable to him if he drew every drop of water. How could you leave one out? Hakubai then asked the man's wife to join in the drawing, which she did, and their child as well. A year later, the family's work was put on exhibition at the Museum.

THE RABARI OF KUTCH

There is no better example of this seamless existence, in which every drop of water matters, than the Rabari community of Kutch, in the westernmost part of Gujarat. Kutch is a peninsula on the border with Pakistan, locked between the great deserts of Sind and Thar, and the Rabari are a semi-nomadic community who travel with their camels for part of the year, and for the rest of the time live in their own villages, which stay empty while they are away.

Every little act in the Rabari world is a celebration of life,

11

and that celebration is in itself the expression of their art and religion. The villages are well kept and clean, but the interior of the houses – which usually consist of just one room – are remarkably orderly and cared for. Their goddess decreed that Rabari houses should only be made of mud, (*mati*, remember, means both mother and clay) and should not contain kerosene or electricity (this last wish is now being disobeyed). The Rabari women are renowned for the creative genius they apply to every aspect of their domestic world. The brass pots, always shining, are arranged above each other on the wall in order of size to create beautiful designs. They fashion cow-dung and clay into porticos, figures of the goddess, toys for their children, and into designs decorated with mirror fragments which they apply to the inside walls. Bead work and embroidery also embellish their camel trappings, and whatever coverings or seats they may have in their houses. Their lives are expressions of living art, without artists.

While the men wear white, with large white turbans and handlebar moustaches, the women wear black woollen skirts with brilliantly embroidered blouses. They learn embroidery at an early age, and soon begin to fashion what will serve as their dowry later. They spend long hours in a magical world of spontaneous design, making garments and quilts with infinitely varied stitches, decorating them with cloth applique work, emblazoning them with tiny mirrors, and using beads to trace shapes of animals and spirit beings. An American anthropologist, Judy Frater, has spent the best part of two decades studying the Rabari way of life, and in particular their embroidery. In 1995, she brought one of the families to Delhi to open an exhibition of embroidery at the Gandhi Centre for the Arts.[4] (Having been considered inferior for decades, indigenous art is now coming into fashion in India.) One of the organizers asked them publicly how they liked Delhi. They looked blank, and then one of them answered, 'We're here. What do you want us to say?' For the Rabari, life is where they are.[5]

The women also decorate the visible parts of their body with tattoos. The back of the hand, the arms, the neck, the feet, are covered with dozens of designs representing temples, altars, symbols of the gods, and protective animals, like the scorpion, to ward off the evil eye.

The great life passages of birth, marriage and death are, for the Rabari as for any Hindu, open doorways to the world of the gods. For some of the Rabari clans, marriages are held collectively on the feast day of the goddess. The preparations begin a week beforehand. The houses are decorated with green branches, and an intricately embroidered *torana* is hung on the architrave of the entrance door. This is one of the most important items in the bride's trousseau, and it symbolizes the welcome to the guests and respect to the divinity. The women, huddled together – you never see a Rabari woman alone – sing propitiatory songs and prepare the food in huge brass cauldrons. The groom remains secluded in his house until the day of the wedding, which often happens at night, and is followed by days of festivities.

As in many villages, and in all tribal communities, the Rabari (who are Hindus, not tribals) have a shaman who serves as a healer and as an oracle to determine the will of the goddess. The Rabari shaman reads her will from the back of a baby she-goat. He rubs the goat along the spine from the back to the front. If the goat shivers, the goddess is answering in the affirmative. They have two goddess festivals a year, during which men get possessed and people come to them for a solution to their problems. The festivals are the only times that children can be named, the naming ceremony being carried out by the shaman on behalf of the goddess. As with other village goddesses, the Rabari's is capricious; sometimes she rises in the air, passes over someone, and leaves them with a kink, or a twisted limb. Then they have to go to the *shaman* to be healed.

Judy Frater followed through one of the cases who was brought to the *shaman* for healing. One of the children had gone mad, and would take on the character of a Muslim who had died. The dead person would tell the boy to act in unsocial ways. The *shaman* said the trouble had been caused when the boy, out herding goats one day, had urinated on the place where the Muslim was buried. The soul was offended, and was taking revenge. His recommendation was to do exactly what the Muslim asked him to do, without the parents restraining him. The family followed his advice, and in days the boy was cured.

Whatever psychological explanation we may rush to give to this anecdote cannot detract from the fact that it is an event which is integral to its context. It makes no sense when lifted out of the magical world of the overall Rabari way of life. How long that world can endure – how long the traditional life of rural India in general can endure – in the era of mass telecommunications and the satellite dish is open to question. The West has produced magic more powerful than any the world has seen before, and it is hard to contemplate the traditional kind surviving much longer anywhere in a global village whose modern sorcerers now have spells which know no limits.

1   Lewis, Norman, *The Goddess in the Stone*. Macmillan, London 1992.

2   Grewal, Rowena, *Sacred Virgin*. Penguin, New Delhi 1994.

3   Annamalai Reforestation Society, c/o John Button, Ramanashram PO, Tiruvannamalai, Tamil Nadu, India.

4   The Indira Gandhi National Centre for the Arts, Janpath Road, New Delhi, published an illustrated book, *The Rabari of Kutch*, in conjunction with their exhibition of Rabari art in 1995.

5   For information on Judy Frater's work with the Rabari and the availability of their craftwork, write to Judy Frater, c/o N. D. Vaidya, Nagar Chakla Bhuj, Kutch 370001. Gujarat, India.

SACRED LAND

Different places on the face of the earth have different vital effluence, a different vibration or chemical exhalation, a different polarity with the stars; call it what you like. But the spirit of place is a great reality.
D. H. Lawrence[1]

2

Wherever a saint is born, walks the earth, works miracles, and dies, there, in India, pilgrims come to worship. Where one of the gods has appeared in their power and glory, or where a sign, natural or otherwise, points to their presence, there too, shrines are built, cities develop, devotees come. A sacred place is one that is graced with the presence of unconditioned being; where, through one agency or another, the unfettered energy and life of the domain of the gods makes itself known in the finite world.

India is a vast network of sacred places. Many mark the spot where one of the great deities is said to have defeated a demon, such as the town of Gaya, which retains the name of the defeated evil power; or where the gods have dwelled on earth, such as Braj, the land of Krishna; or Chitrakut, where Rama stayed at the start of his exile from Ayodhya. A place may have become sacred following the direct benign influence of a god, as in the case of Pushkar, whose lake Brahma decreed would give liberation to all those who bathed in it. An unusual natural formation – the confluence of two rivers, a river source, a mountain, a hot spring – will be a sign of the presence of the sacred.

Fifty-one places across India[2] mark those spots where the different pieces of the body of the great goddess, Sati, fell.

Shiva, mad with grief at Sati's death, wandered around the earth in a solitary dance with the body of Sati on his shoulders. Vishnu, full of compassion, followed him, and cut up Sati's body piece by piece to relieve Shiva of his burden. The myth of the dismemberment of the goddess illustrates the self-sacrifice of Mahadevi into the multiple forms on earth. It is her sacrifice which permits humanity to be nourished by the cyclic return of the harvests.

The most potent of these Shakti Pithas – 'seats of the goddess' – are Kamakhya, in Assam, which guards her *yoni*, vagina; Kalighat, in Calcutta, where her little toe is kept, and Jualamukhi, in Himachel Pradesh, which has her tongue. At Kamakhya, a natural spring keeps a cleft in the rock moist. During the great festival of July/August, the water runs red with iron oxide, and a ritual drink is offered to devotees representing the menstrual blood of Devi. Menstruation is a proof of woman's/the Devi's eternal power of renewal.

Then, as if India needed any more testimony to its sanctity, there are the seven sacred cities of Dwarka, Mathura, Kanchi, Ayodhya, Ujjain, Banaras,[3] and Haridwar; the seven sacred rivers, the Ganga, the Yamuna, the Cauvery, the Narmada, the Godaveri, the Saraswati, the Sindhu (Indus); and the four sacred abodes at the cardinal directions – Badrinath in the north, Dwarka to the west, Puri to the east, and Rameshwarem in the south. The most sacred of the seven mountains, the heavenly abode of all the gods, Mount Kailash, is now in Tibet.

All these power points, and thousands more, are the nodes of an intricate pilgrimage pattern which threads its way all over India. The pattern makes of the sub-continent a body-cosmos in which no local area is without its major and minor sources of sacred power. The entire country is a sacred land, and one of the ancient pilgrimages described in the Mahabharata – undertaken even now by the occasional sadhu – circumscribes almost the entirety of India as it is known politically today. The Devi Bhagavata Purana identifies the earth with the goddess, Mahadevi: the mountains are her bones, the rivers her veins, the sun and moon her eyes. In the central

16

creation myth of the Brahmanas, Prajapati performed great austerities and then released his immense stored up energy to form the underlying substance of the cosmos, pervading it with life and energy. As the earth is a goddess, so the entire cosmos is a living organism. The sacrality of the land of India, not any political vision, is what, still today, gives a sense of unity to this country of so many religions, cultures, races, and factions.

The nationalist movement of the 19th century capitalized on this sentiment by turning the land into a symbol of India as a national entity. They began the modern cult of Bharata Mata, Mother India, and built a temple in Banaras with a map of the country serving as the deity. But traditionally, the land was never seen in this literal way. Nothing in India is literal. It is not arrogance or chauvinism that makes Hindus consider their land to be sacred. It is no more or less sacred than anywhere else: the earth is sacred, and India for them *is* the earth.

William Blake's 'world in a grain of sand' is lived out here on a day-to-day basis. If you would like to circumambulate the Ganges, a well-known sadhu pilgrimage of some 3,000 miles, but do not have the time, you can stand on any spot on the Ganga, with hands raised in salutation, and turn on your axis once. That is the microcosm of the entire circumambulation. All the great sacred sites in India have their smaller counterpart in Banaras, so that city is the microcosm of all India. Make a pilgrimage there, and you have been everywhere.

Some places are more sacred than others, and this is what makes them a node on the pilgrimage pattern. They are called *tirthas*, meaning a ford or a crossing. A place of power is one in which you can 'cross over' from ordinary reality to other dimensions. A tirtha makes this possible because it is a node, or a knot, in the web of creation through which an especially large number of threads are drawn. Each thread is another perspective upon the whole, so a sacred place can connect us to many levels of the one reality.

The sacrality of the place is interior to the pilgrim, as well as being externally located in some physical space. Some pilgrims

17

go here, some there, according not only to the prescriptions of tradition but also to their own predilection. Devotees of Ram will go one way, lovers of Krishna another. A shrine, say, to the goddess, may draw them both into its subtle influence. Actually, we do not choose the place, it chooses us; or rather it is a process that occurs both ways. Nothing more profound than tourism – seeing for seeing's sake – will take place unless the imagination of the pilgrim is sensitized to the deeper realities abiding there. The Hindu has the advantage of being culturally attuned to accepting that, for example, all is in everything, and that one lingam (see page 65 for fuller explanation) in Banaras is actually the essence of all the 12 major lingas in India. This will not be a figure of speech, a metaphor for him, but a reality. Even so, among Hindus themselves, tourism is beginning to rival the traditional motive of gaining merit and blessings by embarking on pilgrimage.

Pilgrimage was at one time no easy affair. Even a hundred years ago – though logging had already begun in earnest to supply wood for railway sleepers – dense forest and jungle covered vast tracts of the land. There were wild animals to brave, brigands, and the dangers of unknown and often hostile territory. The journey would always be made on foot, and this is still the best way to travel to a sacred place. Walking engages the body, sets one in rhythm; it offers one's sweat to the Lord or Goddess of the place; it opens the blood vessels, works the heart, clears the mind, and flushes through the flotsam of collected daydreams. It also has the advantage of taking time. Even arriving somewhere after half an hour's walk gives a deeper perspective than if one piles out of a bus onto its doorstep. With walking, too, it soon becomes clear that the way is the end in itself, which is confirmed in India by the number of pilgrimages which follow a circular route. Where is there to go, in truth, when everything is where you already are? Yet you go anyway, because that is the nature of human existence. Round and round we go; what determines whether it is a sacred journey or not is the quality of our intention. This, as much as any special observances we may adopt along the way, is what can ritualize an ordinary activity into a sacred one.

Some people still climb the Himalaya pilgrim paths to Badrinath, Gangotri, and Kedarnath, but the vast majority of pilgrims now travel by bus. As a result, far more people are travelling the pilgrim routes than ever before. Even in 1976, 20 million people are reported to have visited 150 principal pilgrimage sites.[4] In 1994, two million went to the shrine of Lord Ayappan, in Kerala, alone. If not in such numbers, Hindus have been paying their respects to these sites for thousands of years. Badrinath, a major Hindu pilgrimage centre for at least 1,500 hundred years, was venerated before then as a Buddhist shrine. The places which for centuries have been associated with one or another of the Hindu pantheon, were venerated long before the coming of the gods. They were natural wellsprings of the sacred – not places of 'nature worship', but part of a living theology in which all life was a sacrament. Usually, they were identified in the form of the goddess, who the later Hindu gods took as their consorts as a means of establishing their own sovereignty over the place.

How can a non-Hindu undertake a meaningful pilgrimage in a country whose religious mythology seems so foreign? Some may come to visit a particular saint or guru, while others may be drawn by the natural beauty of the Himalayas, or the Rajasthan desert. The natural world itself is for Hindus the display of the divine. Yet it is so for anyone who can see and hear with the inner senses. Sacred places in the West are undergoing a popular revival. Pilgrimages are becoming a branch of the travel trade. In India, though, pilgrimage is, and has always been, a natural part of life. Even if someone knows little of the cultural context, the land will support them to make their own sacred journey. What matters – what will set apart a pilgrim from the ordinary traveller – is whether you are willing to make the crossing, via the *tirtha*, from this world of mundane reality to one (the same one!) in which the journey, the goal, and the pilgrim himself, are all expressions of the One Divine Whole.

19

PILGRIMAGE THROUGH BRAJ[5]

Those who relate to God as the Beloved are most likely in India to be devotees of Lord Krishna. Krishna's land, where he was born, grew up among cowherds, and became the love of Radha and all the gopis, is known as the region of Braj. For the lover of God, Braj is one of the greatest pilgrimages in India. The circular route that encloses the entire region begins and ends in the city of Mathura. It encompasses all the various sacred sites associated with Krishna's life and exploits.

The entire pilgrimage circuit of Braj covers almost 300 km, though many pilgrims will go to just one or two of the main places – especially Vrindavan, where the child Krishna played with the gopis, and which is now the centre of the pilgrim traffic; Ranakunda lake, which Krishna created from the waters of all the sacred rivers at the request of Radha; Gokul, where Krishna was reared as an infant, and Govardhan. Other places mark the tirthas of Radha and Krishna's sacred play: Ajnokh, where Krishna applied kohl to Radha's eyes; Pisaya, where Radha revived a fainting Krishna with water; Javakban, where Krishna decorated Radha's feet with red Javak dye. Then, Sankari Khor is the place where Krishna demanded a toll of kisses from the cowherdesses, and Chirghat is the name of the Yamuna bank where Krishna stole their clothes and hid in a tree as they bathed.

Vrindavan means 'forest of vrinda trees'. Normally, the forest in India is a place for the ashram and the ascetic, but for Krishna, it is the place of eroticism and an archetypal connection to nature. In journeying from one tirtha in Braj to the next, the pilgrim is instilling the taste of intense devotion and love in his heart by moving in the transcendental world of Krishna's lila, or play, which is anchored in the physical landscape. In this, Braj is unusual: while most Hindu pilgrimages are undertaken for material benefit or spiritual merit, the immersion of the pilgrim's mind in Krishna's pastimes at Braj, and his bodily presence in its physical space, are done for love alone. Love calls to love, and Krishna responds by taking up his abode in the devotee's heart.

1 Lawrence, D. H., *Studies in Classical American Literature*. Heinemann, London 1964.
2 See the Gazetteer for a full list of the Shakti Pithas.
3 This is the common spelling in India, although the most likely spelling in an English Atlas is Benares. Also known as Varanasi..
4 Ghurye, G. S., *Indian Sadhus*. Popular Prakashan, Bombay 1995.
5 This account of Braj owes much to an essay by Amita Sinha, 'Pilgrimage Journey to the Sacred Landscape of Braj'. Published in *The Spirit and Power of Place*, Singh, R. ed. National Geographical Society of India, Banaras 1994.

SACRED RIVER

O Mother Ganga, may your water,
abundant blessing of this world,
treasure of Lord Shiva, playful Lord of all the earth,
essence of the scriptures and
embodied goodness of the gods,
May your water, sublime wine of immortality,
Soothe our troubled souls.[1]

3

The door of our room was open, so we could hear the rush of the river outside. As we were sitting there, watching the day, the cleaner crept in with his brown reed brush. He was stooped, older than his years, a sad little man. I was prompted to ask if he had a family. 'Yes,' he said, and then after a pause, 'but wife sick, and children too. No money for medicines, very difficult.' He spoke without a trace of guile, with no hint of a suggestion that we should give him money. He was just stating the facts of his life. He made to start his work, and then, as if remembering something, he turned and pointed through the door to the river. 'But Ma Ganga will take care of us.' Without another word, he began sweeping the floor.

That exchange took place some years ago in the tourist bungalow at Haridwar. 'Ma Ganga will take care of us' – I had never heard anyone speak of a river in that way before. For this man, the Ganges was a living presence, a protector, a healer of ills. I came to realize during that stay in India that the sweeper was not alone. The Ganges is as alive as it ever was with the hopes and dreams of an entire culture. Even Nehru, that arch-modernist, asked that his ashes be cast into the Ganga at Allahabad. For him, too, the river was India, more than any political party or ideal could ever hope to be. The whole Hindu world still comes to its banks to sing, to pray, to wash, to ask favours and blessings, to urinate, to barter, to die. For the rest of our journey, that great river kept insinuating itself into my thoughts.

It is great, not because of its size (it is 1,500 miles long, but there are many longer and wider rivers) but because, more than any other river on earth, it is a living symbol of an ancient culture's way of life and of the sacred dimension of nature itself. Of all the Hindu goddesses, Ma Ganga is the only one without a shadow. She is the unequivocal fountain of mercy and compassion, here in this world only to comfort her children. Her waters are the milk, the nectar of immortality, source of all life and abundance. She is often shown carrying a plate of food, and an overflowing pot. In Bihar, farmers put a pot of Ganga water in the fields before sowing to ensure a good harvest, while newly-married women unfold their sari to Gangaji and pray for children. It is her physical presence that offers such consolation. The river itself, rather than her image as a goddess, is the one who attracts devotion and worship. Countless flowers are strewn across her body daily; millions of lights set sail every evening upon her waters. While stories of gods and goddesses come and go with the ages, while one myth replaces or rivals another, the organic presence of Ganga continues as ever, absorbing her devotees' offerings and ashes in the same way she has done since time immemorial.

My first contact with Ganga the living Goddess, via the sweeper, and subsequent hours spent by the riverside at Hardwar, fired my imagination sufficiently to impel me to return to India three years later in order to follow its course. I decided to go on foot, by boat, and by bus from its headwater in the Himalayas to Banaras – half the length of the river.

Gaumukh – the cow's mouth – is the source of the river. Hindus carry it with them whenever they go to the Ganga: the spout of the brass pot they use to scoop up holy water for their personal rituals is often in the shape of a cow. Out of the cow's mouth pours the Ganges, by a glacier some 15,000 feet up in the mountains. A sadhu lives there all the year round without a stitch of clothing. It was October when I reached him, and the pilgrim traffic was quiet. I had walked the narrow path from Gangotri, the nearest village, aided at times by the wooden rail that follows the cliff above the stream. The terrain is stark and rocky, with snow-covered peaks looming above on either side. I was cold, hungry, and my head was spinning with altitude sickness. I smiled wanly. He looked at me as if he had seen it all before a thousand times. His matted hair fell below his shoulders. A tiny rag was thrown across his thighs. 'Which country?' he said. 'England.' He nodded. I sat there a few moments longer, trying to feel the sanctity of this source of all mercy and compassion. God knows I needed it; but it was not forthcoming in a way that my senses could register. I sat there an hour with the sadhu, aware through a haze of the austere grandeur not only of the mountains but also of him; aware also that some hours of stiff walking still lay between me and Gangotri if I was to return there by nightfall. Many pilgrims camp at Gaumukh, and still higher up at a spot called Tapovan; but altitude affects me more than most, and the walk down to Gangotri held out more relief at the end than a night with the sadhu.

Such frailties never existed for the likes of Bhagiratha. This ancient king, if we are to believe everything we hear, spent centuries near a Himalayan glacier like this one practising austerities, in order to free the souls of his ancestors. They had all been burnt to ashes by a glance from the sage Kapila, because they had disturbed his meditations. Ganga, the liquid essence of the three great gods, and source of all the heavenly waters, was sufficiently moved by his ardour to appear before him in physical form with the promise that she would come to his aid if he could convince one of the great gods to help break her fall to earth – for otherwise, the force of her waters would destroy the earth. Ganga was stored in Brahma's pot, so Bagiratha prayed to Brahma to help him. 'Go and ask Vishnu to help,' said Brahma. 'I will release Ganga's waters, but Vishnu is needed to help to break Ganga's fall.' Bagiratha prayed with such devotion that Vishnu was satisfied. Brahma blessed Vishnu with a portion of Ganga's power, and as he did so, the essence of Ganga water fell on Vishnu's foot. From the foot of the Lord the waters fell through Shiva's hair, dividing as they did so into many streams, which flowed to different parts of the earth and sanctified them. The main stream flowed through India, cutting a path to where the ashes of Bagiratha's ancestors were piled. It moistened them, and the 60,000 sons were thereby purified and free to undertake the journey to the land of their fathers. The Ganga flowed on across the land, finally to dissolve in the ocean. So it is that the Ganga is graced with the power of the whole Hindu trinity. She is 'the one who flows in the three worlds', heaven, earth, and the underworld below the ocean. She is a liquid axis mundi, the tirtha of tirthas, who unites all the spheres of reality. This is the reason for her central place in the Hindu death ritual. With your ashes in the Ganga, you can be sure, like Bagiratha's forebears, of a safe journey to the land of the ancestors.

It was heaven indeed to see the lights of Gangotri in the gathering dusk, and to slump for a few moments on the wooden bridge that spanned the rushing stream, known up there as the Bagirathi, in honour of the king whose austerities first drew the Ganga down to earth. Even I, with my splitting head, had to pause for a moment to wonder at these pink and white boulders at the foot of the ravine, sculpted with the ages by the river's persistence into living shapes which inspire many a pilgrim who passes this way. James Fraser, the first foreigner to see Gangotri, on his journey there in 1815, immediately set to work with his brushes and easel. By 1820, his watercolours of the Gangotri ravine were already selling in London. Bells were chiming now in the temple to the river goddess, calling devotees to the evening puja. This devotee, however, could think of nothing but sleep, and I saw no more of Gangotri that night than the door to my room.

In the morning I headed off downstream, feeling lighter by the minute as the way fell in altitude. I was following paths that wound through forests of cedar and pine from one tiny hill settlement to the next. The walking, as always, threw me into a rhythm that my body and mind were thankful for. It aligned me with the motion of animals; with the occasional mule or goat that passed me at times on the way. It allowed for conversation in sign language with strangers, for a shared pot of tea with some herders. I could dawdle and watch the birds with tails a foot long, iridescent blue, flutter clumsily on wings too small for their bodies back and forth across the river. And always, I could hear the persistent rush of wild water through the mountain gorges; see its turbulent white tufts, its fierce eddies and whirlpools.

The second morning, I awoke on a ledge of turf by the water to see, here and there at the water's edge, a rock turned on its end and crowned with flowers. A man stood facing the rising sun, still dripping ice-cold water after his immersion in the stream, eyes closed and palms together in traditional greeting. He murmured some prayers under his breath, then turned in a circle on the spot, bowing to the four directions and letting a trickle of water fall back into the river from a brass pot he held out before him. He placed two marigold heads on an upright stone, lit a cone of incense between them, and with a final bow to the flowers and the river, he went on his way. To his tailor's shop, perhaps, or to his field. So simple: no fuss; not even the slightest self-consciousness at the presence of some open-mouthed foreigner. This was his way of starting the day, every day of his life, as it is for millions of Hindus who live near a river, a lake, even a pond.

Some days later, I was camped on a white spur of sand just upstream from Rishikesh, the gateway to the vastness of the Indian plain, the first town the river reaches on leaving the mountains. The stream that had tumbled through canyons and ravines up in the mountains was now a fully-fledged river. Ma Ganga is wider, slower, here; half-tamed already, with the features of a civilization shaping her banks. The straw huts of orange-robed renunciates line the river edge; large ashrams and temples dominate the town. This is where the Beatles came all those years ago to sit with the Maharishi, whose ashram is still one of the largest in the vicinity. People are bathing, doing their laundry, praying, casting flowers on the water, selling pots. Bright swathes of colour fill my eye; fine turbans, yards of cloth, blue and yellow, trailing from a woman's shoulder; eternal gestures, the languid folding of saris, the passing of money, the feeding of children, begging, always the begging, and the placing of the sacred mark on the brow; the grace, wholly unself-conscious, of a woman stooping to place an offering, a leaf-boat of flowers, into the water. Everything, just as it has always been.

Walking along the bank one day, I passed a group of sannyasins in their orange robes chanting over an armchair in which an old woman was sitting. Someone was beating a drum, and a boat was tying up alongside. As I drew closer I realized the old woman was dead. She was tied to the chair, still in her renunciate robes. Next to her was a large box. Chanting continuously, several sannyasis lifted the chair into the box, and began placing stones around the old woman's feet. When they had added enough ballast, they nailed the lid down, and with some heaving and shoving, managed to haul the box onto the waiting boat. The boatmen rowed out into mid-stream, and unceremoniously tipped their cargo over the side. Sannyasis have no need of cremation, since their impurities are consumed while still alive with the fire of their spiritual practice. Small children forego the fire as well, since they are deemed too young to have accumulated bad karma.

Haridwar, half an hour downstream from Rishikesh, is one of the seven sacred cities of India. Two million people visit the town every year, to bathe in the bend of the river known as the Brahmakund, Brahma's basin. This is the place where Brahma greeted the celestial Ganga on her descent to earth; it is also where Vishnu (Hari) left his footprint, so another name for the same place is Hariki-Pairi, Hari's Foot. The footprint is venerated in the Gangadwara (Gate of the Ganga) temple on the right bank. Haridwar's waters are doubly sanctified, then, and it is known as the city of salvation. Criminals come here

27

to disappear into the multitude of renunciates; runaways from ill-fated marriages and family problems, bonded labourers on the run from tyrannical landlords, respectable families from Delhi, businessmen from the Punjab, villagers from Rajasthan, the whole world of northern India throngs in a mass along the river banks, all of them equal at the Gate of the Lord, Haridwar.

At dusk the river at Hariki-Pairi twinkles with a thousand lights. Leaf-boats bob in the water with their cargo of flowers and a camphor flame, sent on their way by pilgrims anxious to secure with their offering the good favours of Ma Ganga. Bells chime across the town, priests are chanting down by the river bank, waving brass candelabra, ablaze with light, in the shape of the sacred sound Aum. Pilgrims throng the Hariki-Pairi ghat, the most auspicious bathing place in the town; the entire river, as befits a goddess, is garlanded with roses and chrysanthemums, and a carpet of petals undulates on the waters.

From Haridwar I took the train to Allahabad, the ancient Prayaga. Another of the seven sacred cities, it in its turn, is doubly holy due to its position at the confluence of the Yamuna and the Ganga. Geographical peculiarities add to the power of the land, and a river confluence is especially holy, suggesting to the Hindu mind the image of the yoni, the vagina, the gate of all life. Prayag is blessed not only with the confluence of two rivers, but three: the Sarasvati, an invisible underground stream, is held to flow into the Ganges at the same point as the Yamuna.

I had met up with a couple of friends in Allahabad, and we intended floating downstream to Banaras, fifty miles on down the road, and three days away by boat. We had an agent arrange the boat for us, and early one morning he ushered us onto one of the small craft that lie in the shadow of the great fort. The skiff we stepped into had nowhere to place the legs, nothing but bare boards to sit on, and scant cover from the sun. In the prow sat a shifty-looking, one-eyed character whose legs were thinner than my wrists. He rowed a few languid strokes, and then gave us to understand that we had to wait for his son. We were still waiting half an hour later. All the boats alongside us seemed sturdier than ours, they all had cushioned seats, and all the other boatmen seemed to be in the prime of their life instead of the eclipse under which our own man seemed to be waning. When I made to leave for another boat, One-Eye immediately discovered a hidden vigour and lurched us into midstream with the assurance that it was unnecessary to wait for his son after all.

His enthusiasm was short-lived. Other boats, far more laden than ours, packed with fat pilgrims from Delhi or Bombay, sped past us towards the confluence, one of the most venerated spots along the whole length of the Ganga. At Allahabad, the Ganga begins to take on the proportions of an epic waterway. At the confluence, the river has the appearance of a huge lake, with dozens of pilgrim boats moored there, out in mid-stream. Our boatman seemed to be taking on this formidable waterway with an attitude more fitting for an afternoon excursion, rather than a trip that was to last three days. At this rate we would be rowing long into the night.

Despite ourselves, we began to settle down to One-Eye's pace, and soon all that could be heard was the creaking of oars (poles with bits of an orange box nailed to them) and the distant chants and calls from a huddle of boats at the confluence, a kilometre or two from the town. As we made towards the main river, the union of the Ganga and Yamuna, I noticed a figure walking in our direction across a curving sandbar on the farther bank. The boatman edged us in the direction of the shore, and the figure walked through the shallow water and out to our boat. It was the son. Everyone smiled; it was all pre-ordained. It was only we who had been in the dark. In every small matter of life, and within the heart of all its chaos and confusion, India has her own inexorable logic that the visitor can only learn to fall into. It is useless, utterly useless, to resist, or to attempt to make things otherwise.

We were almost the only boat on the river. We saw one fishing boat, and just a few small dredgers laden with sand being hauled upstream by men on the towpath who were tied to the end of a long line attached to the mast. The sand had been scooped up from the central channel by buckets on the end of bamboo poles. There were no boats with engines. The one outboard motor I saw in the whole journey was on the ferry at Rishikesh. The only other craft we passed after Allahabad was a small, wide-bottomed boat piled high with reeds. Among them, a flat, high-cheekboned face draped in white cloth peered out from over the steerage.

As we left the city, we wound our way into a land that could barely have changed in a thousand years. In high contrast to the India that most people encounter, the river was silent except for the lap of the water against the boat and the cries of birds overhead. India has to be one of the noisiest lands on earth. Indians are entirely relational: they walk in groups, sit in bunches, travel in families. Their constant banter frequently reaches a decibel level far beyond that of conversational speech. They like to play loud music, of the Indian film variety, to attract customers to their shops, to celebrate a festival (there is always a festival to celebrate), and to call devotees to the temples. The temple loudspeakers begin at 4am and leave no corner of a neighbourhood unscathed. On the roads, day and night, Indian truck and bus drivers, who make up 90 per cent of the traffic, keep their fist permanently on the horn, the volume and pitch of which is at the level of an air raid siren. The river, then, was a sanctuary, an echo, perhaps, of what India might have been like fifty years ago. We passed between high banks, a dirt path spiralling up every now and then to some village above. A woman with a pot on her head swayed up steps that were etched in the mud, children played by the shore, a grandmother washed her linen, buffalo bathed in the river, vultures huddled on the sand.

In the late morning, a band of vultures gathered on the left bank, taking turns at picking the remains from a blanched skeleton which had run aground on the sand. A little later, just before running aground too, One-Eye surprised us with two words of English: 'Dead body!' he exclaimed, pointing proudly into the water. The swollen corpse of a man, bottom up, still

30

clothed, brushed by our starboard side.

Final dissolution in the Ganga purifies on the one hand, yet to the contemporary eye, seems to pollute on the other. Hindus are generally convinced that nothing can pollute their sacred river, and many tests seem to show that Ganga water does seem remarkably capable of retaining its purity. Other tests prove the opposite, that Ganga is as susceptible as any other body of water to the pressures of modern society and a burgeoning population. The matter rests, for the present, in one's own belief system. 'Yes, our water is perfectly good to drink,' my hotel owner in Haridwar had assured me, with a smile. 'It comes from Ganga.' I decided to opt for the bottled water.

Hindus are obsessed with purity, and for them, Ganga is so pristine that the pollution accrued daily through contact with lower castes and other undesirable situations can be erased with a mere handful of river water over the head. To be brushed by a breeze that is carrying even a drop of Ganga water is sufficient, the Agni Purana says, to erase all sins. In temples of the Gupta period, statues of Ganga and Yamuna often grace the entrance, purifying all who pass through the door. The very land the Ganga flows through is purified by her presence, a view more acceptable to the contemporary mind. What defies logic – but then India does not live by Western logic – is that this most sacred of all sacred rivers is used as an open sewer. Cities pour their excrement into it, millions of individuals use it freely as a public toilet, and of course, industrial plants use it to dispose of their effluent. It seems a strange way to treat a goddess. In his first speech to the Indian Parliament, Rajeev Gandhi declared the Ganga a national heritage, and earmarked substantial central funds to deal with its pollution problems. As is the way in India, projects at the local level were hastily conceived and improperly executed; and as always, corruption saw off a large proportion of the allocated funds.

Western countries are more guilty than most for the earth's pollution, a fact I had always attributed in part to the Western dissociation between nature and God. If nature is inert matter, you can treat it with impunity. If she is a goddess, a manifestation of the divine, I would expect her to be treated with more care. Meanwhile, the devotee by the Ganga continues to wash away his sins downstream from the sewer.

As the sun drew near the horizon, the wind died, and dolphins, dozens of dolphins, wheeled and dived alongside us. The boatmen took an oar each. They seemed unable, however, to row in rhythm, so that one soon fell behind, until the other caught him up again. For a few seconds they would row as a team, and then fall out of rhythm again. An hour after dark we saw the flashing light of our agent, who had already set up camp on the bank. Two days later, through an early evening haze, we glimpsed the outlines of the palaces and temples, all pink and brown, that grace the riverfront of Banaras. We were edging our way round the only bend in its entire length where the Ganga makes a turn back towards the north, the direction of wisdom, and away from the south, the direction of death. The bend is in the shape of a half moon, like the one on Shiva's brow. We were finally entering Shiva's city, then, where death is defeated – the one place along the whole length of the river where the great god's fire is cooled by the element of water. In Banaras, the fire and the water, life and death, are reconciled. From the source to The City of Light I had come. I cupped my hand in the water, lifted it to the dying sun, and let it trickle back into the stream. I remembered the sweeper in Hardwar, and knew the water to be on my own breath now.

1   Hawley, John Stratton and Wulff, Donna Marie, eds. *The Divine Consort: Radha and the Goddesses of India.* Berkeley Religious Studies, Berkeley, Ca. 1982.

SACRED MOUNTAIN

When I came to realise who I am,
What else is this identity of mine,
But thee,
Oh Thou who standest as the towering Aruna Hill?
Sri Ramana Maharshi – stanzas to Arunachala

4

Even the mention of mountains in India brings the word Himalaya immediately to mind. Yet while Hindus consider the whole Himalayan range to be sacred in a general way, only one specific mountain there plays a major role in Hindu mythology. Mount Kailash, the abode of the gods and Shiva's favourite home, now lies over the Tibetan border. The Himalayan range as a whole is sacred because it is in the north, which for Hindus is the direction of wisdom and spiritual rebirth. It also includes the highest peaks in the world, which are a sight to inspire awe and wonder in people of any race or creed.

Yet, with the exception of Kailash, none of the main places of pilgrimage in the Himalayas – Gangotri, Kedarnath, Badrinath – honours the spirit of a particular mountain. Sacred mountains are venerated the world over; in India, the best place to witness this living tradition is far to the south, where Arunachala juts out of the Tamil plain, a hundred miles from Madras.

At the foot of Arunachala is the ashram of Ramana Maharshi, one of the greatest spiritual masters of this century. Though he died in 1950, Ramana's ashram today is one of the most potent spiritual places in India, drawing people from all over the world. The only writing Ramana ever did consisted of devotional poems to the mountain. Arunachala, he was to say later, is the physical embodiment of Shiva, of God Himself. Why go anywhere else?

An unusual claim to make for a mountain; but there are many strange claims about Arunachala, and its power to pull towards it those whom it holds dear. I once met a French woman there who had been living by the mountain for twenty-five years. When she was sixteen, she went on a school skiing trip. Out on the slopes, she suddenly felt irresistibly drawn towards a nearby glacier. The teacher told her not to go, but she wandered over to the glacier base. There she knelt down and found a stone which fitted exactly in the palm of her hand. She took it home with her and put it on her mantelpiece. She put some flowers around it. In the following weeks, she decided it would look its best if she oiled it, so she did so every day. She knew nothing of Hindu culture, and had no idea that she was in effect performing puja, devotional worship, to the stone.

Ten years later she went to India, and on the suggestion of a monk she had met in France, she went to Arunachala. All she knew was that it was respected as a holy mountain. She always carried her stone with her whenever she went away from home, and on seeing Arunachala for the first time, she took her stone from her pocket and looked at them both in astonishment. They were exactly the same shape. On her return to France a few weeks later, she put her stone back on her mantelpiece. The next morning it was gone. None of the family could offer an explanation. After the initial shock, she began to sense that the stone was no longer needed, now she had seen Arunachala. Soon afterwards, she came to live by the mountain, and has not left it since.

A financial consultant working in London walked into a bookshop one day and picked up a volume on the life and teachings of Ramana Maharshi. Within the week, he was on a plane to India to spend three weeks in Ramana's ashram at the foot of Arunachala. When he saw the mountain, he knew he had come home. Six months later he was back again for two months. A year later he had sold his various assets in London, New York and Mexico, and had taken up the life of a monk on Arunachala.

What is the call of this mountain, that sages, yogis, and spiritual seekers have been led to it for thousands of years, and continue to be so today, even from distant parts of the world? Arunachala has a story, of course; but before we hear it, we would do well to reflect on the difference between myth and reality. The point is, in India there is no difference. For the great majority of Indians, to believe is to see. Imagination is reality. You have but to think something with full confidence, and it is done. In the West, despite profound changes occurring deep within the culture, the mainstream is still convinced that seeing is believing. When we use the word myth, we automatically think 'story', 'legend', or 'make-believe'. A myth is not true, it is a poetic way of explaining the inexplicable, or of alleviating some collective anxiety or another. This is the 'realist' view.

In India, imagination is the realm of creative will. This is so both in the most elevated and inspired spiritual texts, and in the everyday life of the illiterate peasant. The difference between the two is one of refinement and degree, not of perspective. The imagination is a realm of existence out of which the world of concrete form condenses, so to speak. Forms are brought into being from the more subtle realm of imagination. A myth comes directly from that timeless world of creative imagery. Its logic and truth are the logic and truth of the world of the gods; and that world, in the Indian view, is more real than the physical world about us, just as a cause is more substantial than its effect. Myths are the history not of factual events but of the human condition, and as Eliade points out, in a world founded on religious values, 'one becomes truly a man only by conforming to the teaching of the myths, that is, by imitating the gods'.[1]

Seen in this light, the story of Arunachala is a resonator of living truth. A local version of a story in the Shiv Purana, it has been passed down throughout southern India for centuries. Like any of the great myths of mankind, it must always remain opaque to the linear, conceptual mind. So, to know what really happened, we need to take a step into that time beyond time. This is how it was.

In the beginning, Brahma and Vishnu emerged from Shiva, the Unmanifest Source of all. No sooner had they come into form than they began to argue about which of them had the superior role, as the creator, and the protector of the universe. To stop their quarrelling, Shiva manifested as a column of light so radiant that both Brahma and Vishnu were temporarily blinded, and had to stop their bickering. Now this light was the original manifestation of Arunachala. Shiva told them that the one who could find either the beginning or the end of the column of light would be proclaimed the mightiest. Vishnu immediately transformed himself into a boar, and dug through all the lower realms in search of the beginning of the column of light. For whole ages he dug, but as much as he tried, the source of the light was never revealed. Finally, he was forced to recognize the limitless power of Shiva himself as the true creator and sustainer of the worlds. Full of devotion and remorse for his pride and forgetfulness of his own origins, Vishnu paid homage to the Great Lord.

While Vishnu was digging away in one direction, Brahma turned himself into a swan and flew into the upper regions in search of the top of the column of light. Yet for as long as he flew, the column shone far beyond him into infinity. Brahma could not bear to be defeated by Vishnu, however, so when his wings would take him no further, he returned to tell him that he had indeed seen the end of the light.

At that moment, both in response to Vishnu's devotion, and to confound Brahma, Shiva appeared in his glorious universal form in the midst of the light. Mounted on a white bull, the Lord wore a crescent moon on his matted locks, a garland of skulls around his neck, a serpent in place of the sacred thread, serpents for earrings, an eye in his forehead, five faces, and five blue throats.

Brahma, as you might imagine, was suitably impressed, and knelt before the Almighty One. For his transgression, Shiva cut off Brahma's fifth head, and decreed that no temples were to be built in his name. Even today, there is only one major temple to Brahma in the whole of India, in Pushkar. Brahma accepted Shiva's judgment in good heart, and praised the Lord with such devotion that Shiva restored the role of Creator to him, and allowed him to be worshipped in the Vedic sacrifices.

Then Brahma prayed to Shiva, asking for three boons: that He reduce the radiance of Arunachala Hill so that it might be approached and worshipped by humans; that the hill reveal its glorious light once a year in the month of Kartikai (November-December) on the eve of the full moon; and that Shiva remains for ever in this place in the form of a lingam, so that gods and men can worship His form in the normal manner, with sandalpaste, ablutions, and flowers. Vishnu prayed that all who performed circumambulation (pradakshina) of Arunachala in devotion, with prostrations, dance and song, be liberated.

Shiva agreed to all their requests and disappeared. In his place, a lingam appeared on the east side of the hill. Brahma and Vishnu ordered Visvakarma, the Heavenly Architect, to erect a temple around the self-created lingam in honour of Shiva in the form of Arunachalesvara. They created a tank with the waters of all the sacred rivers, and founded the city that became Tiruvannamalai. Every year in the month of Kartikai, on the eve of the full moon, the Deepam Festival is held to celebrate the full radiance of Shiva-Arunachala. Deepam is still one of the most important festivals in all south India.

I did not know any of these stories when I first arrived in Tiruvannamalai. What I had come for was to visit the ashram of Ramana Maharshi. The mountain, though, was the first thing I saw as we drew near to the town. The surrounding area is a huge flat plain which extends through much of Tamil Nadu. Arunachala looms up from this plain, a solitary pyramid some 2,500 feet high. It was purple and gold in the dusty light. It so dominates the town at its foot that it is difficult to ignore.

I decided to investigate this hill before I did anything else. Behind the Ramana Ashram is a path that leads along the lower slopes. It threads between scrub and huge round boulders, in the direction of the town, some three kilometres away. In the 1930s and 1940s, Arunachala was described by Ramana's disciples as a mountain in the jungle. The ashram itself was carved out of the wilderness, and even twenty years ago, the only transport to it was by bullock cart. Wild animals made the mountain a dangerous place; only yogis lived on its slopes. Now all I could hear was the din of the trunk road to Bangalore, that passes in front of the ashram gates. Not only is there no jungle, there is hardly a tree more than five years old to be found anywhere on the mountain. Even so, the walk is pleasant; it is always a relief to escape even partially the noise and the chaos of an Indian city. In twenty-five minutes I had reached Skandashram, the original ashram of Ramana in the early days. It consists of just one whitewashed building with a courtyard, and overlooks the Arunachalesvara Temple in the city. Here, the path diverges. You can either begin a steep two to three hour climb to the summit, or drop down a few hundred yards, across a stream to the Veerupaksha Cave, where Ramana first lived for sixteen years in silence and solitude.

That first morning, I opted for the easier course. In minutes I had reached the little courtyard at the cave entrance. A single breadfruit tree shaded a tiny lingam set in a circle of water. Someone had left a red rose on the lingam head. The petals of a yellow chrysanthemum were scattered round it in the water. I sat on the low parapet that skirted the tree, and gazed below onto the whole city spread out on the plain. I was looking directly down over Arunachalesvara Temple, all twenty-five acres of it in a single view. Even though motor horns boomed right up the mountain, this courtyard was unusually tranquil. A notice at the cave entrance asked visitors to keep silence. No-one else was there, but there were three pairs of shoes by the tree.

I left my own shoes alongside them and passed through a vestibule hung with pictures of Ramana into the darkness of the cave itself. Three people were sitting motionless in front of a stone ledge. On the ledge, just discernible in the light of a tiny oil lamp, was an elongated mound draped in a faded yellow cloth and a flower garland. I sat down on the floor near the others. The air was hot and thick. The silence and stillness began to enter my mind.

What a relief, to be in darkness, after the glare of the sun. I sensed the wisdom of those builders of old Romanesque churches, which in Europe I had so often passed by in favour of the radiance and soaring of their Gothic successors. This cave, like one of those early churches, was a womb. Its darkness was the darkness of not knowing, of some secret germination beyond the aspirations or grasp of the daylight mind. Maybe I was there for an hour or so, when out of nowhere a voice suddenly rang through the quiet of my body: 'Just rest,' it said. 'Just rest.'

I had thought that I was already at rest, but as I heard these words I was instantly aware of the subtle effort I had been making all along to be aware of the silence I was in. Even that effort was a residual holding back from being there, where I was, in utter simplicity. I let the dark cave take me then, hold me; and in that moment it was as if the mountain moved through me. It was then that I truly felt Arunachala to be alive. It seemed in that moment that the life of the mountain, the cave, and my own innermost being, were one and the same thing.

There are sacred mountains all over the world, and for the local inhabitants, their own sacred mountain is always the world axis. In south India, Arunachala is seen to be the hill that survives the primordial flood from age to age, and that contains all the latent seeds of the future growth of the universe. A mountain, like a pillar, a tree, or a ladder, always signifies the meeting of the worlds. It is the archetypal sacred place, a gateway to the divine and to the nether regions. This mountain really does have a living energy that assists people to enter into the cave of their own heart, into the mountain stillness that stands in and behind every human being.

The cave is called Veerupaksha after a yogi who lived in it some 300 years ago. Ramana was only the most recent in a continuous line of inhabitants who have stretched down the centuries. Veerupaksha gathered his disciples around him one day and told them he would leave this life on the following day. It is a rule on the mountain that no yogis are to be buried there (yogis and small children are never cremated). Veerupaksha, however, did not want his remains to leave the cave. He told his disciples to block the cave entrance, and to open it again the following evening. When they rolled back the boulder, they found a heap of ashes traced on the floor in the shape of their master. These ashes still lie beneath the ochre cloth on the ledge inside the cave. Three hundred years after his unusual departure, Veerupaksha is honoured daily with flower garlands and incense.

Many other yogis and sages live by the mountain today. Some, like Lakshman Swami, and Annamalai Swami,[2] were realized through their association with Ramana Maharshi. Others, like Ramsurat Kumar, who has a large following all over Tamil Nadu, were drawn solely by the presence of Arunachala. On the summit of the mountain lives a yogi who has not taken food for the six years he has been up there. He has a rough shelter of a few branches, and sits in complete silence and solitude. He wears a cloth over his head so that his eyes do not burn those who make the stiff climb up to see him. After a visitor has sat with him for a few minutes, he will gesture to him to be on his way.

To climb the hill, to enter the hill through one of its caves, and to circle the hill are some of the ways of having a physical relationship with Arunachala. Another way was shown me one morning by the shopkeeper who had served me tea the evening before. I was passing his house when he stepped in front of me and prostrated to a roadside figure of Ganesh. Then he got up and, facing the mountain, his palms together in front of his heart, gazed upon it with eyes that were bright with devotion. He turned in a circle on the spot, and facing the mountain again, bowed, and made off for his tea shop.

40

Hundreds of people do pradakshina of Arunachala every day. By tradition, they walk barefoot in a clockwise direction, and keep to the left side of the road, for the souls of the departed also do pradakshina of Arunachala, going anti-clockwise on the right side. The twelve-kilometre route passes through only one village, and except for the last kilometre or two, which takes the pilgrim through the town, the walk is a balm for the soul and for the senses.

It may not have been quite such a balm if I had gone barefoot. I went early one evening with John Button, who has lived by Arunachala for five years as a leading volunteer for The Annamalai Reforestation Society. John is one of those rare people who has the energy and enthusiasm to put his plentiful ideas into action. An Australian, he came to India under the auspices of the Rainforest Information Centre, Australia. The Centre had decided to help fund a group in Tiruvannamalai who were starting a tree planting project on Arunachala. In five years, they have planted more than 5,000 trees on the mountain.

Just two kilometres along from Ramanashram, we left the noise of the main road for a lane that led into the Indian countryside. No more lorries with belching exhausts; just the occasional scooter or buffalo cart, and a steady trickle of pilgrims making their way round the mountain. It was January, but warm air rose from the tarmac, and my shirt was soon stuck to my back. Just a few hundred yards from the main road was the first *Nandi*, Shiva's bull, gazing in adoration at his lord and master in the form of the hill. We paused for a moment to stroke his smooth stone back, black and glistening in the evening light.

'Look at his eyes,' John said. 'Just like the eyes of a lover, and head tilted slightly to one side.'

It was true, I had often been struck by the lover's look in the *Nandis*. Perhaps being a bovine had something to do with it, those large almond cow eyes which never seem to blink or to hold any malice.

We were walking by paddy fields, open land, and fields

where buffalo were heaving a plough through the scrub. The first shrine we came to, in honour of Durga, was by a tree whose trunk was guarded by a tall metal cobra. The shrine was daubed in red, and a *pujari* was squatting waiting to exchange a dab of paste on the brow for some *baksheesh*.

'This shrine is a recent addition,' explained John. 'It wasn't here when I first arrived. Durga is undergoing a general revival now, like Hanuman.'

The Hanuman temple, a little further on, was the only one on the whole route which had a loudspeaker blaring out music. It had evidently gone through a recent metamorphosis, with the original small shrine being extended by a covered area for *darshan*, and the whole complex being plastered with comic book illustrations of Hanuman's exploits. The invest-ment seemed to be paying off: a dozen scooters were parked outside, and every walker we saw stopped for *darshan* of the monkey god.

Soon after the Hanuman temple, we came to one of the eight lingas around the hill which mark the cardinal direc-tions. The lingam was set in a garden which had been restored by the ARS. All the lingas around the mountain have gardens which have long been neglected. Their restoration was anoth-er of Button's schemes which was bearing fruit, along with the renewal of the temple garden itself, which was in the Arunachalesvara temple in the town.

'Temple gardens used to provide all the flowers and fruit needed for the daily *pujas*,' John explained. 'But nowadays hardly any temple in India maintains its garden. The temple authorities saw how we were transforming the lingam gar-dens, so they were only too happy when we suggested we do the same for the main temple property. We collected all the organic manure we needed from the temple towers, which were caked with years of bats' droppings.'

It was evident the more we talked that for John Button and his team, ecology was an inherent part of a spiritual world view. For him, I realized, tree-planting, garden restoration, and the permaculture project the ARS were operating nearby, were activities no less devotional than worshipping the deity in a temple.

'Yes, but we are only bringing an appropriate technology into the service of a view that has been accepted in India for millennia – the view of nature as living spirit. Look at that tree, for example.'

We stopped for a moment by a tree with hundreds of little rag cradles suspended from the branches. I looked into one of them, to find it was holding a rock. Other branches held little cloth bags, and women's bangles. At the base of the tree was a large termite mound, some four feet high, whose base had been daubed in red. Between it and the tree was a metal cobra with a giant hood.

'Trees and termite mounds are expressions of Mother Nature's power,' John went on. 'The local people have hung up the cradles to ask the great Mother for a child; the bags are a request for money, the bangles are put there by unmarried women in search of a husband. For them, Nature is a living intelligence, a sacred realm. That is why so many trees, flowers and plants are sacred to particular gods, such as the banyan and the neem trees for Shiva, and the *tulsi* plant for Vishnu.'

We were arriving in a village now, the only one on the route. Adi Annamalai is the site of a temple of the same name, which is a miniature version of the big one in town. Its name, Adi, 'the original', points to the fact that it is the older of the two. The whole place was festooned in bamboo poles and scaffolding when we arrived. We were met by a large and welcoming man in orange who introduced himself as Ramananda. He had made it his mission to restore the temple to its former glory. Previously, he had been the manager of a nearby ashram, and before that he had spent some years alone on the mountain. Now, he was dedicated to this work of temple renovation, which he had taken up single-handed. He is fundraiser, site foreman and contractor, all in one. Most of his funds come from small foreign organizations. He seemed to have taken on a formidable task for just one man.

'What to do?' he smiled, as we left. 'This is a labour of love.

I love Arunachala, and this is a way I can express it. Come back in a year or two. You'll see. It will all be different.'

We continued for another hour or so, the mountain displaying each of its five peaks as we made the round. After the village we let the walking fill our minds with its rhythm, and words fell away. We arrived in Tiruvannamalai just as the first stars began appearing over the mountain. John went on his way, and I stood for a while in the lee of the great temple, wondering what it must be like to be here during the festival of Deepam.

In November-December, hundreds of thousands of people celebrate this festival in a ten-day re-enactment of the story – or the holy 'mystery play' – of Arunachala. Every morning and evening, great processions of chariots make their way round the outside of the Arunachalesvara Temple, each chariot bearing the image of one of the gods. The temple elephant leads the procession, followed by Ganesh, then Lord Murugan, (these two being Shiva's sons), Shiva, Parvati, and Shiva's greatest devotee among the 63 Shaivite saints of the south. The temple elephant, though, has now been suspended from procession duty because it recently killed a woman. Seeing the elephant as Lord Ganesh himself, she had paid homage to him by waving a lit lamp directly in front of his trunk. The elephant, reacting as an animal, and not as a god, took fright of the flame. He lifted the woman up in his trunk, and then set her down and stamped on her.

For most of the festival, the chariots are made of silver, but on the seventh day, they are made of wood, with Shiva's being five storeys high. This 'juggernaut' is pulled round the temple with two huge chains, hundreds of men heaving on one, and women on the other. The whole event builds gradually to the climax on the tenth day, when a great cauldron of ghee (purified butter) is carried up to the top of Arunachala mountain. Before it is lit with a cloth wick, one last procession makes its way around the temple. During this, Parvati's chariot is rocked wildly from side to side, signifying her burning desire to merge with the unmanifest Lord Shiva.

Thousands of devotees make their way up to the mountain top on Deepam night to witness the lighting of the flame, the re-enactment of Shiva's manifestation as the light of Arunachala. The moment the wick is lit, Parvati's chariot, in the town procession below, ceases its chaotic movement, for the goddess has united with her Lord. In the myth, Shiva appeared as the column of light in response to Parvati's fervent devotions, and declared her his eternal wife. At that moment, she became his left side, and it is in this form, the combined male and female, that Shiva is worshipped in Arunachalesvara Temple.

With my mind still full of the story, I made my way back to Ramanashram. The whole saga of Arunachala, I reflected to myself in the rickshaw, ends in the alchemical wedding of the apparent opposites. The Divine and the natural world, in both the cosmos and in the individual human being, realize their union. Entering the body of the disciple, Mother Shakti leads the devotee through right action to Shiva, her groom, in the cave of the human heart. It is for this alchemy, I suspect, that Arunachala still calls people to her today.

1   Eliade, M. *The Sacred and The Profane*. Harcourt Brace, Orlando, Fa. 1987.
2   See the autobiography of Annamalai Swami: Godman, David, *Living by the Words of Bhagavan*. Sri Annamalai Swami Ashram Trust, Tiruvannamalai, Tamil Nadu 1994.

PART TWO

THE CLASSICAL TRADITION

SACRED WORD

O Mother Word, is there anything in this world which is not praise to your ears, since your body consists of all the words? In all forms I perceive only your body, whether born in mind or manifested externally.
Abhinavagupta, Mystical Hymns, 10th century

5

Though in the beginning, there was the Word, Logos – the Western word – lost half its meaning soon after its utterance. Logos is masculine, and originally it meant both the ordering faculty of the mind – *ratio* – and the revelatory, expressive power that can communicate that order – the spoken word. The revelatory part was gradually eclipsed by an excessive preoccupation with the rational – the conceptual, ordering faculty. This both encouraged – and was in its turn encouraged by – a dominant interest in the written word.

In India, the equivalent for *logos* is Vac, pronounced *vatch*. Vac, however, is a goddess, and she embodies the creative principle of the spoken, not the written word. In the Brahmanas, mind and word are a married couple. In the Tantras, Shiva and Shakti are united to each other as meaning and word. Then, the word *matrika* means both mother and letter: so in India, the alphabet gives and generates life. The combined power of every vowel and consonant comprises the universe, so the Sanskrit language brings everything into being. In this way, Sanskrit is itself an embodiment of the sacred: so much so, that in the Sanskrit grammatical tradition, grammar itself is seen as a way of salvation – if you polish your speech into perfect grammar, you will become one with Brahman.

Unlike the traditions of the Middle East, classical Hinduism is not a religion of the book: it is a 'heard' tradition. Its scriptures are recited, or sung, not read. Though the Rig Veda was known some time before 1500 BC, it was not written down until almost 3,000 years later. The script was available, but the verses were considered so powerful that they were protected from possible misuse by being transmitted orally from master to disciple, father to son. Everything was learned by heart through a complicated system of checks that ensured the verses were not altered by the syndrome of 'Chinese whispers'. Even now, the books are sacred not in themselves, but by virtue of what they contain. They are treated with the utmost respect. Sacred texts are always covered in a cloth, and if they become damaged or worm-eaten, they are not restored, but consigned solemnly to the Ganga.

The most sacred of Hindu texts – the Vedas, the Brahmanas, the Aranyakas, and the Upanishads – are all called *'sruti'*, meaning 'what is heard' from the original Vedic Rishis, whose inspired utterances were passed down from master to disciple. As the oral tradition gradually degenerated, a second body of work developed, called *'smrti'*, meaning 'what is remembered'. While the 'sruti' works are considered to be divine revelations, the 'smrti', though still sacred, are acknowledged to have been crafted by men. They include the epics – the Ramayana and the Mahabharata – the Dharma Sutras (of which the most famous are the Laws of Manu), and the Puranas.

While 19th-century scholars gave almost exclusive interest to texts in Sanskrit, contemporary studies also recognize the profound spiritual and poetic value of many texts that were written in the languages of the south. Of all the Indian languages, Tamil, next only to Sanskrit, has the oldest literary records. But unlike Sanskrit, it is a living language. The Vaisnava Alvar poets, the Shaiva Nayanmars, who were composing their couplets from the 10th century onwards, would still be able to hear their verses being sung in the temples of Tamil Nadu today. Tiruvalluvar's 'Kural', considered the finest example of classical Tamil literature, was composed sometime between the 2nd century BC and the 8th century AD. His work is widely read in the south today, and the shrine in his honour, in Madras, still attracts thousands of pilgrims.

THE MANTRA GURU: SRI VAIMANASA BHATTACHARIAR

All Indian traditions, north and south, make use of the *mantra*, a sacred word of power which connects the inner and the outer worlds. Often, a *mantra* forms the basis of meditation. In Madras, I was introduced to Sri Vaimanasa Bhattachariar, a guru who specializes in *mantra yoga*. My introduction was through a senior civil servant, and I was surprised when my friend told me about his guru; I knew he had a thorough knowledge of the Upanishads, and I expected him to be connected to a more philosophical tradition than a stream which, from his description, sounded more like a branch of the Tantric magical school.

'I'm impressed by the man's integrity,' he explained. 'There are very few who do not use their knowledge for their own ends. He takes no money, and he makes no emotional demands on his disciples at all. And I must say that he has cleared my way of certain difficulties that I could see no way out of by myself.'

'How did he do that?' I asked.

'With mantras. You will see.'

My friend led me to an inconspicuous first-floor apartment in the suburbs of Madras. The door was open. Inside, half a dozen people were sitting around an elderly man in white, complete with the requisite long beard. The atmosphere was relaxed and informal, rather like a grandfather with his grand-children. My friend introduced me, and explained that I was interested to know more about *mantra*.

Without hesitation, Bhattachariar launched upon his subject, using my friend as an interpreter. 'Mantra is sacred sound,' he began. 'When a disciple is initiated into a *mantra*, he is given access to the source of the word's power, its *shakti*.

50

The *mantra* makes him a direct participant in the cosmic power of the deity concerned. Every deity has a different function, and a different *mantra*. The deities reside in your subtle body, the *Antaratman*, so all the mantras are already vibrating in you. It is a matter of making contact with them through concentration. By raising the vibration of the *mantra*, you attune the subtle body to the Absolute, and when you do that, you can leave the body at will. There are literally millions of *mantras*, many of them complete gibberish. But in making non-sense, they bypass the rational mind and access the deeper power of the sound.'

'Why would you want to access these powers?' I asked.

'The ultimate aim of *mantra* yoga,' he replied, 'is *moksha*, liberation. But for that you must be celibate, eat only pure foods, and have pure motivation. Then your food is transformed into blood, which becomes semen, then energy. That energy is drawn up the spine with the use of *mantras*, and manifests itself in the form of a nectar we call amrit, the food of the gods. One drop of this is enough to sustain life for 24 hours.'

'What happens in the case of women?' I wondered. 'How can they attain liberation, since you imply one has to have semen?'

'The same principle operates in women through the ovaries,' Bhattachariar replied. 'But it is true that it does take longer.'

'Is it for moksha that your disciples come to you? Many of them seem to be householders.'

'They are practically all householders. I am a householder myself, though, except for a short period as a priest, I have not worked for a living. I have lived from an inheritance. Now I am in the third stage of life, the vanaprasta ashrama. Vanaprasta literally means 'forest dweller', and refers to that time when a man no longer sleeps with his wife or depends on her to prepare his food. He still lives with her, but as a renunciate, taking care of his own needs. That has been my way of life for seven years now. Very few people today are interested in moksha.

They want success and happiness in worldly life. Spiritual discipline helps them lead an honourable life and still attain their worldly desires. As they become established in the practice, though, some of them become more interested in the spiritual world than material gain. That is my hope.'

I asked him what kind of favour mantras could help one attain.

Bhattachariar laughed. 'Anything at all,' he replied. 'In the Atharva Veda, mantras are sectioned into eight divisions. There are mantras to attract people to you; mantras for fixing someone to the spot; love potion mantras; mantras for curing insanity; for discerning the next step in your life; for making someone go where you want them to go; for protection against murder; mantras to antidote poisons and spiritual obstacles. Mantras can be used for any situation; although they are only effective if received from a guru.'

Bhattachariar reeled off the various powers of mantra without a hint of self-importance, even though his disciples clearly felt that he was able to create any effect he wished through the formulae at his disposal. He was one of the few practitioners, my friend told me later, who knew the Atharva Veda off by heart.

'How do you know when a mantra is working?'

'You will know in various ways,' Bhattachariar replied through my friend. 'At the worldly level, whatever you think will happen. Then, you will see the devata, the godly form of the mantra, and you will also come to see the future. As with everything else, mantras can be used for good or for evil. There are a great many black magicians at work in India, but true Tantra is practised for the benefit of humanity. The quickest results are obtained with the added invocation of Hanuman or Kali, with music and bhajans, as well as the use of their particular mantras.'

When I asked Bhattachariar about his own apprenticeship in mantra yoga, he explained that he had met his own guru forty years ago in Tanjore, and stayed with him for eighteen years, until his death.

'You only have one guru,' he smiled. 'Just as you only have one mother or father.'

Would the tradition continue after his own death, I wondered, in an age like the present one, preoccupied with consumerism.

'I have initiated my sons,' he replied. 'But they are not interested. They have professions, and that satisfies them. I have some serious disciples, but none approaching the renunciate stage.'

As he said this, he nodded in the direction of a man on my left. Anantharam was 38, and had recently left his profession as a lawyer to assist with the administration of the guru's duties. He was unmarried, but had not committed to a renunciate life. Anantharam had been with his guru for six years, and when I asked him about his personal practice, he said he had been given thirteen different mantras for varying purposes. Most of them were protection mantras. He always chanted the Ganesh mantra first, then his root mantra, the Chandi Yajna Mantra. He recited all thirteen a minimum of sixteen times daily.

'Tomorrow guruji is performing a special puja for a family in the city,' Anantharam said. 'If you come, you will see mantra yoga in action.'

The guru nodded his assent to Anantharam's suggestion, and as I got up to go, he handed me a plastic wallet and a small tube of sandalpaste. Inside the wallet was a yantra, a magical diagram of gold interlocking triangles.

'Apply the sandalpaste to the yantra daily,' Bhattachariar said. 'It will help you.'

My friend was busy the following day, and it was Anantharam who led me to the house of the Managing Director of an International Marketing Consultancy. If Bhattachariar's practices were mere superstitions, they were subscribed to by well educated people. The head of the household told me that he had asked for the ceremony in order to deflect evil influences that had been directed towards his family and to his business. It was also designed to ensure the collection of some bad debts.

Bhattachariar sat with two priests who were chanting vigorous Sanskrit mantras over a fire-pit. Kilos of red chillies were piled high by the fire, and as the priests chanted away, they dipped the chillies one by one in a bowl of neem oil and threw them on the fire. The fire was piled high with frying peppers, yet there was no smoke or smell in the room. Bhattachariar noticed my surprise and smiled.

'Burning peppers are often used to drive out evil forces,' Anantharam explained. 'But you will never witness something like this. Normally, this amount of frying chillies would drive us all out of the house. Guruji has neutralized their smell with the mantras. This heightens the purifying power of the ritual. Then, it is very rare to see this ceremony performed in a high caste way, with priests.'

Later, a second puja was performed in honour of the three goddesses, Lakshmi, Saraswati and Durga. The priests re-lit the fire from a spark generated by the rubbing together of two sticks, which took twenty minutes of vigorous muscle work. This puja, said Anantharam, was for the respective blessings of the goddesses – wealth, wisdom and protection. Finally, a third puja was performed in honour of the five-faced version of Hanuman.

The five-faced Hanuman, I discovered later, is to be Bhattachariar's gift to posterity. Aware that his ancient tradition is unlikely to continue for long in its original form of transmission from master to guru, he is raising funds for a unique statue which will enable people to benefit from mantras on their own. Expected to be completed in 1996 outside of Madras, it is to be a 32-feet high idol with five faces on Hanuman's monkey body. Bhattachariar will empower each of the five faces with different mantras. The supplicant will take a ritual bath, and then, standing before one of the faces, will chant the appropriate mantra, which a leaflet will explain to him.

The lion face will protect against murder; the eagle face will clear poisons and spiritual obstructions; the pig will generate wealth; the monkey will dissolve all negative influences, and the horse, on the top, will ensure a good family and education.

In short, Bhattachariar is planting a Wish-Fulfilling Mantra Tree. May all those who sound the true sound receive its blessings.

SACRED IMAGES AND DEITIES

May that Hari (Lord) fulfil all your desires. Hari whom the Saivites
worship as Shiva, the Vedantins as Brahman, the Bhaudasas as Buddha,
the Jains as Arhat.
From the Hanuman Nataka

6

Innumerable gods and goddesses, monkey gods, elephant
gods, four-armed gods, wild-eyed goddesses with necklaces of
skulls and gnashing teeth, radiant goddesses with fulsome
breasts and undulating forms, are showered daily with hon-
orific baths, perfumed, dressed in fine silks and cloths, sung
to, wept before, pleaded with. In India, the heavenly family
extends to thousands of different names and forms, and to
complicate things further, many of them are variations on a
single theme. A single deity can become many, and the many
can also become one. As in a dream, the multiple forms flow
in and out of each other, one or another becoming prominent
as the occasion, time of year, or mood of the moment,
demands.

The same description could also apply to the day-to-day
functioning of an individual psyche, which we know to be
composed of an entire series of characters, any of which may
take centre stage depending on circumstance. With this view
of the human personality, Carl Jung has done much to rein-
state the value of the Greek pantheon for the monotheistic,
Christian West. People in psychotherapy now commonly
identify their various moods and tendencies with one or
another of the Greek gods and goddesses. Jung, though, saw
the gods as far more than symbols for parts of the individual

psyche. He looked upon them as archetypal forces that are actively alive in the collective mind of a culture. He considered these forces to have both a creative and a destructive potential for the culture as a whole and on individuals. Whether their influence was benign or otherwise depended on the degree of consciousness of those concerned.

This is how the gods are seen in India: as personifications of forces which are active both within the individual psyche, and on a collective and universal scale. Time, for example, is intimately connected with the goddess Kali, which partly accounts for her destructive nature. Energy – in Einstein's equation, $E=MC^2$ – is personified in India as Shakti in her various guises. Any of these forces can be benign or malevolent, and much of the worship paid to them in their personified forms is to ensure they bestow the former, rather than the latter favours. Christian missionaries, and Muslim invaders even more so, were naturally shocked at the profusion of 'idols' they found in every town and village in the country. Their distaste, however, was caused more by their own literalist manner of thinking than by any intrinsic inadequacy in the Hindu religion. The three religions of the Near East are all religions of the book. The word, which they all depend on, tends inevitably towards concretization: this is the truth, so that must be false. Once cast in stone, the truth has no freedom of movement. It becomes linear, set down for all time, and casts a shadow as dark as its words are bright. Hinduism had no founder, and no single book, foundation, or organization to set uniform standards and rules. As in life, all the subtle variations of light and dark thrive there, and are indeed encouraged to do so.

One particular deity can appear in one area under one name, and in another name or form somewhere else. At one temple or festival, Shiva is the wild and dancing ascetic who delights to live in the graveyard; in another, he is the yogi of immense erotic power, gained through millennia of spiritual discipline; in the form of Bhairava, he is the destroying demon, and elsewhere, he is the glorious lord of light and beneficence. So, too, in one celebration the Goddess will be the dark and bloodthirsty Kali, in another her name will be Gauri, meaning golden radiance. To make matters more subtle (or more complicated) still, most Indians will assure you that there is in reality only one God, though you may worship Him in the form of your choice. This is one reason for Hinduism's ready acceptance of the divinities of other religions. All the names and forms of the Lord are His primary manifestations from out of the Absolute Silence, which is, always, in the beginning and now.

That Silence exists, not in some transcendent Heaven, but here, in the hearts of human beings. For the Hindu, the human being is also a form of the Supreme, and there is no clear dividing line between the realm of the gods and of men. This is the meaning of the gesture of greeting, Namaskar, the two palms held together in front of the chest. Namaskar is made both to gods and to men, meaning, in the latter case, 'I salute the god in you'. Traditionally, a wife would see her husband as a god. Today, still, every Hindu couple is worshipped as a divine couple at least one day in their life, their wedding day. The bride and groom are treated by the family and guests as embodiments of the divine couple, Rama and Sita. In the large Shiva and Vishnu temples, the priests carry out a rite to make themselves a form of the god during the public worship, for it is said that only Shiva can worship Shiva. In this context, an individual claim to divinity does not cause the sensation it might in the West. People frequently become possessed by gods, and there are always a few great souls in India at any one time who are generally assumed to be direct incarnations of the Supreme. Jesus Christ would have had a smoother passage had he been born in India.

God's innumerable forms, and the acknowledgement of His Presence in everything, are an expression of the extraordinary vitality of India's collective imagination down through the ages. Countless local beliefs and customs have fed their way into the more orthodox, Brahminical tradition of the Vedas. This accounts for many of the animal gods, such as Hanuman the monkey, and Ganesh the elephant, which probably had their origins in tribal India. It is also an explanation for the paradoxical faces of Shiva who, over the millennia, has absorbed various minor and local deities into his worship. The Brahminical and the local folk traditions have always fed into each other, so that the classical theologies of Hinduism have continuously reflected the evolving needs of the times and the people.

This is as true today as it was in the past. In the face of growing consumerism and Western values, the spiritual streams of India still, as yet, retain their fertility. They continue to give birth to new deities, and to revolve other, ancient ones, around from relative obscurity back into renewed popularity. A few years ago, I used to wonder who these bands of men were that could be seen tramping along roads all over south India at the end of the year. They were – and still are – always dressed in a single colour, often black, sometimes green or orange. They would look intent and travel-stained, eyes pressed to the road, bare feet moving fast over the hot earth. There are so many unusual-looking characters on the pilgrim routes of India that at first I assumed them to be members of one of the innumerable sects of sadhus. Yet these people still had the look of the world on them; their uniforms, though dusty, were not time-worn, and they were not the dress of the sadhu. It was a while before I realized they were all pilgrims on their way to pay homage to Lord Ayappan.

Until fifteen years or so ago, Ayappan was a minor deity whose principal temple at Sabarimalai, in the hills of Kerala, was visited only by the hardy few who were willing to make the arduous trek up the mountain. Ayappan is the son of Shiva and Mohini, a female form of Vishnu. In the last ten years or so, his popularity has grown to such a degree that in 1994 literally millions of pilgrims made the journey to his shrine in the particularly auspicious month over December-January. This is all the more impressive when one knows the requirements of the journey. Pilgrims should have no sex, meat or eggs for the 41-day period during which the pilgrimage should take place, and should also sleep on the bare floor.

The six-mile trek is made barefoot.

The devotees are almost entirely males, since women of menstruating age are not permitted into the temple. Busloads of them are to be seen all over south India in the winter months. Why this particular god should suddenly receive such favour is not clear, although Ayappan is credited with great physical power, and his cult clearly appeals to younger and middle-aged men. They are mostly from the urban lower-middle classes, which accounts for much of that large group in India which is educated to degree standard and yet can find no work.

The same social group has also played a part in reviving the fortunes of Hanuman, the monkey god who is also accredited with supernatural strength. He is once again a favourite object of devotion. In the Minakshi temple at Madurai, which has no official shrine to Hanuman, a cult has started round a figure of him which is sculpted in one of the temple pillars. Even though most of the temple priests do not approve, since the statue has not been consecrated as a proper idol, a light burns before it continually, and a steady stream of both men and women walk round the pillar in honour of their hero. Ten years ago, nobody noticed him.

Similar developments have occurred among the female deities. In the last few years, the head of the Kali temple in Madras has popularized a rite to Durga, the warrior version of the goddess, involving the offering of a flame in a lime fruit. The rite occurs on Fridays, and is almost exclusively carried out by women. Another goddess who has recently found favour again in the south is Adi Parashakti, a form of the Great Goddess. Her recent ascendancy, however, is due to her possession of a particular individual in Tamil Nadu, who will be discussed in the chapter on the Divine Mothers.

Out of this teeming mass of heavenly beings, only a few will be likely to strike the foreign eye again and again. No-one can fail to notice Ganesh, with the elephant head and the happy belly. He is the most frequently honoured god of all. This is because he is the lord of new beginnings. Before you worship any other god in a temple, you start with Ganesh, who is usually at the temple door. He removes the obstacles that might be in the way of a devotional frame of mind, and thereby assures you a smooth passage through the rest of the temple. Hindus usually have an image of him in their homes, so that they can bow to him at the start of a new day, or before they begin any new venture. He must be propitiated at a wedding, at the new year, or at the beginning of any new business undertaking. The sophisticated Bombay businessman with international interests is as likely as anyone else to make an offering to Ganesh before signing a new contract.

He is also likely to honour Lakshmi, goddess of wealth, at the beginning of a new accounting year. Every night millions of Indian housewives light a lamp for Lakshmi in their homes, to bring her protection and well-being to their family. I was in a grubby little restaurant one evening recently, the kind that opens directly onto the road and the diesel fumes, when the owner came waddling in with a greasy tin plate in his hands. In the middle of it was a cloth wick which sent up a smoky flame. He offered it to each of his employees in turn, including the diminutive cleaner who normally cowered at the mere sight of his patron. Each of them scooped the flame up eagerly and put their hands to their heads. It was the only time in a week that I saw the cleaner look happy. Diwali, the autumn festival of lights, is dedicated to Lakshmi, and is one of the greatest celebrations in the Hindu calendar.

The reach of the most important gods of all, however, extends far beyond the others. While most of the lesser gods are called upon to intercede in daily affairs, the major gods are the lords and creators of the universe. They are Brahma, Vishnu, Shiva, and Mahadevi, the Great Goddess. The first three are the trinity of Hinduism. Brahma creates the universe, Vishnu sustains and maintains it, and Shiva draws it all back into the Primordial Zero at the end of each world cycle. For the devotees of the Divine Mother, the actions of these three come into form through the power, the shakti, of Mahadevi. Brahma has only one main temple in the whole of India dedicated to him, (in Pushkar, Rajasthan) and plays almost no part in the devotional life of popular Hinduism. Worship in India is fairly evenly offered to Shiva and Vishnu, and somewhat less to Mahadevi in her various forms. For their own devotees, each one – especially Shiva and Vishnu – is considered to contain all the other gods, and is thus the manifest form of the One Supreme Being.

LORD SHIVA

No-one can catch Lord Shiva with words. Divine trickster, he may appear as a beggar – that one in the street now, maybe – to see how you treat him; as ecstatic dancer, he is worshipped in the great southern temple of Chidambaram; most one-pointed of all ascetics, he sits on Mount Kailash in deep absorption for whole ages of time; master of all erotic power, his phallus remains constantly erect without the stimulus of desire; as Dakshinamurti, he is the greatest guru, who teaches by silence; as Bhairava, the embodiment of ferocious anger; flaunter of social convention, and yet glorious, compassionate Lord of all. Shiva is all things to all men. He passes beyond distinctions and reconciles all opposites. Being beyond description, he may be revered in any number of ways. Some take no chances, and offer their devotion by chanting all of his 1,008 names in turn. For Lord Shiva, of all the gods, is the one who points to the great space beyond names and forms.

In Chidambaram, he is worshipped as the Akash lingam as well as in the form of Nataraja. Akash, or ether, is the first element of manifestation. It spreads in all directions and makes space possible. Akash permeates the other four elements, and all that is manifest, while itself remaining invisible. In the holy of holies in Chidambaram, the lingam is said to be created of this element. It is therefore invisible to the eye, and the inner sanctum appears to be empty.

The akash lingam would not, however, be invisible to the third eye in the centre of the forehead. This, the eye of insight, is the true eye of Shiva, who is known as the three-eyed Lord. Shiva's left eye is the moon, his right eye is the sun, his third eye is the arrow of truth. This is the eye that burns away the veils of egoism, ignorance, and apathy. The fire that burns there is the inner fire that Shiva has generated through his rigorous asceticism. It is the eye which burnt Kama, the Lord of Desire, as he was about to fire his arrow at Shiva with the intention of dissolving his yogic powers.

Shiva is widely worshipped as Bhairava, who was generated miraculously from Shiva's anger as he was forced to listen to the vain boasting of Brahma. Bhairava sprang forward and cut off one of Brahma's five heads. As penance, Bhairava was destined to wander endlessly with Brahma's head stuck to his hand. Only when he reached Banaras did the head drop away and give him liberation. He is portrayed as a wild young ascetic with matted hair and an erect penis. The Kapalika sect of sadhus follow him as their principal deity. They, too, wander aimlessly with a skull (kapala) for a begging bowl, certain they will, like Bhairava, reach liberation in the end, with Shiva's grace.

Shiva's origins reach back to the pre-Aryan peoples, though the earliest existing figures of him in a purely human form, found in north-west India, date only to the first century AD. He was certainly honoured long before then in the form of the phallus, an object of devotion which is frowned on in the Vedas. Lingam shapes as old as 3,000 years have been found in Mohenjo Daro and Harappa. In the Vedas themselves, the word Shiva, meaning 'auspicious one', or 'blessed one', first appears as a description of Rudra, the storm god. Shiva is recognized as the Supreme Being for the first time in the Svetesvatara Upanishad, around 300 BC, when his original association with the fierce Rudra was developed to make him also the god of love and the source of all.

Shiva's lingam

For more than 2,000 years, Shiva has only ever been worshipped in the inner sanctum of his temples in the form of the pillar, or erect stone. This is the lingam, the uncarved block which is the closest one can come to having an image of the formless. Since remote antiquity, people not only in India, but throughout the world, have honoured pillars, or standing stones, as representations of the divine. When Jacob in his dream saw a ladder ascending to Heaven, he awoke and felt himself in the presence of God. To commemorate the occasion, he took the stone that had been his pillow, raised it up as a monument, and poured oil over it. A Buddhist text refers to the appearance of the Buddha in the form of a pillar surrounded by flames. At Amaravati, the great Buddhist temple site in Andhra Pradesh, a pillar sculpted to represent this scene is enthroned and venerated.

The vertical axis is a lightning rod: it draws down the powers of heaven to earth, joins the worlds, and thereby preserves the world order. For earthly life can only be sustained along the model of the realm of the gods. If the above and the below are separated, chaos will reign on the earth. When a person is in the presence of one of these stones, he is at the centre of the world, and his life can be harmonized according to the pattern of the divine order. For a Shaivite, this pattern is the emanation of Shiva, which acts upon the worshipper in such a way as to synchronize – and temporarily identify – god and devotee.

The original meaning of the word lingam is a 'sign', a mark which proves the existence of something. The word was first used in sacred tradition in the Svetesvatara Upanishad, which says that Shiva had no lingam, no mark – meaning that he was transcendent, 'beyond any characteristic' (*The Presence of Shiva*, S. Kramrisch). The main distinguishing mark for a human being is the sex organ, and later, the lingam also came to mean the phallus.

The phallus, though, represented not only sexual power, but the essential seed, or essence of the human being. The lingam, then, signified the existence of perceptible things, but also the imperceptible essence of something, its inherent potential. Shiva, as lingam, is essence of all, the source of all life and blessings. As such, the lingam reflects the devotee's own unmanifest nature back to him – the essence which is behind the face in the mirror.

The lingam has three parts. The root, which is in the ground, is oriented to the four directions, and is the creative force of Brahma. The base, just above the ground, usually in the form of an elliptical dish, or yoni (vagina), is Vishnu, who sustains the structure. The stone itself is Shiva, his power being gathered in behind all conceivable representation. Thus the lingam contains the power of the Trinity in One. When I visited the ancient temple of Adi Annamalai, at the base of Arunachala, there was a mirror in the inner sanctum, behind the lingam. The priest explained that this was because restoration work on the temple was being carried out. The mirror withdraws all power from the building back into the lingam. Once the restoration is finished, the mirror is smashed, and the power of the Three in One can radiate back out from the lingam to the whole temple.

The celestial pillar of light, or flame, described in the story of Arunachala mountain, is Shiva's first level of manifestation down into the material world. The pillar condenses further into pure crystal, and further still into the lingam that is found in the inner sanctuary. These lingas, which mark the direct presence of Shiva in a particular location, are known as *jyoti* lingas – lingas of light (the light of wisdom). There are twelve of these in India, listed in the Shiv Purana, though other places – like Arunachala – make their own claims to being the site of a *jyoti* lingam in other Puranas and Mahatmaya texts. Among the twelve accredited *jyoti* lingas is the one in the Vishvanath temple in Banaras; the Omkara lingam on the banks of the Narmada; the one at Kedarnath, in the Himalayas, and the one in the Shiva temple at Rameshwaram, Tamil Nadu.

The most revered of all lingas are the 'self-created', *svyambhu* – immovable natural formations which are spontaneous, miraculous manifestations of Shiva. At the human level, the self-created lingam can mean nothing less than the alchemical transformation of the devotee, with the grace of Shiva. As the light descends from above to infuse matter with being, so the individual can reverse the process and reabsorb his grosser elements into the body of light. This is the inner message of the myth, which, as always in India, assumes no separation between the divine and the human worlds.

The Lingas of the Five Elements

The other miraculous lingas are those five which are considered to represent the eternal elements of Shiva. These are all in temples across south India, and together, they form an ancient pilgrim route. The five elements constitute the known universe; as the matrix of all, they are the primary manifestation of the all-pervading power of Shiva. The fire lingam is in the temple at Tiruvannamalai; earth is manifest at Kanchipuram, water in Thiruvanaikaval, air in Kalahasti, and ether in Chidambaram. Parvati herself made the Kanchi lingam during her penance for darkening the universe by momentarily covering Shiva's eyes. She made it out of sand near the river, and prayed to it ardently for reunion with Shiva. It now stands in the sanctuary of the Ekaambareshwarar temple there. These five lingas represent the vital energies which make up our own being, and through contemplation of their significance, the pilgrimage to them is intended to deepen our awareness of our own nature, which resides ultimately in Shiva.

Shiva: Lord of the Dance

Shiva never ceases from dancing. He dances for the Goddess in her three forms of Uma, the Earth, Gauri, the Radiant One, and Kalika, the Dark One. He danced as a beggar for Parvati's hand, and he danced as Bhairava when the skull dropped from his hand in Banaras. In his ten-armed form, he dances with Kali in the cremation grounds. He is in the whirl of the atoms, in the turning of the planets, the stars and the galaxies, and above all, in the beating of the human heart. There is no end to Shiva's dance, and in his ecstasy, he flings his fiery energy and glory across the worlds.

Shiva loves the burning ground. He himself is the fire that consumes the body. What he destroys in his dancing flames are not only the worlds, but the fetters that bind the human soul. The burning ground upon which Shiva most loves to dance is the heart of his devotee. With his illusions in ashes, the lover of God has nothing else to hope for but the imminent presence of his lord.

A medieval text, the Unmai Vilakkam, (V. 32, 37, 39), says of Shiva:

> The Supreme Intelligence dances in the soul ... for the purpose of removing our sins. By these means, our Father scatters the darkness of illusion, burns the thread of causality, stamps down evil, showers Grace, and lovingly plunges the soul in the ocean of Bliss. They never see rebirths, they who behold this mystic dance.

The dancer in the heart is none other than Shiva in the form of Nataraja, the most reproduced image in all Indian art. He dances inside a circle, and the whole figure is usually cast in bronze. Despite his world-wide recognition, Nataraja is only found in the southern state of Tamil Nadu, or in temples which have come under a Tamil influence. His principal place of worship is Chidambaram (Chit, consciousness, Adambaram, boundless), which is generally recognized to be the supreme temple of Shiva. This can only be so because the essence of Chidambaram, the place of dance, the centre of the universe, is within the individual heart. The outer Chidambaram is a model of the heart, and so great is its standing, that in Tamil Nadu it is simply known as 'the temple'. The symbolism of Nataraja is explored in the chapter on Sacred Art.

LORD VISHNU

In the Hindu trinity, Vishnu ('The Pervader'), embodies the role of the sustainer of the worlds, the preserver of cosmic order. He is always associated with kingship, and usually wears a crown. People look to Vishnu for stability, certain knowledge, and the security of a solid community. He represents all the qualities most highly valued in an orthodox Hindu household, where the good of the family and the caste are more important than the individual. Only rarely is he conceived as an ascetic, although there are some ascetic orders who worship him as their principal deity.

Like Shiva, Vishnu appears only in the later Vedas, and his image first appears in the 1st century AD in the Ghandara area of north-west India. Though they may appear to have opposite roles, they frequently take on each others' attributes. The Alwar poet-saints of the south, while being staunch Vaisnavites, made no fundamental distinction between Shiva and Vishnu, while the Nayanmars, who are fervent devotees of Shiva, see Vishnu to be the left half of Shiva's form.

The major difference between Shiva and Vishnu – and the most significant fact about Vishnu himself – is that the latter takes human birth as an avatar during particular periods in the Earth's history. Shiva, although he may spontaneously appear to his devotees, never descends to earth in human form. Vishnu has come to earth in nine different incarnations which trace the span of evolutionary growth from his fish incarnation, through various animal incarnations, to his best known forms of Rama, Krishna and the Buddha. The incarnation process has enabled other gods to be subsumed into Vishnu's cult, and allows for endless new names and cults to be added. Christ is often named as an incarnation of Vishnu today, and the tenth avatar is expected at any time.

The Bhagavad Gita gives the reason for Vishnu's descent onto Earth as an avatar, when Krishna explains to Arjuna:

Though I am unborn, imperishable, and the Lord of
beings, yet, subjugating my own Prakrti, I come into
being by my own Maya.
Whenever there is a decay of dharma and a rise of
adharma
Then I embody Myself, O Bharata.
For the protection of the good, for the destruction of

the wicked, and for the establishment of dharma, I am
born age after age.

The Gita, the most widely read of all Hindu texts, forms a small
part of the huge epic, The Mahabharata. The Mahabharata is
three times the size of the Bible. Known as the fifth Veda, one
of its intentions was to bring the ancient vedas into a new for-
mulation for a new era. The Mahabharata was – and still is –
the veda for the masses, and for all castes. When it was serial-
ized on television in the early 1990s, crowds spilled over into
the streets from every cafe and public place that had a television. For that half hour every week, India fell unusually quiet.
Its message is a devotional one, centring around the idea of
god as saviour, in the form of Krishna.

The Mahabharata, and the other great epic of the same era,
The Ramayana (the story of Ram) evolved something over
2,000 years ago. This, in the Hindu conception of ages of time,
was the beginning of the dark age, the Kali Yuga, when men
and God are least able to be in communication with each
other. During such a time, which we are still in now (though
the next age is approaching), the way most open to God is
Bhakti, devotion. Vishnu's descent into human form makes
the object of devotion more tangible. Some time before the
Christian era, then, bhakti cults became increasingly popular
across India, and they continue to be the most widespread
form of worship today. Devotion is accessible to everyone,
does not necessarily require any specialist, esoteric knowledge, and is not dependent on the services of a priest. It is the
personal relationship with god that is at the heart of Vaishnavism, along with its doctrines of monotheism and divine grace.
Today, Vishnu is known and loved primarily through his incarnations of Rama and Krishna.

Yet the richest and most popular Vishnu temple in India is
dedicated to neither of these incarnations. That honour goes to
the temple of Vishnu in the form of Lord Venkateshwara, near
Tirupathi, in southern Andhra Pradesh. An average of 30,000
pilgrims a day pour through its gates, the temple serves over

3,000 free meals a day, and its annual income is in excess of five billion rupees. The temple staff number more than 6,000, and most of the funds are ploughed back into the infrastructure – pilgrim's rest houses, orphanages, homes for the poor, schools and colleges. One of Vishnu's titles is 'The Bestower of Boons', and in his form of Venkateshwara, he is the supreme fulfiller of wishes. This is why thousands flock here daily from every corner of the country. Vishnu has a different name here because of the common practice of associating Shiva and Vishnu, lords of the cosmos, with a specific location in time and space. Since they are beyond time and form, the difficulty is resolved by the development of a mythology which combines them with a local god, who then assumes all the powers of the great god. The mythology is that Venkata hill was brought to its site at Vishnu's command, because he decided to rest there when, in his boar incarnation, he had rescued the earth from the waters covering the universe after its dissolution.

LORD RAMA

The Ramayana is as popular in India as the Mahabarata. It is a glorious tale of a kingdom lost, a wandering in exile for fourteen years, a wife abducted, the lord of devils overthrown, and the eventual regaining of wife and kingdom. It is the true hero's journey, with the difference that this hero is a god in disguise. Vishnu incarnates as Prince Rama in the kingdom of Ayodhya. No-one, not even Rama himself, is aware of his true identity, though his perfection of character marks him out from everyone else. Everyone loves and admires him, and looks forward to the approaching time when Rama shall be King of Ayodhya.

By a trick of fate, however – which allows the whole story to unfold – Rama is banished from the kingdom for fourteen years, and only regains his throne after defeating Ravana, the Lord of the Devils, and freeing his wife Sita, whom Ravana had abducted.

70

Despite all Ravana's attempts to seduce her, Sita remains faithful to Rama. She insisted on accompanying Rama into the wilderness in the first place, despite his attempts to persuade her to remain in Ayodyha, with the argument that a wife should always be by her husband's side. In the patriarchal society which India continues to be, Sita is the ideal model of the perfect wife. She is one incarnation of Lakshmi, Vishnu's consort, who accompanies him in all his earthly forms. As Rhada, consort of Krishna, she will play a very different role.

Rama is the very embodiment of virtue, regality, patience and single-mindedness. He never questions what destiny places before him, he is utterly committed to his duty as a husband and as a king, fearless in battle, and so modest that he is unaware of the greatness that all others see in him. Rama is the ideal husband and head of family and kingdom.

His faithful servant, Hanuman, is the model of selfless devotion and superhuman strength. The devotees of Rama, who are mainly in the north of India, adopt Hanuman's style of devotion in the worship of their Lord. The mood is one of servant to master, a respectful distance taking precedence over the ardent lover relationship which is often assumed by the devotees of Krishna. Rama's name is said to have been inscribed all over Hanuman's heart, and chanting the name of Rama is the most common practice among his devotees today. One great saint, Neemkiroli Baba, who died in the early 1970s, is said to have had the faint imprint of Rama's name miraculously inscribed all over his body.

The various places that Rama passed through on his wanderings are today his principal *tirthas*, the places of pilgrimage for his devotees. Rameshwaram, a small town on the southern tip of Tamil Nadu, has the good fortune to be the legendary spot on the mainland from where Hanuman set about the construction of a bridge across to Sri Lanka, enabling Rama's army to cross over and face the hordes of Ravana. A chain of reefs, sandbanks and islets does in fact stretch from Rameshwaram to Sri Lanka, almost connecting them. The Ramanathaswamy Temple is the main focus of attention for devotees, who travel

71

there from all over India. The temple is equally sacred to both Shaivites and Vaishnavites, because it marks the spot where Rama, on his return from defeating Ravana, gave thanks for his victory by worshipping Lord Shiva – another instance of the mutual admiration and kinship of Shiva and Vishnu.

The two other main *tirthas* sacred to devotees of Rama are Sita's birthplace, which is in Nepal, and Rama's legendary birthplace and kingdom, the city of Ayodhya. On *Ramnavami*, Ram's day, usually in April, hundreds of thousands of pilgrims converge on Ayodhya from all over north India.

LORD KRISHNA

Krishna and Christ are the world's most refined expressions of the religion of love. Though the way they embody that love differs markedly, Lord Krishna's story, in some of its essentials, is remarkably similar to that of Christ. The birth in poor surroundings, the flight of the parents with the child, and the massacre of the male children are all features shared with the story of Christ. The traditions are also similar in their worship of the child, and the stress on complete devotion.

After that, though, the stories diverge. Krishna was so beautiful and radiated such a powerful quality of spiritual love, that all the cowherdesses – the gopis – fell in love with him. Krishna was a mischievous young man, and would not be averse to playing tricks on his devotees. On one occasion, while they were bathing in the river, he stole their clothes and draped them in a tree. He would play his flute, and they would drop whatever they were doing, steal out of their houses without their husbands knowing, and gather round him. One time, when they were at play with him in the river, Krishna disappeared. They sought him everywhere, but, unable to find him, they began to imitate his movements and exploits. This is the beginning of what is known as the Krishna lila, the 'play' of Krishna. Then they saw his footprints, and were dismayed to see that someone else's footprints accompanied him. Counting

72

their number, they realized that one of them, called Rhada, was missing. Krishna, however, had disappeared from Rhada too, and the gopis found her among the trees. They all returned weeping to Vrindavan, and there Krishna appeared again, and began the rasa lila, the famous circle dance. He played his flute in the middle of the circle, and all the gopis turned around him, each one of them convinced that he was dancing with her alone.

The rest of Krishna's life concerns his devotees little from then on, except for the magnificent portrayal of him in the Bhagavad Gita (The Song of the Lord), when he appears to Arjuna and gives him the most profound of spiritual teachings. He also appears to Arjuna in his full resplendent form, making it clear that by his grace the Lord can bless his devotees in this way. Here, Krishna is the embodiment of nobility, extolling the virtues of duty, service and, above all, devotion. The devotee's attitude in the Gita is one of respectful distance, that of the servant to his master. From the medieval era onwards, and still today, it is Krishna's early life in Vrindavan – and especially the love play of the rasa lila – that is at the heart of his devotees' philosophy and worship.

What starts out in earlier texts as child's play becomes in the 10th-century Bhagavata Purana the play of love.

Without the bristling of the hair on the body, without the mind dissolving, without being inarticulate because of tears of joy, without bhakti, how can the heart be purified?

To fan the flame of love within the hearts of his devotees, not the killing of demons and the restoration of order, is the real purpose of Krishna's descent to earth. He wants to make possible a full revelation of the godhead in the experience of his lovers.

The whole story of the Bhagavata Purana is one of complete surrender to the Lord. To be with Krishna, the gopis drop all their earthly duties, and are willing to risk the wrath of their husbands. Krishna's flute, a phallic symbol, appears for the first time in this Purana. Before then, Krishna enchanted the gopis with his voice. The play, lila, of disappearing is his way of increasing their longing for him to such an intensity that he is bound to appear before them again. Krishna purifies their desire through his separation from the gopis, and when he reappears, and the rasa lila begins, the whole dance is performed in pure spiritual love, prema.

Although Radha is barely mentioned in earlier texts, the Gita Govinda, written down in the 12th century, makes her, of all the gopis, the paradigm of devotion and the embodiment of bliss. In the 16th-century Brahmavaivarta Purana, she has become the left side of Krishna, and in the Radha Ramana temple in Vrindavan, there is an image of Krishna, but only Radha's crown, for she herself has merged into Krishna's form. In India, Krishna and Radha, above all others, are the model of spiritual love, of the new birth that comes from the union of the inner male and female. In the celestial realm, a constant stream of bliss flows between them which is the source of all the pure love between men and women on earth.

THE DIVINE MOTHERS

I'm sweating like the slave of an evil spirit,
Flat broke, a coolie working for nothing,
A ditch digger, and my body eats the profits.
5 elements, 6 passions, 10 senses –
Count them – all scream for attention.
They won't listen – I'm done for.
A blind man clutches the cane he's lost
Like a fanatic. So I clutch You, Mother,
But with my bungled Karma, can't hold on
Prasad cries out: Mother, cut this black snarl
Of acts, cut through it. Let life, when death
Closes down, shoot rejoicing up
Out of my head like a rocket.

L. Nathan and C. Seely, trans. Grace and Mercy in Her Wild Hair:
Selected Poems to the Mother Goddess

'Cut through this black snarl of acts,' the poet cries: cut through this constant idea that I am the one leading my life, running the show – that my whole existence depends on my efforts alone. Death to that idea – this is your show, not mine. I place my head in your lap. Only with your grace will life shoot through my veins again. The poem above is just one of many examples, in poetry, literature and psychology, as well as in socio-cultural affairs, of the renaissance of Western interest in the theme of the feminine, and specifically in the personified form of the goddess.

The two themes that the poet addresses – the power of the goddess to kill the ego, and her power to bestow new life – are the same threads that run through goddess mythology the world over. That contemporary writers should want to address the same themes in their own language should be no surprise, because myths are eternal: they are the ever-recurring, collective dreams of mankind. To place these themes in the context of the goddess is one contribution among many to the recovery in the West of her mythology. For centuries now – for most of the Christian era – the knowledge of the feminine mysteries of life and death has been repressed and even, in the body-spirit polarity, equated with evil. Consequently, the earth itself, the embodiment of all things feminine, has been severed from the realm of value and meaning.

Two and a half thousand years ago, the goddess was the principal deity all over the world. While signs of her presence persist everywhere in all the major religions, only in India is she still honoured and revered with a similar vitality and diversity of forms as she was at the dawn of the Christian era. For early agricultural societies, as we have seen, the fertile earth was an endless source of awe and wonder. The earth was – and in India, still is – worshipped in the many local forms of the goddess discussed in Part One, 'The Popular Tradition'. Nature's forms, being expressions of the earth's life-giving

75

powers, had their own sanctity and were worshipped in their own right. Also, right across India, there are megalithic sites which have personified the Great Earth Mother in her universal, rather than local, aspect, dating back at least as far as 8,000 BC. A prehistoric megalith in Bolhai, Madhya Pradesh, is still being worshipped today as the shrine of the Earth Mother. It is a 7-foot long, oval stone, coated in red, which rings like a bell when struck. In the Kaimur region of central India, there is a monument dating from the Upper Paleolithic era which is known locally as the shrine of Kalika Mai, Mother Kali (see *Kali, The Feminine Force*, Mukerjee). Fifteen hundred years ago, the Mother of the Universe began a progressive retreat before the advance of the patriarchal Aryan culture, only to emerge again several centuries later as the object of Shakti worship in the Tantra treatises, suitably modified for the changed times. Like all gods and goddesses (in distinction to the Supreme Godhead, which is changeless), she is a process, not a fixed event.

A current example of the vitality of The Great Goddess is her renewed popularity in her ancient form of Adi Parashakti. Under this name she is once more attracting thousands of pilgrims; this time, to an inconspicuous little village south of Madras, called Melmeamathur. The origin of this extraordinary interest lies in the tale of a man called Bangaru Adigala, who lives in the village. The story goes that at the age of ten, Adigala was walking through the fields feeling very thirsty, when he had a vision of Adi Parashakti, who came and gave milk to him. Some years later, a storm felled a neem tree in the village, and a lingam was discovered inside it. For some days after the storm, milk seeped from the tree's branches. At fifteen, Adigala had another vision of Adi Parashakti, who told him his father, who was a well-off landowner, should build a temple in her name of Mariamman. The temple was built, and Adigala worshipped there daily. By the time he was twenty, he claimed to have oracular powers, and people began to visit him for his help. He continued his profession as a schoolteacher until, at around 30 years of age, Adi Parashakti entered him permanently. He then became a full-time guru, and ever since, he has never looked back.

Now, at 53, he is regularly consulted by high state officials, and by influential figures from all over India. The village was on the main Madras-Trichy highway, but the crowds have become so great that a bypass has been made to skirt the village. Apart from the attraction of the oracle, the temple, which is now a huge affair, is rare in allowing people of all castes and creeds to enter the sanctum sanctorum. Women are allowed entrance even if they are menstruating, against which there is a strict taboo in Brahmin temples. Adigala is a non-Brahmin and the temple, as is often the case with temples dedicated to the goddess, is also non-orthodox.

As a by-product of his popularity, the Adi Parashakti shrines in the major south Indian temples, overlooked for decades, have all become the focus of a new lease of devotion.

Mahadevi is the creative energy that whirls the particles of the atom, turns the galaxies, and causes the dance of the male and the female. The electric fan in my room, as I write, has the brand name 'Devi' inscribed on it. In relation to the god, who is the supreme stillness, Devi as consort is the means by which he is able to generate the worlds. For Shakti devotees, she is not simply one of a polarity, but as Mahadevi, is the entire reality, complete in herself.

The shakti of the Mother, which whirls in and out of form in a perpetual dance, is the cause of Maya, the mystery which appears to separate us from true reality. The usual translation of Maya as illusion casts the phenomenal world in the negative light commonly attributed to it by the world's religions. The world of the senses is unreal, the world of the spirit real. This is not what is meant by Maya. It is not the flower, the sun, the moon, our wife or husband, our daily life in the world, that is unreal: everything is a manifestation of the goddess, the one reality. The mystery of Maya – her conjuring trick – is that reality is everywhere, breathes in everything, yet cannot be pointed to or named. Our urge to name and to point to answers – to try to fix the reality of something in time and space – is the illusion. The entire phenomenal world, with all its pains and all its joys, is the garden of truth; but no one flower goes by that name. Mahadevi tricks us time and again into knowing the answer – this theory, that guru, this problem, that spiritual experience – until, exhausted with our own explanations and discoveries, we fall silent. Then the world becomes whole, and everything remains as it always was.

THE BRIGHT GODDESSES

Mahadevi in her radiant, beneficent forms, is almost always the consort of one of the great gods. Parvati is the wife of Shiva, Lakshmi the wife of Vishnu, and Sarasvati, of Brahma. Parvati and Lakshmi assume many forms, according to different localities and myths, and are almost always worshipped alongside their husbands. Sarasvati, goddess of wisdom and learning, is worshipped far more than her consort, who hardly gets any attention anywhere.

The Goddess in any form, light or dark, represents power, shakti. The gods need their consorts in order to act, since by themselves, they are prior to all manifestation, the still point at the centre. 'Without you,' says Krishna to Radha, 'I am lifeless in all actions.' Only through the power of his shakti, the goddess, can Shiva bring the universe into being. In her relations with human beings, the bright goddess uses her powers to bestow life, well-being, happiness, fertility, beauty and nourishment.

In her role as consort, the goddess rarely stands alone. The fierce and dangerous characteristics of her dark sisters have, in her, been 'tamed' by her marriage to the Lord, and as such, she is the ideal Indian housewife, always at her husband's side.

THE DARK GODDESSES

Durga

I watched them for an hour or so, poor women in grimy saris, tiny women with children at their breasts and around their feet, grandmothers stooped with a lifetime of drudgery, teenage girls with oiled hair in bunches, better-off ladies in bright, ironed colours, coming and going in gaggles and streams – never alone – before the shrine of Durga in the Meenakshi Temple at Madurai. They would arrive with a lime fruit, cut it in half, fill one half with oil, and light a wick in it. Placing the lamp on the ground before the shrine, they would circumambulate the image of Durga before joining the crowd seated before Her. It was a Friday, Durga's day, and the crowd was spilling along the corridor on either side of the shrine. A few men had come along to join in the worship. Some families had brought their lunch, and the air was thick with the smell of incense, burning oil, curried vegetables and mangoes. The walls around the shrine, and much of the floor in front of it, were daubed in red paste with the sign of the trident, Shiva's emblem, but appropriate for Durga, since she is Shiva in his fierce feminine form. Now and then, one or other of the women would get up and smear another trident over the existing ones, muttering the name of the goddess to herself as she did so. Someone started up with a pair of hand cymbals, and in a few moments the crowd was swaying to the rhythm of devotional song. One woman began shaking uncontrollably, releasing every moment or so a piercing cry. Then, as suddenly as it had started, the chanting ebbed away, and people returned to eating their sandwiches, lighting another lime lamp, feeding and scolding their children.

I came away with my mind and senses alight. I had just witnessed a tiny display of the renaissance of Durga, and the power she now holds for women in India. Unlike their bright counterparts, Durga and Kali are fiercely independent goddesses. The name Durga means 'beyond reach', in the sense of virginal autonomy. Durga is nobody's lady but her own. She entirely contradicts the model of the Hindu woman upheld by the consorts of the gods. She is not subordinate to any male deity, she has no household, and far from being submissive, she excels in battle. She lives on the edge of normal society; the places She is most associated with are the wild mountains of the Himalayas, and also the Vindhya range of central India, where She is the preferred deity of many of the remote tribals.

Instead of lending her power to a male consort, Durga actually takes power from them in order to perform her warrior duties. Mythologically, her principal role is to defeat the demons who threaten the stability of the cosmos. She is a great battle queen with many arms, each one bearing a weapon. Her steed is a lion, and Her greatest victory is over the buffalo demon, Mahisa, whom none of the gods are able to defeat.

The gods are obliged to sacrifice their inner fire and heat to the creation of Durga, so that she might achieve what they alone are incapable of. She embodies their potency, and clothes it in her own form of feminine beauty and attraction. As a result, her enemies, which are always male, fall in love with her. She tells them that in order to win her, they must defeat her in battle, which they are never able to do. Durga's beauty, then, instead of serving the usual purpose of attracting a husband, entices her victims into battle, which is always fatal for them. It is difficult not to avoid the thought that Durga the Man-Eater must, at least in part, represent the vast storehouse of power and resentment which is still deeply repressed in the consciousness of traditional Indian women. It would be simplistic, however – and an insult to the goddess – to attempt to reduce a great archetypal force such as Durga to a single psychological complex.

Later on in her evolution, Durga came to assume the role of Shiva's wife, and also of a mother, though this has never compromised her independence. She has also had an ancient association with fertility and crops, for, like all the goddesses, her deepest roots are in the tribal and peasant cultures of rural India, which are still the principal source of her vitality today.

80

Sharing the ambivalent, trickster-like nature of Shiva, her male counterpart, Durga embraces the opposites. She is the Wild Woman on the edge of the world, but She is also the protector of the cosmos, in her role of destroying the demons who have usurped the position of the gods. She pervades the cosmos, She creates, maintains, and destroys it, and like Vishnu, She manifests in form in times of unusual darkness. She is a personal saviour, too, and part of the reason for her popularity is that She is willing to intercede on a devotee's behalf in times of trouble. Every goddess will play this role, in every tradition in the world; for the mother is closer than the father, always more available to soothe her child's sorrows.

Kali

In the Meenakshi temple are two larger-than-life figures of Kali and Shiva in the Tandava, the dance competition to which Kali challenged Shiva. One afternoon I sat at the foot of Shiva and watched as couples and families came by and purchased pats of butter from a man with a stall to the side of Kali. Giggling in the shy way of Indians, they stood in front of the dancing Kali and threw their butter at the statue. Kali was covered from head to foot in dripping fat. A priest's assistant was up on a platform at the level of her neck, adding to the goo by pouring coconut water over the head of the goddess, including an offering now and then of a flower. I was there for a while before I realized that butter is a coolant in the Ayurvedic system of food categorization. The devotees were helping to cool Kali down, lest, in the heat of her dance, she burn the world to a cinder.

The Tandava, in which Shiva and Kali incite each other to dance ever more wildly, has inspired a thousand songs, especially in Bengal.

Crazy is my Father, crazy my Mother,
And I, their son, am crazy too!
Shyama [the Dark One, an epithet of Kali] is my
mother's name.

My father strikes His cheeks and makes a hollow sound:
Ba Boom! Ba Ba Boom!
And my Mother, drunk and reeling,
Falls across my Father's body!
Shyama's streaming tresses hang in vast disorder;
Bees are swarming numberless
About Her crimson lotus feet.
Listen, as She dances, how Her anklets ring!

Gospel of Sri Ramakrishna, trans. Swami Nikhilananda

In Bengal (though not in the Shaivite south), Kali is usually the victor of the dance, and iconic representations show her dancing or standing on Shiva's prone body. When they are portrayed in sexual intercourse, she is usually in the superior position. Like Shiva, she loves to dance in the cemetery, all black and naked, her hair dishevelled, with a necklace of freshly-cut heads, a girdle of severed arms, children's corpses for earrings, serpents for bracelets, surrounded by jackals and goblins. Long fangs protrude from her lips, which are covered in blood. On the battleground, she is shown drunk with the blood of her victims.

Kali is the blackest of black, the hottest of hot. The essence of Durga's fury, the Devi Mahatmaya tells how she sprang from the brow of Durga to decapitate the demon generals. She is the supreme independent goddess. At the same time, she is, with Durga, one of the dark manifestations of Parvati, Shiva's wife. As consort of Shiva, she is as dangerous as ever, because she incites Shiva himself – and he needs little encouragement – to acts of wildness that threaten the stability of the universe. One can appreciate, then, why she needs all that butter, and why that priest is up there all day pouring water over her head.

Kali summons up everything that the orthodox, purity-conscious Hindu – and most of the rest of us – would rather not contemplate. She is that aspect of existence which is all-consuming – her hallmarks are death, destruction, fear and terror. She is the forbidden territory, the impure par excellence. She lives in all of us, and she perpetuates herself through the entire universal process. She represents everything beyond the pale of orthodox Hinduism, and undoubtedly she is a way for the culture to come to terms 'with the built-in shortcomings of its own refined world view. She is an escape valve, an acknowledgement of the unpredictable, the un-purifiable, the eternal threat to society's attempts to order what is essentially disorderly – life itself.' (*Hindu Goddesses*, D. Kinsley)

Kali is the preeminent deity of the Tantra school, as well as the many forms of Bengali devotionalism. What her devotees seek through their practices is her unlimited power and energy. Another name for Kali is Vama, meaning 'she who is on the left', and the left-hand school of Tantra follows Kali's example and flouts all social convention. Their guiding principle is, 'you stand by what makes you fall'. By undertaking the pancatattva ritual of the five forbidden things – wine, meat, fish, parched grain (hallucinogenic drugs?) and sex – they generate Kali's power, her shakti, and overcome the dualistic perception of clean/unclean, sacred/profane. Thus they affirm the essential unity of life; for the divine, they say, includes everything – there is nowhere and nothing in which God is not.

For the spiritual practitioner – the one who practises inner, rather than outer sacrifice – both the way of Kali and of Shiva is that of negation. Their devotees may suffer, and be disappointed in worldly affairs and desires. Neither Kali nor Shiva are ones to grant wishes – unless the wish be for an inner emptying that lays the soul bare for them alone. Only then may they come and dance there, and bestow the ultimate boon of self-knowledge.

PRIESTS AND TEMPLES

As house of the gods … the temple continually resanctifies the world, because it at once represents and contains it. In the last analysis, *it is by virtue of the temple that the world is resanctified in every part.* However impure it may have become, the world is continually repurified by the sanctuary of sanctuaries.[1]

7

To step over the threshold of a Hindu temple is to enter the half world between sleeping and waking. Even now, on approaching the main gateway of a south Indian temple, I have the sensation of entering a domain where different worlds merge. I gaze up at the huge towers, or gopurams, that stand over the four entrances, and wonder at those figures, dancing, playing the pipes, making love, defeating the demons, singing songs. They all flow imperceptibly into and out of each other, with the same creative genius that spins our dreams every night.

Then there is the shape and direction of the towers themselves. They scroll upwards for twelve stories or more, not in the way of a gothic spire that goes straight to the point, but in a circuitous, roundabout way that needs a sculpture, a figure, a scene from scripture on every square inch of the structure to validate its upward movement. The purpose of the gopuram is not in where it is going, but in the tales it tells on the way. Unlike the spire which is aspiring to Heaven, the gopuram has nowhere to go because for the Hindus, Heaven is right here, where we are, in the middle of everything else.

On the way in through the temple doorway dozens of vendors try to sell the devotee whatever he might need for his worship of the gods – coconut halves filled with bananas and

flowers to make as their personal offering; camphor to offer a
flame to the Lord; sandalpaste; red kum-kum powder; picture
postcards of the supreme deity of the temple; but also an
incongruous assortment of anything from plastic toys, buckets, brooms, aluminium frying pans, pots, bangles, beads, to
cassettes and even transistor radios. At the doorway itself the
line of beggars sits on either side: twisted bodies, scraps of
sackcloth, leprous stumps for hands, feet in bandages, limbs
like twigs, impervious to the swarming flies – yet smiling at
times with toothless grins, life undefeated by the proximity of
death. Behind the withered beggars the voluptuous form of
the goddess, Ganga, with the most ample of breasts, holds life-
giving vines which twist their way upwards in fruitful plenty
to the vault above.

Just beyond the beggars, there, on the left over the threshold, is Ganesh the elephant in a niche in the wall, a camphor
flame at his feet, oil over his blackened body, the remains of a
flower in his lap. The Remover of Obstacles, just three feet
away from the last outstretched hand in the line. I have
stepped over the threshold into the first great courtyard of
Arunachalesvara temple in Tiruvannamalai. On the left is a
large rectangular water pool – the Brahma Tirtha tank – with
three steps leading the worshipper down to where he may
bathe his impurities away before proceeding any closer to the
sanctum. Huge fish leap out of the water to catch the puffed
rice thrown to them by the devotees. In front of me is the next
gopuram, its archway an invitation to the second courtyard,
another step closer to the Lord. Huddles of people sit before
one or other of the shrines of this first, large open space; some
are eating, playing with children, others are prostrating
towards the inner sanctum, or towards one of the shrines in
the courtyard itself. Hawkers are selling postcards still, sadhus
in orange are lounging along a wall.

Five rectangular courts in all draw the worshipper in ever-
decreasing circles – he should circumambulate each one before
proceeding into the next – towards the garba-grha, the womb
house, where the worshipper is reborn. In the fourth court,

the temple elephant takes offerings, rolls his trunk in a salute, and places it gently on the head of the devotee in blessing. Every evening, he kneels before the shrine of Ganesh and trumpets his praise to the deified form of his own kind.

On the way to meet the supreme King and Lord, the devotee will pay his respects to the King's family and retinue, each having their own shrine, and often more than one, in the various courtyards. Ganesh will be worshipped first in any temple, since he gives access to the rest of the court. Then, in a Shiva temple, Lord Murugan is usually next, while in a Vaishnavite temple, the goddess Lakshmi is likely to take the place of Murugan.

Ganesh and Murugan are Shiva's two sons. To place Ganesh first in order of worship has an inherent logic. As the personification of auspicious beginnings, he also represents the capacity to succeed in the world, and the fulfilment of worldly desires. Hinduism recognizes that a person cannot proceed very far on the spiritual journey until – either in this birth or in a previous one – he has satisfied his search for worldly fulfilment. Only having done this, and recognized that he is still not content, will he search for happiness at a deeper, more spiritual level. Then (in the south, where practically all the major Shaivite temples are) he will see Murugan, rather than Ganesh, as his personal deity. For Murugan is the Warrior Lord of Yoga. He is both the energy of will required to practise the disciplines of raja yoga, and the esoteric knowledge of yoga itself. In other courtyards, the shrines of the saints may help him further on his way to the ultimate guru, Lord Shiva himself, and his consort, the Universal Mother, Queen Parvati. On the way to Shiva, the planets of the solar system will also be honoured. Any Hindu, whether a nominal devotee or a spiritual practitioner, will recognize the power of celestial influences over his destiny, and will smooth his own passage through life by paying homage to the Navagraha, as the shrine to the planets is called.

A southern temple such as Arunachalesvara is a sophisticated diagram of the spiritual journey of the worshipper towards the centre of his own being. The journey from one courtyard to the next is a progressive interiorization, away from the daylight world of ordinary affairs through arrangements of space that become ever more closed and dark; so that when you eventually reach the inner sanctum, you are in a small, cave-like womb, where the only light is from the flame that is offered to the Lord. The entire ground plan of the temple is a mirror not only of the human body but also of subtle anatomy. The five courtyards represent the Hindu conception of the five bodies of the human being; so the journey from the outer courtyard to the sanctum is a passage from the physical level of existence, through the subtle realms of being, to the bliss body of the inner sanctum, where you come face to face with God. The sanctum has two side entrances, representing the ears, and the god is seated in the place of the third eye. In a Shiva temple, the image of Nataraja, The One who Dances in the Heart, is to the left and below the main deity, just as the human heart is below and to the left of the head.

From the 5th century AD, the first free-standing temples began to appear in the north, which had international contacts with the temple-building peoples of Western Asia. In time, with the exception of Khajuraho, all these great temples were sacked by the invading Muslims, so that those which remain today are mostly of regional importance. It was only some centuries later that temple building began in the south. There, however, the culture was spared the invasions suffered by the north, and the temples founded 1,200 years ago are still flourishing today.

Temples in the south evolved distinct features which have never been part of the northern tradition. By the 15th century, the gopuram, the temple gateway, had become the most visually dominating feature of the entire temple. Not long after that, gopurams were being built in a series, one over the entrance of each successive courtyard, such as can be seen in Srirangam, Minakshi, and Arunachalesvara temples. As well as being symbols of royal power, the gopurams were also representations of the feet of the divine being, which could be

87

seen and remembered throughout the surrounding area. The feet of the god, and also of the guru, are considered to be the source of a continual stream of blessings.

In the north, on the other hand, the shikara, the tower over the sanctum, has always been the dominant feature. It represents Mount Meru, the Centre of the Universe. The sanctum is the 'cave' at the foot of the 'mountain'. Whereas, in the south, all major temples are built on a grand scale, there was never the confidence in the north to make such dramatic statements. By the 16th century, temples in the south were urban units in their own right, with a huge staff, successive enclosure walls one within the other, and their imposing, brightly-painted gopura which could be seen for miles around. At one time, Chidambaram temple had 3,000 priests actively engaged in service. Now, there are 300.

Through all the vicissitudes of history, the temple has retained characteristics from the earliest period of the Vedas. The design of the temple, ordained with precision in the shastras at around the time of Christ, was a representation of the form of Purusa, the first human being, and of the cosmos, based on the original construction of the sacrificial altar. God was at the centre, surrounded by the concentric squares of his creation. The square, the archetypal pattern of order, was oriented to the cardinal directions. The macrocosmic plan was mirrored in the microcosm of the human being, so the temple is a map of the different levels of consciousness both in the human being and in the cosmos.

The early cave temples have also left their mark in the temples of today. Temples constructed from caves continued the principles of the ancient cult of the Mother Goddess. The worship of the Goddess centred around the theme of fertility, and by extension, the rites of death and rebirth. These same themes were taken up by the devotionalist Buddhist movements, and in their turn by the Hindus. The devotee is reborn by his pilgrimage to the temple. Insemination happens in the dark, in mystery, and the central shrine of the Hindu temple is called 'the womb house', a small black cave from which new life is born.

Love of the Mother Goddess has continued unbroken in India for thousands of years, and devotion to her still continues today in the outer courtyard of the temple. There you will see clusters of snake/naga figures in a corner, or under a tree. Or there may be some upright stones, daubed with a red eye, near a well, or the sacred tank. One or more trees will be laden with the rag cradles that women have put there to express their desire to the Goddess for children. All levels of activity and worship take place in the temple simultaneously. Animism continues in the outer courtyard, business deals are struck in a corner, streams of people come to worship in the normal, orthodox manner, and here and there, at the foot of a pillar, a yogi or a sadhu will be seated in deep contemplation.

In the West a sacred place is usually a haven of quiet where, if people speak at all, they do so in hushed tones. In India, the temple is designed to draw you out of yourself, into ecstasy, rather than encourage a personal withdrawal away from the world. Those who want to sit in silence are free to do so, but they must immunize themselves from the noise around them, an ability which all Indians seem to be born with. The garish colours, the images – by turns fierce, voluptuous, contemplative, dancing – the flames of the lamps, the smoke, the incense, the drums, the pipes, the Vedic chanting, the heat and the press of the crowd – the whole experience makes for sensory overload, an ecstasy which literally shocks you out of your mind and into the realm of the gods.

DARSHAN, PUJA, AND PRASAD

Somehow I had managed to squeeze myself into the small antechamber that just precedes the dark sanctum of Lord Arunachalesvara, in his temple at Tiruvannamalai. It is utterly blackened in there with the smoke of centuries. No ornament or statuary diverts the eye from the image of the deity. The tiny room was thick with heat, smoke, the clanging of bells and the flicker of flame. It was dark, just a few moments before the curtain would be drawn back to reveal the Lord to his disciples. This was one of the last *pujas* of the day. *Puja* generally refers to ritual worship of any kind, though when I turned back to look behind me, I could appreciate its literal meaning of 'adoration': hundreds of people were straining forward for a glimpse of their god. The men were on the right, the women on the left, of a narrow corridor of space that had been left empty. Shiva's mount, Nandi the bull, was at the entrance to the sanctum, and the corridor enabled him to have a clear view of his beloved master. I was huddled in among the others who had managed to secure a ringside place. We had received the ash and the red kum-kum powder from the priest, smeared the first across our foreheads, and applied a dot of the kum-kum between the eyes. I had just, to my shame, let the offering of sugared water the priest had poured into my hand slip through my fingers. The banana and coconut goo he handed out next caused me a second inner struggle.

My back was turned to him – it was the crowd I was in awe of. They leant far over the rails of Nandi's corridor for a clearer view. Some even climbed on the rails and hung by an arm and a leg in the way of Nandi's gaze, but they were quickly put back into line with a swish of the peon's cane. Suddenly, a great bell was struck; immediately the devotees became like one body: crying out the holy mantra, Aum, in chorus, all stood on tiptoe in one motion, and those by the rail, the peon helpless now, strained in front of Nandi, eyes bulging out of their heads at the sight of Lord Arunachalesvara. Somewhere outside, firecrackers were exploding.

I turned back to face the sanctum. The curtain had been drawn back and the lingam of Shiva, magnificently costumed in flower garlands, jewels, and fine cloths, was revealed. More than all his other finery, the gold visor that was wrapped around his eyes captured the gaze of all. *Darshan*, the seeing of the Lord, had occurred. I was in the presence of genuine and fervent devotion, and for all my Anglican cultural heritage and my personal predilection for silent, imageless contemplation, I was shaken and moved.

Foreigners have scorned the Hindu love of idols for centuries. What they have never understood is that the Hindus are not idol worshippers. They know as well as anyone – probably even more so – that God can never be reduced to an image. What the devotee's gaze is fixed on in darshan is the eyes of the idol. Through those eyes streams the power that lives in the image through the grace of the god and the invocations of the priesthood.

This is why the eyes are always larger in proportion than the rest of the image, and why a red eye is daubed on the stones that are sacred to the goddess of a village. It is not the image, but the power in the image, that is worshipped by the devotee. Through the ritual of its creation according to precise instructions in the shastras, through the invocatory rituals of its installation, the image becomes the home of the god, who, while existing throughout time and space, and beyond, agrees to dwell in the temple image with focalized power. This is indeed the realm of magic, which can only be intuited by one who accepts the reality of the subtle worlds, and their influence upon the physical domain. The quintessence of the magic, and the whole purpose of a pilgrimage to the temple, is the darshan of the lord.

The seeing is a two-way process: the god sees the devotee, just as the devotee sees the god. In this meeting of eyes, devotee and lord become one. For a brief span, the devotee is identified with the god who, in the deepest sense, is his own life source. The entire puja is a progressive identification of man and god, culminating in the meeting of eyes and the passing of the flame, the arati, that ends the ritual. The flame is passed before the image of the god, and then brought to the devotees for them to pass their hands through and put them to their eyes. The god sees the face of the individual in the flame, and his power is transmitted through the flame into the person's eyes.

'Don't forget, though,' said Professor Saraswati, when I discussed the subject of darshan with him back in Delhi, 'that even a blind man goes to the temple for darshan. It is not the physical eyes, so much as the inner eye, or the third eye, that receives darshan of the lord. The meeting happens in the intuitive, supersensible realm. And since that realm is not limited to time and space, this allows the untouchables, who were traditionally never allowed into the temple, to have darshan merely by looking at the temple from the outside; while someone living some distance away can have darshan by looking at the tall gopurams. The essential exchange goes on in the mind.'

It is difficult for a foreigner to appreciate how deep the importance of darshan is for the ordinary Hindu, unless perhaps he wakes early on the first day of a month and attends the first puja, for the wakening of the god. This is the most auspicious time for darshan, and streams of people are to be seen making their way to the temple. On the first morning of Margali, the Tamil month that spans December and January, huge crowds press through the darkness for the first darshan. In Madurai, outside the Minakshi temple, police have to order queues desperate for their prasad of milk. By dawn, 20,000 devotees will have been to the temple.

The daily round of pujas in a temple only makes sense to an outsider when they realize that they have entered a royal palace, of which the god is the living sovereign. The other gods in the temple are part of the lord's family and court, and the priests are the servants to the royal household. The pujas follow the rhythm of the king's day. He is ceremoniously awakened in the early morning, bathed, clothed, and fed. He is fed at other times in the day, and then put to bed in the evening. The awakening and bed rituals are usually carried out with smaller, doll-like figures of the king and his queen, rather than with the main idols. Often, each doll has its own royal apartment, the king and queen only being brought together for the night, when they are seated together on the royal swing. Each temple has its own variation and particular customs. Typically, there will be six or eight main pujas during the day, which are offered separately to the king and then to his queen.

The puja is a public opportunity to make offerings to the king and to have his audience. The fruit and flower sellers, the shopkeepers at the entrance to the temple, depend for their livelihood on the pilgrim's generosity to the god of the temple. He may buy a plant sacred to that lord, a flower garland, fruit, camphor, a small basket of food, a tray of sweets, or even some fine cloth or a piece of jewellery.

The deity first receives a number of dousings – abishekam – of saffron, riceflour, sandalpaste, rosewater, lime, honey, coconut water and milk. Each abishekam serves to cleanse the souls of those present. Outside the sanctum is a spout in the form of some animal through which the liquid offerings drain away into a tank. I watched entranced one day as a five-year-old boy sat beneath this spout in the Minakshi temple drenching his head in the god's holy left-overs, totally absorbed in singing the name of the lord in a high staccato voice.

After the abishekam, the deity is dressed in fine cotton, silks, and gold, the food offerings are made to him, and are then distributed among the devotees in token quantities. This receiving of *prasad* – the food which has already been offered to the deity – is the first communion between god and devotee. While the Shiva temples lean more towards the abishekam ritual, the temples to Vishnu are more fond of food offerings. In the Jagganath temple to Krishna at Puri, the deity receives 52 food offerings a day!

Flower garlands are draped over the image, and finally, just before the drawing back of the curtain and the darshan, special lamps are waved before it in the form of Aum. Throughout the ceremony, the priests are intoning sanskrit mantras and verses from the *Agamas*, bells are tolled periodically, and the whole spectacle ends at the darshan with firecrackers.

Nothing in these ceremonies happens fortuitously. The physical actions, materials and offerings all have a significance beyond their appearance. The perfume of a flower is its spiritual essence. The devotee will never smell his own flower offering, since to do so would be to deprive it of its essential quality before the deity has received it. The ash you are given in a Shiva temple to smear across your forehead is a reduction of wood to its purest form. Ash cannot be made any purer than it already is; it is the same with a devotee in the presence of the god. The sandalpaste you are offered, a gift of the sandalwood tree, is a symbol of supreme compassion; for the tree exudes its scent even to the axe that fells it. The red kum-kum powder, a gift of the goddess, is the sign of her power of wisdom. The camphor which is used for the arati flame leaves no sooty residue. Its intangible display of light and fragrance represents the god's transcendence of form, as well as its embodiment. It symbolizes the transcendence of the devotee, too, since in the flame, god and devotee become one.

With such generous blessings bestowed on the devotee, why should he need to keep coming back for more? The entire drama is re-enacted just a few hours later in a slightly different format because Hindus have an innate sensitivity to the impermanence of everything. The liquid offerings drain away,[2] the flowers fade, the camphor flame quickly goes out, the ash rubs off, the oil dies in smoke. All this points to one thing: the devotee's identification with the deity is fleeting, and the puja must be repeated over and again for him to maintain his connection with the divine.

He can also do this in a private puja of his own. Families may come for a blessing of a house move, for the curing of sickness, or for divine assistance in any undertaking. The simplest offering is a camphor flame which they can light for themselves before their chosen deity. Or they may buy a small basket of coconut and fruits to give to the priest of the main deity.

The large temples have a scale of offerings from a fruit basket up to donations sufficient to make the priests toll the bells and walk in procession round the outside of the temple. 'Donate liberally and get goddess blessings,' it says in large letters in the Minakshi temple. And people do. In the large temples of the south, the number of devotees is increasing, along with the scale of offerings. While 20,000 people visit Minakshi temple daily, at Tirupathi the crowds are in hundreds of thousands, and the gifts pouring in are worth millions of rupees a day.

When I conveyed to Professor Saraswati how impressed I was by these figures, he quickly put them in context. 'Remember,' he said, 'that the temple is not a church. Hindus do not need to go to the temple to be Hindus. Worship for us is not primarily a collective affair. It is individual, and as many as go to the temple, a hundred times more practise their worship in other ways. God is everywhere for us. He can be in a tree, a stone, or a river. We can interact with God through our relationship with our parents, our marriage partner, and also by the giving of gifts – even to animals. Vishnu incarnated as a fish and a boar; the gods and goddesses are always being born in animal as well as human form; so in offering a gift to another, we are honouring the divine. Traditionally, the guest is a manifestation of god for us, which is why, if you go to a devout Hindu family, you are treated so well. Instead of being central, the temple is one part of the mosaic of life in which everything is seen to be sacred. That is the inherent freedom of the Sanatana Dharma – you can go to a temple or not, on pilgrimage or not, worship some deity or not: everything is within, and what you do externally is a matter of your individual choice.'

THE PRIESTS

Priests in India have always had a bad name. Even 2,000 years ago, they were denounced in the laws of Manu as money-grabbing incompetents. Like any closed shop, they incur the jealousy and resentment of outsiders who begrudge having to pay for their services. Not all Brahmins are priests, but all priests belong to one or another of the sub-sects of Brahmins. Their positions are passed down from father to son, guaranteeing employment in a society in which millions eke out a subsistence living, and millions more, highly educated, can find no work. Hindu priests have married since Vedic times, with the rationale that only man and woman together constitute a unity, and that the man needs the shakti, energy, of the female in order to properly serve the deity. The result is that a particular family is guaranteed a living into posterity. In reality, most of those livings, in the thousands of small temples across India, are meagre. Only those born into the more famous temple complexes can hope to earn a decent wage.

The claim of incompetence is more widely true. Each large temple uses its own selection of the agama texts for its worship, and at their simplest, the agamas rival in complexity the Book of Revelation. Few of the older priests today have any idea what they are chanting, and some of them even make up gibberish, knowing full well that the pilgrims will be none the wiser. Hardly any of the older priests have even a rudimentary knowledge of Sanskrit.

Happily, the picture is changing. Over the last ten years or so, at least in the larger temples of the south, the younger priests have become more educated, and some are learning Sanskrit. Whereas in the eighties it was politically expedient to be anti-Brahmin and anti-religion, the Tamil Nadu government (Tamil Nadu is 'the temple state')is now actively encouraging temple worship. The Chief Minister, who is herself a Brahmin (any connection?), has set up a Temple Renovation Fund and has begun opening Sanskrit schools. The first priest of the Minakshi temple to begin a formal training in the Vedas and Agamas did so only in 1976. By 1994, ten of Minakshi's 80 priests had completed a course at a Sanskrit college, while ten others were also enrolled. Some of them also have degrees, and they now see themselves as professionals. Their self-image is improving, and they are better off financially due to the increase in the middle classes, who constitute a large percentage of the temple's devotees.

Sadashivam, one of the priests in the service of Minakshi, is a member of the Adisaiva caste of Brahmins, who have had exclusive rights to the Minakshi priesthood for over a thousand years. I met him in his tiny house near the temple. He told me he had been a telephone operator until the death of his father, whose position as a priest of the temple needed to be taken up by a member of the family. His elder brothers, all of whom were in the professions, chose him for the job. Sadashivam was 32, and happy enough to oblige, since his prospects in the telephone company were not bright. Now, at 57, he is a respected member of his family and community, and when I met him, he had just spent a year in Canada serving in a new temple there. Many temples are now being built abroad to cater to the needs of the large Indian expatriate communities, and they offer increasing opportunities for a lucrative career move for priests of a large temple in India. Sadashivam, like any other priest who has spent a term in the West, returned laden with consumer durables that a priest of an earlier generation could only have dreamed of. His son, a man in his twenties, assured me he would be following in his father's footsteps.

The priests at Chidambaram temple are an exception to the rule in every way. To begin with, their haircuts rival the more outrageous ones to be seen in London or New York. Half their head is shaved, while the left half is allowed to grow into a long black mane which is tied into a top knot. In this way they embody both male and female, the union of Shiva and Parvati. They all belong to the Dikshitar community, which claims it was brought to Chidambaram 3,000 years ago by Nataraja to serve in his temple (which in fact is no more than 1,500 years old.) The Dikshitars still live by traditions that have remained unchanged for centuries, rather like the Amish in North America, or the Hassidic Jews. All marriages occur within the clan, and at an early age, usually when the children are around seven years old. The couple live together when the girl has reached puberty, and from then on the woman will wear a nine-yard sari, and live her life between the kitchen and the family puja room. As soon as a male child can speak, he attends the home prayers, the temple pujas, and all religious festivities. When he is seven, he begins regular Vedic classes. A Dikshitar priest is unusually devout and highly knowledgeable, both in the scriptures and in the traditions of his temple.

How long their way of life can survive, however, remains uncertain. Their birthrate has fallen drastically in the last few decades, almost certainly the consequence of their strict inbreeding. Their exclusively religious way of life is also under severe economic pressure. Chidambaram is the only temple in Tamil Nadu to remain outside of state control, thanks to a legal battle in which the Dikshitars claimed that the temple and its lands had always been the personal private property of the clan. The Dikshitars retain their pride and control of their temple, but they forfeit the rights of state and government aid, even though Chidambaram is known as the temple of temples. Despite its reputation, Chidambaram is off the main tourist routes, and the small town provides only a trickle of local devotees. Already many of the younger priests are finding part-time employment to supplement the subsistence living they make from the temple offerings.

The one area of public life where Brahmins still enjoy all their old privileges is religion. Thanks to the legal reforms and political pressure on them during the 1980s, they no longer retain the socio-economic power that enabled two per cent of the population to dominate the culture for centuries. Caste quotas now ensure that most of the university places and government posts go to members of the other castes, who represent the vast majority of the population. But only a Brahmin can be a priest, and only a specialist sub-caste can be a priest of a large and important temple. The other castes have won many victories over the last decade, although they still have a long way to go before India has a society of equal opportunity, or even a genuine democracy. Even so, Indians in general are willing to concede that religion is the rightful domain of the Brahmin. The priest, I was assured, will always remain a necessary evil.

1   Eliade, M. *The Sacred and The Profane*. Ibid.
2   This description of the impermanence of the puja owes much to *The Camphor Flame*, C. J. Fuller, Penguin, New Delhi 1992.

FESTIVALS

8

Just as the temple is a sacred space, a festival is an emergence of sacred time into the ordinary temporal flow. In India, a festival is being celebrated somewhere every week. The Hindu festival is sacred because it re-enacts in the present a primordial mythical time. It is a sacred drama which is not remembered, but reactualized; everyone who takes part is renewed by a return to the timeless 'beginning' – the eternal present – in which the myth has its roots. The festival relives a particular myth which either has relevance to a specific location, which celebrates the dawning and passing of the seasons, or which is the passion play of one of the gods or goddesses. The sacred time of the festival re-establishes the community within the divine order of the cosmos and, in asserting its divine origin, reaffirms the sanctity of human existence.

Just as every village has its own festival, so does every temple and region. The festivals which most closely resemble the ancient art of sacred drama are those of the major temples. Some of these, like the Car Festival of the Jagannath temple in Puri, which takes place in June or July, have an international reputation. Celebrating the journey of Krishna from Gokul to Mathura, the images of Jagannath ('Lord of the World') and his brother and sister are taken with great fanfare out of the temple and dragged in huge 'cars' through the city to the garden house of the gods. The main car of Jagannath, riding on sixteen wheels and fourteen metres high, is hauled along an inch at a time by 4,000 temple employees and even early in this century devotees frequently threw themselves in front of the 'juggernaut' (the English word was originally a term for Jagannath's 'car') so that they could die in the god's sight. Hundreds of thousands of pilgrims flock to Puri from all over India for this spectacular festival. When the gods reach their garden house, they take their summer break for a week and are then wheeled back to the temple and the festivities reach a climax all over again.

The Meenakshi temple in Madurai holds its festival on the full moon day of the month of Chittirai (April-May). The entire city turns out throughout the day and the night to celebrate the marriage of the local goddess Meenakshi with Shiva in his form of Sundareshwara. Like any marriage celebration, it is a joyous and often wild affair. Devotees dress in yellow and dance for hours in the procession that follows the couple round the outer walls of the temple in the middle of the town. The goddess is decked in fine jewellery, adorned with a pearl crown and brought out from the temple on a golden bull, the mount of Shiva. 'How beautiful she looks!' the crowd exclaim. Meenakshi is given away by her brother, with a fine trousseau of gems, studded jewel crowns and sweetmeats.

Maha Shivaratri, the main festival dedicated to Shiva, is celebrated all over India, but nowhere with more fervour and devotion than at the Matangeshwara temple of Khajuraho. Shivaratri occurs every month on the dark night of no moon, but the great festival is in the month of Phalgun (February-March), the last month of the Hindu year. Since this period is the most inauspicious time of the year, the festival of Shiva, whose name means 'The Auspicious One', counteracts the dark forces of that time. Some 20,000 people descend on the village of Khajuraho for the annual celebrations, which at this temple are centred on the divine marriage of Shiva and Parvati.

In her book, *Divine Ecstasy*,[1] Shobita Punja has shown how the erotic sculptures of Khajuraho are an illustration in stone of the Shiv Purana, which narrates the story of how Shiva reduced Kama, the god of desire, to ashes and then went on to marry Parvati, free of all longing. Far from being in honour of Kama, the sculptures depict his defeat and celebrate the consummation of the divine couple. The lingam in the Matangeshwara temple – one of the largest in India, some eight feet high – is said to be a swayambhav lingam, one which manifested spontaneously at the moment when Shiva destroyed the god of desire. The various temples at Khajuraho were built, Punja contends, as the abodes of the gods on the occasion of the divine wedding.

The wedding is re-enacted each year during the night of Shiva's festival. The eleven Brahmins chosen to serve as the marriage priests gather at the pandit's house and from there the procession begins towards the temple, led by a band. A great crown, symbolizing Lord Shiva, made by the local bamboo weavers each year, is borne along in state on the roof of an Ambassador car, which has come to replace the traditional elephant. The streets are thronged with devotees and thousands more wait at the entrance to the temple, waving flags and chanting wedding songs. Far from being onlookers, the pilgrims consider themselves to be the couple's wedding party.

The crown is carried ceremoniously up the steps and placed on the top of the Shiva lingam, while the Brahmin priests who are to conduct the ceremony sit around the lingam in a semicircle. Local Brahmins who are the 'family members' of the bride, sit on the other side. The 'father of the bride' wears a turban as a mark of respect for the visiting dignitaries. The chief priest plays the role of Lord Brahma, who performed the rites at Shiva's marriage in the Shiv Purana. The night is divided into four parts and each one begins with devotions to the lingam, with bathing, washing and the applying of ash from the burial ground at Banaras. The lingam is dressed in a white dhoti with a yellow sash and during the course of the night is transformed into a handsome bridegroom. A chillum of hashish is offered to the Lord and the wedding party follow his example. Throughout the entire ritual, the Brahmins are chanting prayers, until finally, at around 4am, the wedding completed, the couple are taken to the temple steps to see the pole star, 'the only constant in the universe, a symbol of the steadfastness of conjugal love'.

Soon after Shivaratri, the spring festival of Holi is an excuse for wild abandonment and revelry all across India. Bonfires celebrate the passing of winter, people paint their faces and gangs of youths run through the cities throwing bags of coloured water or red powder over anyone who happens to be passing by. Holi commemorates the time when Krishna and his cowherd friends visited Radha's village and challenged the girls to match their skill in showering one another with coloured powders and water. The tradition began in Braj, the area around Vrindavan sacred to Krishna and was probably absorbed from a local festival into the Krishna story during the medieval era, when the bhakti movement was at its height.

In Braj, Holi continues to be a sacred as well as a joyous occasion. On the first day of spring, forty days before the full moon of Phalguna, (February-March), when the rest of the country celebrates Holi, the temples in Vrindavan have their first sprinkling of colour and the singing of Holi songs begins. Each temple has its own tradition of samaj, the sung recitation of Krishna's exploits, and during the forty days of Holi is the best time to hear these ecstatic expressions of sacred music. Each day, in the temple of Radha-Madanamohana, exquisite-ly refined colour decorations are drawn for the deities by the temple priests during the samaj.

Holi only officially begins in Vrindavan on the eleventh day of the waxing lunar fortnight, when the temple priests squirt coloured water over the devotees. In the streets no-one is spared, not even the animals, for in Vrindavan, everyone takes each dousing to be the blessing of Radha and Krishna. Festivi-ties begin in earnest three days earlier in the temple on the hill of Barsana, Radha's village. A messenger is sent from Krishna's village, Nandagaon, informing the gopis that Krishna will be coming the following day. Devotees throw colours over each other and over the musicians singing the samaj. The temple staff fill cloths with large quantities of coloured powder and repeatedly throw them over the singers, who quickly come to resemble rainbows. Sadhus dance in wild abandon and even some of the women join the dancing, which they would never do except during the sacred time of Holi.

Holi in Braj is an extraordinarily rich and layered mythic event, with many social, spiritual, cultural and artistic dimensions. The huge bonfire which marks its culmination, like every other detail of Holi in Braj, has its mythological background which is beyond the scope of this brief account. That night of the Holi full moon is one of unbroken revelry and gaiety, which continues through until noon of the following day, when everyone goes to bathe in the Yamuna river. In the temples, Radha and Krishna are seated on a swing, decorated as if in a flowery grove, quiet at last after days of unceasing play.

At the other end of the year, in September-October, the festival of the goddess Durga is the most popular one of the season, especially in northern India and Bengal. In its own way it is as raucous as Holi. Its name, Navaratra, signifies its duration of nine nights. The first three days are dedicated to Durga, Goddess of Protection and Valour; the second three days honour the goddess in her form of Lakshmi, Bringer of Wealth; and the last three days are given to Sarasvati, Goddess of Wisdom and Letters. The tenth day, the Day of Victory, celebrates with wild revelry the myth in which Durga slays the buffalo-demon, Mahisa. A male buffalo is still sacrificed on that day to commemorate the event.

Traditionally, Navaratra celebrated royal and military power and in later versions of the Mahabharata and the Ramayana, the Pandava kings and Rama invoked Durga before battle. The festival's origins, however, lie in the fertility rites common to harvest festivals everywhere and this is still a central feature of the rituals today. Nine plants are identified with Durga, as is a pot filled with Ganga water. The priest scatters five grains around the pot and honours it as the source of the nectar of immortality (amrit), which the gods churned from the ocean of milk at the beginning of time. Durga, then, is invoked both as the power to promote growth in the grains and as the power of life through which the gods achieved immortality. At one stage during the temple rituals, she is addressed as 'She Who Appeases the Hunger of the World'.

In the villages of Bengal, the women sing songs of welcome to Durga at daybreak for several days before the beginning of the festival. In many parts of north India, clay or plaster objects, gaudily painted with floral and faunal designs, are placed in the central hall of the house. Paper garlands decorate the homes and meals are made from all the pulses and cereals of the nine holy plants. Elderly ladies offer their neighbours betel, kum-kum and other things sacred to married women, to wish them a long and happy married life.

The largest celebration of any kind in the world takes place in India once every three years. The site of the Kumbh Mela rotates between the four cities of Haridwar, Allahabad, Ujain and Nasik. In 1989, some 18 million people converged on Allahabad, for the Great, or Maha, Kumbh Mela which happens every twelve years. They all come to take their bath in the Ganga on the same auspicious day and though the bathing area around the sangam, the confluence of the three rivers, permits 300,000 to bathe in an hour, twice as many actually scramble into the water in that time. The temporary township of tents and huts that springs up around the sangam during the Mela covers 3,600 acres. The fair has been celebrated since the 2nd century BC. The first written record of it was by a Chinese traveller, Hiuen Tsiang, in the 7th century, who mentions the presence there of Buddhist and Jain monks as well as Hindus.

The origins of the Kumbh Mela are founded, predictably, in myth. Long ages ago, the gods and the demons fought a great battle for possession of a khumb, or pitcher, which contained the nectar of immortality. Together the gods and asuras raised the pitcher from the depths of the ocean, but as soon as it was in the light of day, Vishnu grabbed it and ran off. After a battle lasting twelve days, the gods finally defeated the demons and drank the amrit. During the battle, four drops of nectar fell to earth where the four cities are now. The Kumbh Mela

104

celebrates the victory of the gods.

Shankara is said to have asked the heads of his four maths, or monasteries, to always meet at the Kumbh Mela to discuss the mutual affairs of their monasteries. Whether he did so or not, the Mela has long been the occasion when sadhus of every denomination come from all over India to meet and to re-establish contact with their Orders. Most of the great gurus and teachers also attend the Mela. Many Orders perform their initiations during the fair and for the Naga babas, the Mela is the only time they are initiated.

The Mela is above all for the benefit of the sadhus, who are always the first to bathe in the river at the most auspicious moment. There is a strict order of precedence, with the Shaiva Nagas going first, then the Vaishnava Nagas and so on. They march to the river in full regalia, announced in advance by loud bands, while the gurus and heads of the Orders are brought in palanquins pulled by the sadhus themselves. On the eve of the fair, each Order announces its arrival with a grand procession headed by a brass band, with the monastic heads riding on elephants and many sadhus riding horses or camels. With all the fanfare, the highlight of the mass dip in the Ganga and the presence of millions of sadhus in one place, the Mela has no rival anywhere in the world for sheer spectacle and colour. It also happens to be the one occasion when more saints and sages are gathered together in one place than at any other time or place on earth.

1   Punja, Shobita, *Divine Ecstasy: The Story of Khajuraho*. Viking, Delhi 1992.

SACRED ART

9

The arts, like any other aspect of life in traditional India, have been practised within a world view that weaves the sacred and the secular into one indivisible whole. Art in India, far from being for its own sake, or a means of personal expression, has always been inextricably related to a wider function in the world. The word for art, *shilpa*, embraces a vast range of activities that include not only what in the West would be called crafts, but also skills such as cooking, perfumery, making love, and engineering. The Sanskrit word *shilpin* covers the English terms 'artist' and 'craftsman', but also includes the concept of priest, or magician – for in India the artist's role is to bridge the worlds; to offer in his creation a door through which man might be led to the realm of the gods.

This is why an Indian sculpture or painting does not engage the viewer in the personal realm. Since the Renaissance, Western art has been conceived within a world view which places man at the centre of the universe. Man in his physical and intellectual prowess has been seen as the 'measure of all things', the supreme achievement of Creation. Michelangelo's David glorifies the male body; Botticelli's La Primavera celebrates feminine beauty; Leonardo da Vinci's Mona Lisa looks directly at the viewer, inviting a personal response. Indian art, on the other hand, does not address a personal viewer at all; it is not made for looking at, for appreciation, or for reflecting back to an observer the glory of his human condition. It is made to be worked with in meditation and contemplation; its function is to take the devotee beyond the surface world of form to the eternal world of essence. The Divine, not the human, is at the centre of the Indian universe, and all painting, sculpture, music, dance and drama traditionally took place within the temple, at religious festivals, or within the precincts of the royal palace.

What matters for the shilpin, then, is not that he expresses his personal view, but that he transmits eternal and collective patterns of energies which act on human beings today as they have always done, irrespective of the vicissitudes of history. Unlike the West, which lives in a historical world, India is rooted in a timeless universe of eternal return: everything which happens has already done so many times before, though in different guises. It is the *pattern* of events that matters and the artist follows the pattern because it is that which is immutable and eternal. His work is therefore anonymous and follows the strict codes of practice laid down in the Shilpa Shastras, the classical texts that have determined the rules of painting, sculpture and architecture for more than 1,500 years.

For each godly form there is a *dhyana sloka*, a verse which describes the precise image of the figure to be carved. The sculptor fixes the image of the god in his mind by reciting the *sloka* and then performs a puja to that particular deity. Instead of working from a model, the artist follows the prescribed proportions in the shastras and creates an idealized image which is shaped by a poetic, rather than a realistic, conception of the human form. The image is divided into 124 sections: four for the forehead, 13.5 for the face, 4.5 for the neck and so on. If the formula is strictly adhered to, the image will be in perfect proportion, whatever the distance it is viewed from. Other scriptures detail the depth, thickness and elevation, which give the image its three dimensionality.

Like all traditional artists in India, the sculptor comes under guidance from a very early age. He will learn the ten vocations (working in metal, clay, stone, gems, etc.) and will also know Sanskrit and the four Vedas. When a sculptor and architect are asked to work on a new temple, they will perform special pujas, observe fasts and spend nights on the site where the temple is to be built. Prayers will be said to ask all evil spirits to leave and if a tree needs to be felled, they ask its spirit for forgiveness and promise to use the wood to good purpose in the temple.

What the sculptor or painter is seeking to give form to in their work is shakti, the primal energy which shapes itself into all the myriad forms of the physical world, including the human being. The whole of Nature emerges and falls back into this creative matrix, which is the life principle in any given form. Indian art expresses the vitality of shakti through a kind of aesthetic rapture which unifies the sacred and the sensuous. The physical form is celebrated, not for its own sake, but for the principle that brings it and everything else to life. Godly forms twist their hips and curve upwards like plants because they, like the vegetable and animal worlds, live and have their being in the same exuberant and vital force that generates all things. Whereas in Western art, the human figure stands out supreme against the background of the rest of Creation, in India it unfolds out of its natural context in the same organic way a plant does.

Shakti expresses herself in a spectrum of feeling tones and each subject has an essential tone that the artist tries to convey. These essence qualities are the rasas and the work of any artist, whether sculptor, musician, painter, or dancer, is coloured by them. The nine basic rasas, or feeling tones, are the erotic, comic, pathetic, furious, heroic, terrible, odious, marvellous and peaceful. In *The Hindu Vision*,[1] an excellent introduction to Hindu art, Alistair Shearer explains that 'each rasa elicits its appropriate emotional response (bhava) in the viewer: respectively love, mirth, sorrow, anger, energy, fear, disgust, astonishment and tranquillity.' Rasa, as an expression of shakti, also came to mean the current of bliss that is the source of spiritual love, which can be stimulated by yogic practices and meditation.

This more esoteric application of the rasa theory lies at the heart of Tantric art, which has been a major force in painting and sculpture for centuries. Imagery really rose to prominence in India between the 2nd and the 7th centuries, when the rise of the bhakti movements popularized the forms of the gods and goddesses. For the Hindu and for the Tantric practitioner in particular, shakti can be symbolized through different names and forms of the goddess. Each of these devatas points to a different level of energy up a scale from gross to fine, culminating in the formless, which is Brahman. The image expresses the energy of the devata, who in her turn points to an ultimate truth beyond herself. At Hirapur, in Orissa, there is a circular temple dedicated to the 64 yoginis. The practitioner will meditate on each of these forms, which are symbols for energies that live in his own being, in order to finally move beyond the visible and the imaginal worlds altogether, to the formless domain of creative silence. The images are packed with symbols evoking the attributes of the deity, which the meditator contemplates in order to identify with the godly power and to move from physical reality through the different levels of the invisible realms.

Vishnu, for example, is always represented with four arms, suggesting God incarnate as the four directions of the universe. In one of his hands he holds the revolving sun disc, circling round his right index finger. The discus symbolizes the unlimited agility of his mind, but it is also a weapon which he uses to combat evil and ignorance. In another hand he holds the mace, symbol of authority and in his third hand he has a conch. Originally used as a horn in war, in Vishnu's hand it is an object of generative power. When Vishnu blows his conch, it produces the primordial sound of the universe, in the same way that Shiva's drum does. In his lower left hand, Vishnu holds a budding red and white lotus. In Tantric art, red and white symbolize the female and the male in union. Vishnu's divine consort is the lotus goddess, Padma, otherwise known as Shri, the resplendent Earth Mother, or Lakshmi, goddess of wealth and fortune. Vishnu, like his incarnation as Krishna, is always coloured dark blue or black, to indicate his quality of infinity.

NATARAJA: THE DANCING SHIVA

Nataraja, Shiva as Lord of the Dance, is one of the most familiar figures of all Hindu deities. His image – the one of a male dancer with a foot in the air, surrounded in a ring of flame – is sold in tourist shops all over India. Yet an entire cosmology, theology and way of salvation are embodied in this single form. No gesture or component is without its layers of significance. To really see the meanings of Nataraja is to see into the inner workings of our own existence. Though all sacred art in India is deeply symbolic, the one figure of Nataraja can lay the workings of our life before us.

The fiery arch[2] around the central figure is the dance of natural forces, of the material and individual energies which constitute our daily experience of the world. Shiva-Nataraja's own dance in the centre is the dance of freedom, of the omnipresent spirit which secretly sustains the outer dance of nature. Between these two stands the individual soul, who can choose to dance to either tune.

The drum in Nataraja's upper right hand sounds the note of creation, for sound is the first element of the universe, represented as ether, akash. The flame that flickers in his upper left hand ushers in change and can be seen as the force of withdrawing, returning to centre. His lower right hand is in the abaya mudra, the 'fear not' gesture, which grants freedom from the fear of repeated births and deaths. The lower left hand, in the posture of the elephant trunk, points to the lifted left foot as the refuge of the devotee. This foot is being worshipped to gain union with Shiva and represents the bestowal of grace. The right foot is Nataraja's sublime force which drives the individual soul into the sphere of matter and illusion. The

110

two feet together represent the continual circulation of consciousness into and out of the condition of ignorance. Ignorance, or forgetfulness, is personified in the dwarf (ie. stunted
development) under the dancer's foot.

The whole figure is a model of the eternal play of energy
upholding the universe through its five activities. Those activities, which are continuously at play in all things, are (as out-
lined above) creation, or unfolding; withdrawing, which may
have the appearance of destruction; maintenance, or upholding; concealing, or veiling reality through the force of ignorance; and favouring, or bestowing grace, through the
acceptance of the devotee's longing for truth. Finally, the whole
form may be read as the sacred sound, AUM, which is the sum
totality of the world and the psyche in all their varying levels of
consciousness. AUM in its expanded form is the mantra of
Shiva – Om Nama Shivaya – the five syllables of which corre-
spond directly with the five elements of Nataraja. The symbolism of the number five extends even to the materials with
which the figure is made – a temple figure of Nataraja, such as
the one at Chidambaram, is usually made of an amalgam of the
five sacred metals – copper, silver, gold, brass and lead.

INDIAN DANCE

Just as the Shilpa Shastras determine the form and proportions
of an image, so the Natya (dance) Shastras have defined the
gestural language and grammar which is the basis of the various Indian dance forms. Eye movements, mudras (hand gestures), feet placements, the movement of the upper torso in
relation to the lower, are all determined by the codes of practice
laid down in the sacred texts. At Chidambaram temple, the
classical poses are portrayed in a series of dancers sculpted
along the wall of the south entrance. Even recently, Dr Padma
Subrahmanyas, Director of Nrithyodaya Dance School in
Madras, has designed for sculptural codification 108 karanas –
hand and feet combinations – for a new temple to be dedicated

to Lord Nataraja. She based her work on the techniques described in the Natya Shastras.

Dr Subrahmanyas is an exponent of Bharat Natyam, the southern dance form which until the early years of the twentieth century was inseparable from the life of the temple. Bharat Natyam was originally performed exclusively by the devadasis – servants of the goddess – who danced before the deity in the temple and offered themselves to male devotees as a means (the story goes) for them to enter into union with the divine. These temple dancers 'belonged' to the temple and its deity; they were often highly refined, skilled in the arts of music, aesthetics and love-making. By the 1920s the devadasi tradition had almost died out and Bharat Natyam was continued only for the enjoyment of a small number of high society aficionados. Then an extraordinary woman called Rukmini Devi founded the Kalakshetra International Centre of Dance in Madras. With the help of a former devadasi, Bala Sarasvati, Rukmini Devi began to refine the Bharat Natyam form and to stage public performances. Now Bharat Natyam is performed all over the world, with the same characteristics – fanned fingers, deep knee bends, vigorous foot stamping, sensuous body and arm movements – which have been its hallmark since its origins in the temple.

The sacred dimension of those origins is still evident in the dance today. At the beginning and end of every programme, the dancers will touch the earth and ask forgiveness for stamping on her. Then they will bring their palms together above their heads and offer their performance to God; with the palms in front of the third eye, they will honour their guru; and with palms together before the heart, they offer their respects to the audience. As they begin their dance, they will sing a prayer from the Natya Shastras.

All Indian dance is performed as an offering to God. Just as ghee (purified butter) is used to fuel the fire of a sacrificial offering, so the dancer's energies are offered up in the dance. The dance itself is a poetic glorification of reality, an evocation of the ideal state of the gods. By reflecting the divine in the earthly realm, it explains in the Natya Shastras, the dance serves to elevate the state of mind of the audience by revitalizing its moral values and inducing a condition of santi, spiritual peace.

Another Indian dance style is known as Kathak, which means storyteller. The word points to the original function of the dance, which was used with music in the temples of north India as a means of conveying the myths of the gods to the local people. In the beginning, only male brahmins were permitted to perform Kathak. Then, in the 17th century, the Moghul emperors wanted women to perform Kathak for them in their courts and today, the great majority of dancers remain women.

Saswati Sen is widely respected as the finest female Kathak artist in India. She is the principal disciple of the legendary Birju Maharaj, who has done so much to revitalize the Lucknow style of Kathak. When I met her in London in the summer of 1995, she was in the middle of an intensive teaching and performance schedule. I would not have suspected it: she strolled into the Institute of Indian Culture with two laden shopping bags, apologizing for her delay with a side remark on the length of the check-out queue. A relaxed, small woman of considerable beauty, she filled with an immediate presence as soon as she began to speak of her dance.

'I am a science graduate,' she began, 'and it was only when I was twenty-five that it became clear to my parents as well as myself that I should take up Kathak professionally. I had been dancing since I was six years old, but for the sheer love of it – I had never thought of dance in terms of a career. My father was a doctor and for a while it seemed I would follow in his footsteps. Then I won a National Dance Scholarship and destiny seemed to take over. I am one of those artists who lives in two worlds. I am an urban intellectual, yet I spend my life performing the stories of the Hindu gods.' She paused for a moment, as if wondering which way to proceed.

'I shall never forget the time when I saw some young boys dancing one of Krishna's lilas in a temple in Vrindavan,' she continued. 'They must have spent three hours going over the tiny episode of Krishna taking food. I couldn't believe the concentration they maintained from beginning to end and when they eventually finished I expressed my amazement to the person next to me. An elderly woman overheard me and said, "You don't understand. They are not performing Krishna: they are Krishna."

'I know now what she meant. Through the dance, the gods really do come to life. I know them now to be real presences, even though my rational mind prevents me from being religious in the conventional sense. Sometimes, when I am dancing for Krishna, the audience disappears and I am there with Krishna alone, the world's love personified. Kathak has awoken a deep faith in me and I think you have to have that faith if you are to dance convincingly – especially since the very basis of all traditional Indian art forms is a religious view of life and the world.'

I asked her if she ever felt constricted as a contemporary artist by the stylistic conformity of Indian dance.

'I have chosen a traditional form which allows for a lot of improvization,' Saswati explained. 'Though the gestures of Kathak are defined in the Natya Shastras, they are more natural, less stylized, than in other forms. We use many everyday gestures which anyone can understand. We tend to improvize both with technique and narrative. In my performance last night, for example, I collaborated with a Karnatic vocalist, whose tradition is quite different from my own. As he sang, I danced his narrative. And we never rehearse. We just agree on the general story and take it from there.' Saswati paused for a moment. Her eyes lowered, then raised again. 'Many artists and promoters in India today feel we should make the traditional forms more contemporary,' she went on, 'to suit current tastes and interests. But how can you make Krishna contemporary? He is eternal; love is always the same in any age. Our myths speak from a place beyond time and I think we should believe in their messages enough to realize they are as relevant now as they ever were.'

INDIAN MUSIC

As with dance, classical Indian music was once the preserve of the temple and the court. Few temple musicians and singers survive today, however, except in the Krishna temples of Vrindavan and in parts of Rajasthan. Personal success and reputation, rather than religious service, is the common aspiration of artists in India today as it is everywhere else and India's classical music tradition now survives thanks to the concert hall and television. It does not, though, seem to enjoy the home following that its counterpart does in the West. Indeed, along with everything else Western, Bach and Beethoven are even winning over audiences in India. In Bombay there is a popular FM radio station devoted exclusively to Western classical music, while there is no similar station for the Indian variety.

While the emphasis on personal public performance has diminished the unselfconscious expression of a sacred tradition, the very nature and structure of Indian music tends to draw the listener into subtle states of body and mind which can lead one from the outer ear to the more interior vibrations and currents of shakti. The many ragas are attuned to the energies of the different times of day and are designed to evoke the various rasas. The professional musician will have learned his art from early childhood, will have given unswerving obedience to his guru and in a traditional setting would have lived, studied and practised in the guru's house.

Shubha Mudgal, like many artists under the age of 45, has managed to cut her own path while still remaining within the broad tradition of her particular style. She is a highly acclaimed singer of Khyal, a north Indian branch of popular classical music which had its origins in the Moghul courts. We met over coffee one morning on the terrace of the Imperial Hotel in Delhi, Shubha's home city. She told me that she had studied with several gurus, rather than one and that she had spent eight to ten hours a day for years singing or conversing with her teachers. She was first taught to sing nothing but one raga for three years, without ever being able to question the teacher. The effect, she said, was to humble her completely.

'There is a beauty in that kind of surrender,' she mused. 'The ego is tamed and that is necessary for an artist. But you lose something as well. I always wondered how dialogue could be omitted from what was understood to be a relationship of love. It is love which is meant to unite guru and disciple, whatever the art form. So I began to repeat exactly what they asked of me during the lesson, but outside, I would change it. I was brought up in a modern, English-speaking family, you see. Such rigidity was foreign to my background, which was non-traditional and non-ritualistic.'

Shubha now has students of her own, who she treats as equals, even though she is guru to them. In 1992, she was introduced to the Radha-Ramana temple in Vrindavan where the art of singing as an act of devotion has been studied and practised for centuries.

'I saw how the priests there were singing not as a performance, but as a means of worship,' she said. 'They made me even more aware of what I had been feeling for some time – that singing for an audience without a conscious spiritual perspective brings a huge focus and strain on the individual personality. I longed to know the feelings of reverence and self forgetfulness that these priests conveyed so naturally in their temple. So I began to study with them through the channel of a cultural institute which is attached to the temple, the Shri Chaitanya Prema Sansthana.'

Shubha went on to explain that the priests gave her ancient texts which sing the praises of Radha, Krishna's consort. 'Sing these for Radha,' they said. 'But don't perform for us. We are not interested in your virtuosity; we want to hear the quality of your spiritual feeling.'

Shubha has been a regular visitor to Vrindavan ever since. The priests have given her 14th-century texts to study and sing which praise every one of Krishna's lilas, as well as the songs which accompany all the pujas to the deity.

'They say that only two offerings are truly appropriate for God,' she said as we got up to leave. 'Food and music. The offering of music is known as the rag seva. I am still learning to make that offering without holding anything back.'

1 Shearer, Alistair. *The Hindu Vision: Forms of the Formless*. Thames and Hudson, London 1992.

2 For a full explanation of the symbolism of Nataraja, see Kramrisch, Stella *The Presence of Shiva*. Princeton University Press, Princeton, N.J. 1981.

SACRED CITY

Banaras is wherever you are.
Old Benarsi saying[1]

10

Banaras, City of Light, City of the Dead, The Forest of Bliss, The Never-Forsaken, The City of Shiva: call it what you will – and it is known by all these names – it has to be one of the maddest, holiest, ugliest, most entrancing cities on earth. Every deformity imaginable is displayed in the queue of beggars lining the road to the main ghat. Every trick in the book is used by the touts, the rickshaw wallahs, the boatmen, the hangers-on, to part another fool from his money. The assault is continuous, and only ceases when one flees to the river on a boat of one's own. Then, the light falls on the temples, the palaces, the water, with a radiance that is equalled nowhere. The whole place takes on a dream-like air, with nothing moving faster than the pace of an oar. Buffalo lounge in the water, a man meditates by the shore, sadhus walk by with their staff and water pot, people squat having their head shaved; a woman bathes in the silky water, gluing her sari to her graceful frame; children play chase among the funeral pyres, a dog snatches a foot that has slipped from the fire. It was little different a hundred years ago, when W. S. Caine wrote:

> Up and down the ghats, all day long, but especially in the early morning, stream the endless course of pilgrims, ragged tramps, aged crones, horrible beggars,

hawkers, Brahmin priests, sacred bulls and cows, Hindu preachers, wealthy rajas or bankers in gay palanquins, Fakirs, pariah dogs, and scoffing globetrotters from Europe and America.[2]

There are seven major sacred cities in India – Banaras, Mathura, Puri, Ayodhya, Dwarka, Haridwar, and Kanchi – and many more smaller ones. Normally, a city is sacred because of its direct association with a major deity: Mathura, for example, is where Krishna was King, while Ram had his court at Ayodhya. Banaras, however, is associated with all the gods, as well as being on the Ganga river. It is a city-cosmos, conceived as a reflection on earth of the divine order above. Banaras is at the heart of the longest unbroken tradition in the world. Its spiritual/religious culture has a history of at least 3,000 years. It is 'older than history,' said Mark Twain after his visit there, 'older than tradition, older even than legend.' Even before the gods came to claim her for their own, Banaras was there, up on the high plateau to the north of the present rail and road bridge that crosses the river; skirted by the Ganga on one side and the Varuna river on the other. Around her, to the south and the west, spreads the 'Forest of Bliss', a land of pools and jungle that harboured ascetics and their disciples. It was also the place of spirits and nature deities, who are still venerated everywhere in the city today in much the same way as they were 1,000 years before Christ, with flowers, water libations, and incense.

Many of the great spiritual teachers down through the centuries have lived or taught in Banaras. Buddha gave his first sermon in nearby Sarnath; Parshvanatha, the first historically dated master of the Jains, was born in the city in the 8th century BC. Patanjali came here in the 2nd century BC, as did Shankara nearly 1,000 years later. Ramanuja, Tulsidas, Kabir, and countless lesser-known masters lived and taught here. Today, all the major monastic orders are represented in the city, and sadhus of every denomination are always to be seen along the river bank in the early morning. Diana Eck, in her excellent book on Banaras,³ tells us that in some parts of India, even today, the initiation ritual for young men includes a symbolic journey to Banaras. In the rite, the young man is 'led forth' to the guru, from whom he receives his sacred thread and initiatory mantra. Then he takes seven steps in the direction of Banaras, 'a ritual enactment of the ancient journey to the fountainhead of all wisdom'.

As the city moved south in the wake of Muslim invasions, its shrines and temples were rebuilt on new sites and the cosmic centre of the town took on different names and forms. But always, throughout history, Banaras has been a physical expression of cosmic order. Though it is the dwelling place of all the gods, Banaras is a sacred city first of all because it is the embodiment of heaven on earth, as Jerusalem is for the Middle-Eastern traditions. It is a cosmogram which weaves together nature, humanity, and the cosmos in an intricate web of 56 pilgrim circuits. Banaras is what it is today because of the Ganga and because of its pilgrim circuits.

When you enter Banaras, you are reborn into a sacred cosmos. Another name for this cosmos is India. India was always conceived by its inhabitants to encompass the universe. So Banaras is India, and you will find in Banaras an exact, scaled-down version of every major sacred site in the country. The seven sacred rivers are all represented here – Godaulia, for example, the main street of the old town, used to be a stream whose name was Godaveri, after the sacred river in Andhra Pradesh. There are seven replicas in the city of the great temple of Rameshwaram, in Tamil Nadu. All the twelve major lingas are here; the shrine of Badrinath is here, and so on. Banaras is India – not just in some poetic, or mystical sense, but in a tangible dimension of energy. Come here, and you can forego all other wanderings.

Of the 56 pilgrim circuits in Banaras, five surround the city in irregular concentric circles, and the inner four of these are still in common use. Dr Rana Singh, who is a lecturer in Geography at Banaras Hindu University, and President of the Indian Society of Pilgrimage Studies, has probably done more research than anyone on the sacred geography of Banaras. Rana Singh has lived in the city for more than 20 years, and his fascination with it is as passionate as ever. He explained the basic plan of the circuits to me as we walked along the river one day.

At Assi Ghat we watched a crowd of pilgrims marching up from the river towards the town at a determined pace. 'They're just starting out on the Panchakrosha Yatra,' commented Ranaji as they passed out of sight. 'That's the fourth of the five circles, the most popular pilgrimage in Banaras. It's a fifty-mile journey, and it will take them five days. They have 108 shrines to venerate along the way, and they will end up in the centre of the town at the Jnanavapi Kupa, the Well of Wisdom which sits between the Great Mosque and The Golden Temple. The Well has been the axis mundi of the city for centuries now, and the other three yatras end there too. You know the story, don't you, where Shiva dug into the earth with his trident and offered the water he found to another of his forms, Avimukteshvara. Shiva took up his abode in the well he had dug and promised to stay there and grace Banaras with his presence forever.' He went on to explain that the Panchakrosha Yantra, like all of the yantras, is ancient, and that it was already well documented in a 12th-century text. The third circle, he said, called the Nagara Pradakshina, marks the city territory. That one takes two days to complete, and has 72 shrines. The second circuit, with a radius of just over a mile, marks the zone which is 'Never Forsaken' by Shiva-Avimukteshvara, He who dwells in the Well of Wisdom. Unlike the outer three, it moves in a spiral to the centre, the Well. The inner circuit, the Antargrha, takes the pilgrim seven times round the Vishvanath, better known as the Golden Temple, in reference to its splendid roof.

'The whole cosmogram is a beautiful but also precise weaving together of the different worlds,' Ranaji enthused as we stepped into a boat to take us farther downstream. 'The five circuits represent the five elements, Ether, Earth, Air, Water, and ending in the centre with Fire. But they also connect to the human head, legs, face, blood and heart. You see how the whole thing brings together the human and the divine? Then, throughout the system of five circles, there are 56 Ganesh shrines along the eight radial directions, the main routes into the city. These are to protect the pilgrims as they approach and enter Banaras. Now just think; why 56? 56=7x8: they protect the eight directions not only on the earthly plane, but on all the seven levels of reality, or layers of the atmosphere.'

My head was beginning to spin with all the numbers, and I lay back to contemplate the extraordinary panorama of the Banaras waterfront. The ghats, colossal flights of stone steps leading down to the water's edge, were pink and gold in the afternoon sun. On some of them, the washermen had laid out their day's work to dry: yards of sari, blue and bright yellow, stretched down towards the water. Here and there people were squatting watching the river go by; dogs ran between them, snapping at each other; a huddle of people, all in white, gazed on as the body of one of their relatives cracked and dissolved in the flames of a great fire. Somewhere, bells were ringing, and firecrackers were being set off. Overhead, two vultures circled. Palaces and temples line the entire curve of the river for some four miles as it passes through Banaras. Many seem to be falling down; but even their decay only adds, somehow, to the dream-like sensation of floating in a boat through the city of the gods. I ended that day back on the ghat at Assi, alone with a new moon.

ASSI GHAT

The universe, India, Banaras, and Assi Ghat, the microcosm of the microcosm. The city is so drenched in flowers and incense and bulging with temples and shrines to every possible deity that one could probably take any few square hundred yards in the old city and find a miniature of the whole. I explored the small area around Assi and Tulsi Ghats, the southernmost ghats of the city, and found 3,000 years of living tradition right there in all its layers and incredible variety.

On the ghat itself is a pipal tree. A barber sits next to it in the morning, ready to serve those on their way down to bathe. On the other side a panda, a priest of the ghats, sits on a wooden platform with a large pot plant by his side, a bowl of vermilion to dot on the devotee's forehead, and a book of scriptures. Someone else has a little table with a mirror and a comb on it. The table is surrounded by bunches of clothes which he is tending for the bathers.

Around the pipal tree are several lingas, a Ganesh, a few snake deities, and one or two black stones. On their way back up from the river, the bathers come straight to the tree and circle it, placing flowers, rice and a sprinkling of Ganga water on each of the sacred objects. They smear vermilion on the trunk of the tree, throw a few grains of rice at it, and put the same hand to their foreheads. Every gesture has a purpose, a meaningful intent. Some stand for a few moments facing the tree with palms together in the namaskar, praying intently to their chosen deity. This tree is as sacred as any temple.

Ranaji and I wandered up the steps through a narrow alley to the first lane that parallels the river. A corner of one of the steps was wet with offerings of Ganga water, and strewn with flowers, I don't know why. A few yards along the lane on the left is a green-walled shrine topped with a dome. Inside is a marble enclosure on the floor, surrounding a lingam with its accompanying mount, Nandi the bull. 'This is the sangam lingam,' Ranaji explained. 'Sangam means the confluence of two rivers, and this lingam marks the confluence of the Assi river and the Ganga. See the white flowers on the lingam, they are from the marijuana plant. They are offered to Shiva because he can absorb all poisons without being affected. When the devotee offers Shiva these flowers, he is offering him his own impurities.'

A man and two women were sitting in front of the lingam, their lips moving in silent prayer. Every few minutes, one of them would sprinkle the deity with Ganga water from their brass pot, or lay another flower or leaf on its head. At the door, a stone receptacle overflowed with earlier offerings, the white marijuana, bilva leaves in sprays of three, chrysanthemums.

We walked back along the lane, in the other direction. In five minutes we had reached Lolarkakhund, one of the most ancient sites in Banaras. Three giant stairways led steeply down to a well which was in the shape of a keyhole. Sheer walls enclosed the barrel part, which from the top looked like any other deep well.

'First mentioned in the Rig Veda, 2nd century BC,' Ranaji said with a feigned show of casualness. I knew of his particular interest in this well. 'This is the most southerly of the twelve sun shrines along the Ganga at Banaras. It's incredible to me that the ancients could have exercized such scientific precision. Each of the twelve marks the exact spot of the cusp between one zodiacal sign and the next – a time which in India is considered highly potent and auspicious. Recent astronomical observations have shown the sitings to be absolutely correct. In June the sun is directly overhead the middle of this well, and that is the most sacred time for this Surya shrine.' Surya, I knew, is the god of the sun, worshipped daily by millions in the Gayatri Mantra.

'Surya has his festival here twice a year,' Ranaji went on. 'Women fast for three days and pray to Father Sun where he lights on Mother Water. It's an energy cult: the women seek impregnation. Those with no children pray for a male son, those with children pray for long life, those whose prayers were answered in previous years return in thanks. At the end of their fast they make offerings first to Ganga and then to Lolarkakhund. The children who were born as a result of previous offerings are tonsured and their hair is dipped in the well. Surya still has a strong hold on people's minds here.'

At the top of one of the flights of stairs was another lingam by a tree, its trunk daubed in red. We walked round it, turned a corner, and there was a shrine to the goddess Durga. No-one had paid their respects to the well while we were there, but this red-faced goddess with staring eyes was drawing a steady trickle of devotees. Her little shrine was of red brick, and a red flag fluttered from a bamboo pole on the roof. By her side, a brass cobra protected a lingam under its hood. A few days later I passed by here again to discover it was the day of Durga's festival. Then a priest was sitting next to his goddess in the little box of a shrine, daubing red paste on the brow of anyone who could make their way to the front of the crowd. Music blared from a makeshift system, and the area round the shrine was fenced off with brightly coloured cloth.

Ranaji and I walked a few steps back towards the river, and stopped at a narrow doorway which opened onto a steep flight of steps leading down into the basement of a house. I peered in. Below me was another lingam set in a marble surround, with men packed in on all four sides chanting in unison.

'The jyoti lingam,' Ranaji explained. 'All the twelve jyoti lingas of India – the lingas of light – are represented in Banaras. But this one is the essence of all the twelve.'

Whatever the official story, all I could see was a huddle of men down in the womb of Mother Earth, in semi-darkness, all paying homage to a phallic symbol. If that isn't for the generation of vital power, I don't know what is. We climbed down to join them, and squeezed in a corner of the tiny room. In minutes, the chanting had lulled my thoughts away. Every now and then one of the men would pour rice over the lingam. Another would light a camphor flame. The chanting grew to a pitch, a large conch shell was blown, and suddenly it was all over. Everyone got up and filed up the steps, leaving Ranaji and I in an empty room with a lingam covered with rice. As we got up and slowly made our way to the daylight, I felt we were coming out of some burial chamber, and we were the risen ones.

I was beginning to think that was enough for one morning, but Ranaji hadn't quite finished with me yet. Round another corner we went, and suddenly we were overlooking the river bank. To one side was a huge Ganesh.

'That is not just another elephant guardian,' he said with undisguised pride. 'This one is the Mother of all the 56 Ganesh shrines which, as I told you, guard the eight directional entrances into the city. Pay your respects to this one, and you satisfy them all.'

Another essence shrine: there must be enough essence in Assi to make it the holiest place in India. Before we turned to walk down the steps to the river, I heard a shout from across the lane. Glancing through an open gateway, I saw young men tussling with each other under an open roof. I stepped nearer, and realized I was having my first sight of a Banaras wrestling arena, for which the city is so famous. Two pairs of wrestlers, caked in white clay from the floor, were locked in complicated holds in the middle of the arena, while others looked on.

'The Tulsi wrestling ground,' Ranaji said. 'We are above Tulsi Ghat, and it is said that Tulsidas himself used to wrestle here. The ground belongs to the Tulsidas Acara, the institution he left behind him. Actually, the word acara refers to the wrestling ground. The difference between an acara and a math, a monastery, is only that the acara traditionally included this kind of body work along with its spiritual practices.'

As we made our way down, I decided to return later on my own to visit the Tulsi Acara. I knew and loved some of Tulsidas' poems, and was aware that his 17th-century rendering of the Ramayana, the Ramcharitmanas, was the most popular text in all India.

'It seems we are not quite finished yet,' said Ranaji as we reached the pipal tree at Assi Ghat. A group of men were sitting by the tree in front of a priest. All dressed in white, and tonsured, they were cleaning the ground in front of them with Ganga water from their pots. Onto the cleared area they were placing offerings of barley and oats.

'What you are seeing is a rite for the ancestors. At only three places in India – Prayag, Banaras, and Gaya – can such a ritual take place. They are invoking the souls of their ancestors to come and dwell on the spot before them. You see, the priest is giving them kushi grass to make a bed for the soul, and to make a ring which they will put on their finger to symbolize union with the ancestors. Now he is giving them flowers to put on the bed as an offering. Look, you see how they are making balls out of the barley, mixing it with Ganga water. They will make 21 of those balls, representing the past 21 generations. The whole point is to ensure a good seat in heaven for those generations. They don't want any of them running around as ghosts. If the ancestors are happy, so will the living be. Most foreigners think that the ideal of Hinduism is moksha: freedom from the round of birth and death through the relinquishment of all desires. That is true only for the tiny minority of serious practitioners. The great majority of people do not understand what moksha means. The point of leading a good life, for them, is to go to heaven, and not to wander in the nether worlds. This is what they are concerned with here. In Kartikai, your month of October, everyone venerates the ancestors. Then, you will see tall bamboo canes all along the river with a small woven basket suspended from them. Families light a lamp in the basket to call their whole family line, who will recognize the light of their family and bathe with them in the Ganga.'

Later that day, when Ranaji had gone off to put in an appearance at his university, I made my way back up to the Tulsi Acara. I could hear the drums beating before I even set out: they were performing the Hanuman puja, and I reached there in time to see the last few minutes. I was astonished to find that all that noise came from just one assistant priest who was hitting a double-ended drum as if his life depended on it. The main priest was attending to the deity, a huge red Hanuman, in a room which gave out on to a balcony overlooking the river. On the balcony a man was cleaning brass pots with mud, seemingly oblivious of the din by his side. By the deity I could see a pair of wooden clogs which I knew to be those of Tulsidas. There was also a bit of wood, reputed, in the way of the relic trade, to be a piece of his boat. It stood up against a portrait of Tulsidas, along with a translation of his Ramcharitmanas.

When the puja had ended, I asked the priest if I could see the head of the acara. He led me through a tiered courtyard into a room with a large bed in it. Instead of a mattress the bed was covered with a cloth. Its purpose, as in any house in India, is to receive guests, to lounge, to be at leisure on. On the bed sat a striking man in his fifties, wearing a dhoti. Two or three visitors were sitting with him already, and he motioned me to join them.

'As the Mahant, I am the spiritual and temporal head of the acara,' he said, when I asked him about his role. 'One of my ancestors was an initiate of Tulsidas, and my family moved here from Gorakhpur some 170 years ago. The acara itself has several thousand disciples, though my personal role as a spiritual adviser is minimal. Tulsidas is the guru, Hanuman the deity. Tulsidas was a lover of Ram, and Ram's greatest devotee was Hanuman. So our practice is the recitation of the Ram mantra, and kirtan, devotional singing, of the Ramchirat-manas. That is what I do myself, and my early morning dip in the Ganga is part of my spiritual practice along with every-thing else.'

This Mahant spoke with a rare combination of fluency and warmth. 'Have you spent your life in the acara?' I asked.

He smiled. 'No. Tulsidas was not a renunciate. In fact it is not even known if he was in any order or tradition. He didn't distinguish between monk and householder, and it is a tradi-tion of the acara that the Mahant cannot spend the temple offerings on his own family. He must earn his own living.'

'What is your work?' I asked.

'I am at the university,' he replied.

I imagined he might be in the Philosophy Department, or the Sanskrit Department, perhaps.

'He is Professor of Hydraulic Engineering,' one of the other guests said.

'It seems to be my role to try and bridge the traditional and the modern worlds,' the Mahant went on. 'It is also an inter-nal work. On the one hand, I have faith in the purity of the Ganga. On the other, the scientist in me knows it is polluted; yet I bathe in it all the same. You may have noticed the Ecolo-gy Centre just along the ghat from our acara. That is our work. It is a project to determine the pollution levels in the Ganga, and to seek funds for practical solutions.'

Two hours later, full of respect for the Mahant and his vision, I left the acara and stepped into the night. One or two lamps were floating on the Ganga. Shrouded bodies lay snoring on the ghats. Some Naga babas, the ones who go naked, covered in ashes, were sitting by the Ganga smoking a chillum of dope. Someone was playing tabla at one of the windows of an old palace. A group of 20 young men were chanting softly up on a step. I remarked to one of them how unusual it was to see people of their age singing devotional bhajans.

'We call ourselves the Vivekenanda Club,' he replied. 'We are all in the Engineering Faculty at the university. Yes, it is very rare. We just feel there is more to life than films and career. We want to address the deeper questions of life, and we feel our old traditions can help us, without having to join some traditional religious group.'

I sat with the Vivekananda Club for a few minutes, filled with a new appreciation for engineers. Only at the persistent prompting of the mosquitoes did I finally end the day and walk back to my hotel by the pipal tree.

THE JEWELS IN THE CROWN

Everywhere in Banaras has its unusually holy temple, well, relic, or tree; but the sites that have attracted the myths on which the reputation of the city stands are all in the labyrinth of lanes that weave between the main ghat, Dasasvamedha Ghat, and Panchaganga Ghat, several hundred yards downstream. Ranaji and I landed at Panchaganga below the great mosque that Aurangzeb built on the site of an ancient temple of Vishnu. The ghat gets its name from the story that five rivers meet here, including the Sarasvati and the Yamuna. A bath at this ghat is auspicious beyond measure in the month of Kartikai, for then, all the gods, including Shiva Vishvanath, come to bathe here daily.

Wrestlers were doing their press-ups on the steps. A sadhu

passed by. 'Sri Ram, Sri Ram,' the wrestlers puffed in greeting, without ceasing from their labours. A large Ramanandi Math is just here by the ghat, and legend has it that it was on these steps that the poet Kabir was initiated by Ramananda, founder of the order.

Ranaji led me up to the gate of the mosque, which is rarely used today. The largest honeycombs I have ever seen, six feet across and clouded with bees, hang from the delicate arches. Across the lane from the mosque is an old people's home. When the original Vishnu temple was destroyed in 1669, the deity was hidden here. Ranaji led me up some stairs to an empty room with paintings of Vishnu's incarnations in panels along the walls. At the end of the room was a grilled area, with a priest and the idol of Vishnu, known as Bindu Madhava, the Drop of Krishna. The original Vishnu temple was built at Panchaganga because this was the spot that the god chose for his permanent abode in Banaras. He had few devotees that day; just a couple of old ladies, residents of the home, and us.

'Even so,' Ranaji said, almost, it seemed, by way of apology, 'Bindu Madhava is the most powerful form of Vishnu in Banaras, and one of the most auspicious in India.'

I nodded, and we left to make our way to Manikarnika Ghat, known to everyone as the burning ghat. It is not the cremation ground that gives it its sanctity; rather, it became a burning ghat because of its proximity to one of Banaras' most sacred pools, the Manikarnikakhund. It was the pool that gave the ghat its name. Benarsis will tell you that Manikarnika was the world's first pool and tirtha, dug out by Vishnu himself with his discus, and filled with his own sweat. His work completed, Vishnu sat nearby for aeons performing fierce austerities. One day Shiva and Parvati came that way and Shiva was so impressed by Vishnu's devotion that he shook with delight and dropped one of his jewelled earrings – manikarnika – into the pool. That is what the legend says, but as Diana Eck reminds us, the word mani, jewel, is commonly a prefix given to the nagas, the snake guardians of the treasures in the earth. The pool, then, was almost certainly sacred to the nagas long before Vishnu and Shiva came along.

The pool is a rectangle whose sides lead down to it in a series of steps. Today, a water pump sits idly at the edge of the water. In front of the pool, under a roof supported by four pillars, are a set of Vishnu's footprints, marking the spot where the god did his austerities. When we were there, the footprints were surrounded by women selling bangles, and nobody seemed too interested in Vishnu. Customers were what mattered, and they were thin on the ground that day.

A few yards away was a temple which was doing more business than the pool and the footprints. The Tarakeshvara Temple, a single red tower above the cremation ground, is the most important one on the ghat because it holds the form of Shiva who imparts the liberating taraka mantra, the 'prayer of the crossing' at the moment of death. Lord Shiva whispers the mantra into the ear of the deceased to ensure a good place for them in heaven.

We passed through stacks of wood ready for the fires below along the lanes that led to the Golden Temple. The Banaras lanes teem with life. A perfume seller wiped the stopper of a bottle on my arm as I passed by his stall. I turned to see rows of bottles of coloured liquid arranged in a semicircle around a basket of flowers. I sniffed my arm. Jasmine. A buffalo lumbered towards me, head bucking, it seemed, in a fit of ill temper. I pressed my back to the wall, feeling the warmth of his flank as he passed. At my feet was a rubble of broken pots, palm leaf plates, and squeezed out sugar cane. The sugar-cane wallah was opposite, pressing the last drop out of a pulverized shoot with an antiquated machine. He handed a glass of grimy green liquid to a customer who drank it with relish. Ever-boiling teapots steamed away on all sides in little booths with a chair or two outside. Clay dishes, a yard across, held the delicious curd for which Banaras is famous. 'Sit down, baba, you like tea?' Every shop and booth was decorated with gaudy posters of Ram, or Krishna, or some other favourite deity. Most of them had a lamp burning before a makeshift shrine. These simple demonstrations of faith, it seemed to me, were as close to the living religion of the Banaras people as any big temple or historic shrine.

'Look Golden Temple and Moxque on my Roof. No Money. Rajesh Silk House.'

'Mr Ajit Singh, King of Varanasi Silk.'

We were clearly approaching the sacred heart of the city. Wide plaited straw baskets filled with garlands lined the street now. Soldiers were on every corner. The lane was thick with people. On the right was a door through which much of the crowd filed. Ranaji motioned for me to look: this, I realized, was the entrance to the most venerated place in Banaras, the Shiva temple of Vishvanath – 'The Lord of All'. With so many shrines and temples in every street, there was nothing to mark this one out as anything special, except for the volume of devotees who were so keen to get in there. The complex is surrounded by a wall which gives it the outer appearance of any other building in the street. I peered through the door, unable to go in because entrance is restricted to Hindus. It is a small place, not to be compared in grandeur to any of the temples of Orissa or of south India; and the present temple is recent, constructed only in the 18th century. Yet it contains perhaps the most revered jyoti lingam in all India, a small black stone set in an altar of solid silver. The air in there was thick with incense, devotion, the clanging of bells, and streams of people circumambulating round the shrine.

The earlier Vishvanath temple was destroyed by Aurangzeb, and the mosque built on its site is just behind the present temple. The proximity of the two explained the heavy army presence, since tension between Muslim and Hindus frequently runs high here. Ironically, the Well of Wisdom lies between them, and we set off towards it down the lane.

Just along from the temple door was a shrine which was attracting almost as much attention as the temple itself. Behind a grill, up on a cloth-covered bench, was a deity with a large silver mask and a splendid Rajput moustache, draped in dozens of marigold garlands. The ground at his feet was sparkling with hundreds of clay lamps. People were pressed to the railings muttering their prayers. This was the great Sunni Maharaj, better known as the planet Saturn, who can cause you a hard time unless you smooth his path with devotions. As we turned to go, I bumped into a Naga baba, grey with the ashes smeared over his naked body, who was stepping up and down on the spot right behind me, waving a peacock feather in one hand, and holding out a begging bowl in the other. He was one of those who had taken a vow not to stand still, and every day he did his begging and blessing rounds through the lanes. People seemed to regard him much as they did Sunni Maharaj, and no shop failed to put something in his bowl.

The Jnanavapi Khund, The Well of Wisdom, was said to have been dug by Shiva himself in order to cool the lingam of Vishvanath. The waters that sprang up were the first pure waters, the liquid form of jnana, the light of wisdom. In the past, devotees have been convinced enough to throw themselves into the well and to certain liberation. The top is now covered with bars to prevent further 'liberation suicides'.

The water is still hauled up daily and ladled out to all devotees before they enter the Vishvanath temple, so their eyes might be clear enough to behold the mystery of the black lingam. The dispenser of the waters is known as the Vyasa. He was sitting by the well on his throne seat when we arrived: an elderly man who looked so at ease on his stone chair, dispensing mantras and water to all and sundry, that he could have been the original sage and compiler of the Vedas, Vyasa himself.

'His family have supplied the Vyasa of Jnanavapi for five hundred years,' Ranaji commented. 'It's a good living. And the title carries a lot of respect. That man is more in touch with the traditions of Banaras than almost anyone else in the city. Every Banaras pilgrimage starts here with a ladle of wisdom water. The Vyasa knows all the mantras associated with every yatra; so if, for example, you are beginning the Panchakrosha pilgrimage, he will recite all 108 mantras connected with the 108 shrines along that route, asking that you be blessed and protected by those deities. Then when you return here at the end, the Vyasa will ask that any omissions, or incorrect puja

133

that you have performed, be excused.'

By the well a group of men were chanting some verses from the Puranas; others were lying under the open roof that shaded the area. A few sadhus had set up camp some yards away, and were boiling tea on an open fire. In front of us was the mosque, built onto the ruins of the original temple, which were integrated into the new building by Aurangzeb as a final insult. How strange we are, I pondered as we made our way back through the lanes; we human beings, who know the taste of love and wisdom, and long for it sufficiently to cover the landscape with wells, with temples, mosques, and shrines – images, all of them, of our desire for love, if not truth; and yet who continue to be possessed by some ideal of the mind and strike out on its behalf, in defiance of the very waters we long for – at our wife, our neighbour, at another caste or creed. None of us is innocent.

CITY OF DEATH AND LIBERATION

Drifting down the Ganga from the main ghat towards the great cremation ground at Manikarnika, you will notice a palace right on the water with an open parapet on the top, guarded at each end by the statue of a prowling lion. You are looking at the Dom Maharaja's palace. The Doms are the untouchable caste who have been in sole charge of the Banaras cremation grounds for centuries. They set the charges for each individual cremation, and if you don't like their price, they will tell you to take your corpse somewhere else. The head, or king, of the Dom clan handles all the rich clients. In the 1920s, when a family member of the Maharaja of Banaras died, the Dom Maharaja asked for the palace by the water in payment for his services. The Maharaja accepted, and the building still houses the head of the clan today, who numbers among the ten richest people in Banaras.

One family holds the hereditary post of Dom Maharaja, and seven families oversee the cremation business as a whole.

Around a hundred families comprise the clan; together, they control the selling of the wood, collect a tax for each corpse, and tend the ever-burning sacred fire which gives the flame for the funeral pyres. They also rake up the ashes, and sift them for valuables before pushing them into the river.

It's a lucrative, but hard life. Apart from the drudgery of stoking the fires of the dead, and living your day among ashes and scavenging dogs in temperatures often well into the hundreds, the Doms have the pressure of a deeply ambivalent role in society. On the one hand, they perform a duty that makes them the most polluted of all the untouchables. No-one would ordinarily keep their company. Yet at the same time, they are indispensable for the most sacred ritual in Hinduism. Everyone from the Maharaja down has to argue a price with them for a service they can get from nobody else. The power of the Dom is unassailable, yet the combined pressures of their unusual occupation has turned many of them into alcoholics.

A few boats of Western tourists lie alongside the ghat, their passengers gawping at the scene before them. Half a dozen fires are burning near the water, and other corpses, trussed in yellow and gold cloth on bamboo stretchers, are waiting their turn nearby. The family members are sitting up above, watching the proceedings in silence. Mourning is considered to be bad luck for the dead, and no-one is shedding a tear. Rather, the atmosphere is casual, almost routine. A wide-bottomed boat heaves to with another mountain of logs. An eldest son, head shaven, clothed from head to foot in a white robe, walks down to one of the fires that has done its work, throws a pot of Ganga water over his shoulder onto the embers, and without looking back, rejoins his family. The last rite completed, they all troop off to bathe for a last time in the Ganga. On returning home they will offer water and light to the deceased for ten more days, to ensure the person has completely left this realm and joined the ancestors.

The fires burn day and night, consuming bodies that have been flown in from all over India, and even from as far away as London, by relatives anxious to smooth the passage of their loved one to heaven with the most auspicious end conceivable, in the Ganga at Banaras. Those who want to make certain of a happy fate after death come here to spend their last days in the city, and Banaras is full of people waiting to die. Old people's homes, run by trusts which take care of the last rites, line the river bank at Manikarnika, ensuring the inmates have not far to go.

The most unusual cremation ceremony I ever saw was at the other burning ghat further upstream, Hariscandra Ghat. As I passed by, a procession of drummers and pipers came down to the water leading a flower-covered bier, chanting 'Ram, Ram, Satya He!' the mantra that accompanies every corpse to the fire. Just before the fire they stopped, and two young men leapt out in front of the body, which was still on the shoulders of the bearers. To the encouragement of the beating drums, they threw themselves into a wild sexual dance, one with a stick in his trousers that seemed to give him a massive erection, the other gyrating his pelvis like a woman, with his arms and forefingers prodding the air. Round and round each other they turned, totally given over to what I assumed to be some ancient evocation of fertility and new life. The musicians circled round them, drumming the dancers into an ecstatic frenzy. By now everyone was clapping and laughing, and as the dancers' exhaustion slowed them down, they motioned to me to come and join them. I had never been to a funeral like this before, and I backed away, embarrassed. Later, too late, I wished I had danced that cremation dance.

1   Quoted in an unpublished manuscript on Banaras by Richard Lannoy.
2   Caine, W. S. 'Picturesque India'. Quoted in *Banaras: City of Light*, by Diana Eck. Penguin, New Delhi 1993.
3   Eck, Diana, *Banaras: City of Light*. Ibid.

PART THREE

THE INNER TRADITION

SADHUS AND RENUNCIATES

Whoever honours his own sect and disparages that of another man, whether from blind loyalty or with the intention of showing his sect in a favourable light, does his own sect the greatest possible harm. Co-operation, concord, is best, with each hearing and respecting the other's teaching.
12th Rock Edict of Emperor Ashoka, 3rd century BC[1]

11

Like any other religious tradition, popular and classical Hinduism is based on external forms of worship which require the intermediary of a priest, a holy place, or a ritual for communication with the divine. The intermediaries are accepted unquestioningly by the devotee. You do what your father and his father before him have always done: you fulfil your social and religious obligations by following the prescribed forms of worship. Your practice depends more on received custom and belief than on some inner call or prompting. This does not necessarily mean that the worship is empty of personal significance – far from it, as we have already seen in previous chapters – but the motivation arises more from external conditioning than from within.

Yet exoteric Hinduism has also been a fertile ground for something far more than itself: out of it has grown the most sublime spiritual wisdom that the world has ever known. India is the motherland of the spiritual quest. Her ascetic tradition is older than history itself. For millennia, individuals on the sub-continent have stepped outside of the conventional norm to conduct their own personal search for the divine. The inner tradition relies not on outer observances so much as verification through personal experience and experiment. Its practices are esoteric, less because they are hidden to outsiders – though this may also be true – than because they take place internally, in the mind and heart of the practitioner. The body becomes the temple, the heart the altar, one's attention the offering.

The early ascetics described in the Vedas differ little from the *sadhus* who walk the roads of India today. Known by the Greeks as 'naked philosophers', the Vedas speak of renunciates with long matted hair, covered in ashes from head to toe, with just a scrap of rag or an animal skin for clothing, and distinguishing marks on their forehead. Among their only belongings were a staff and a water pot. Vaishnavites may also have possessed a conch and a replica of Vishnu's discus; Shaivites would have carried a trident, a skull, a drum, and a small lingam.

These possessions still characterize the two main branches of Hindu ascetics today. Their distinguishing marks have also remained the same: Shaivites take ashes from the cremation ground and daub three horizontal lines across the forehead, or two with a red dot between the eyebrows. Vaishnavites stripe their forehead with vertical lines. For their *mala* (rosary) beads, the Shaivites use rudraksha seeds; while Vaishnavites use *tulsi* wood, from the tree that is sacred to Vishnu.

There are somewhere between four and five million ascetics, or sadhus, in India today, perhaps ten per cent of whom are women. Most of them wear orange robes, though a few sects, like the Nagas, go naked. Broadly, most of them are Shaivites; only two of the four Vaishnavite sects, the Nimbarkas and the Ramanandis, have many ascetics, while some sadhus are Shaktas, worshippers of the goddess. These general categories embrace a wide variety of sects and sub-sects who may worship different forms of the main deities, have different texts for their source material, and different gurus whose inspiration was the origin of the sect in the first place. Sometimes, as in the case of the Goraknathis, the founder himself is worshipped as an expression of God.

Between them, they represent the whole range of inner

disciplines and spiritual practices that have developed in Hinduism through the centuries. Many Shaivites, following the teachings of the Upanishads, will be non-dualists, and will spurn any outer ritual or worship of any kind. One of their main practices will be the mantra, *Shivo'am* – 'I am Shiva'. Others will be non-dual in principle, but will still incorporate ritual and worship into their discipline. While the Shaivites tend towards an impersonal view of the cosmos, the Vaishnavites will all be devotionally inclined, with one or other divine incarnation of Vishnu serving as their personal deity. Their mantra will be the name of their lord, *Hare Ram*, or *Hare Krishna*. Poetry and song is often central for the Vaishnava. The Sri Vaishnava sect, for example, which is centred on the Shrirengi temple in the south, was inspired by Ramanuja (1050–1137), the great exponent of qualified dualism who first introduced the songs of the Dravidian poets, the Alvars, into the temple ceremonies. Sri Caitanya, the founder of the Gaudiya Vaishnavas, was also an ecstatic poet. The manifestation and intensity of devotion, though, will vary considerably between the different Vaishnavite sects. While some, like the Hare Krishna followers who are known so well in the West, will dance and sing in ecstatic union with the Lord, others look down on any display of the intensity of interior feelings.

Some sects, both Shaivite and Vaishnavite, as well as the Shaktas, have a strong tantric influence in their practices. *Tantra*, from the root 'tan', 'to expand', literally means nothing more exotic than 'exposition': it refers to those texts which, coming after the Vedas and the Upanishads, sought to translate their philosophies into an active path of practice. In Tantra, the world is not *maya*, illusion, but power, *shakti*. Far from being seen as an obstacle, shakti is the fuel for tantric spiritual practice, enabling the dark forces of the instincts to be faced and absorbed instead of being rejected. The sacred and the profane are all one in the eyes of the tantric practitioner, whose discipline aims to make him free and invulnerable even while enjoying the world.

A few sects, like the Vaishnavite Sahajas, have female

140

consorts with whom they act out the union of the male and the female principles. The Sakhis are a transvestite sub-sect who literally take on the role of the mistress of the lord. These are exceptions, however: the usual tantric practice is to seek to unite the male and the female principles internally by visualizations of the different goddesses. Tantra became integrated into Shaivism primarily through the dark goddesses, and into Vaishnavism through the bright goddesses. Connected to these practices is Hatha yoga, which does not mean in India what it has come to mean in the West: rather than a series of physical postures, it signifies a powerful means of raising energy – kundalini – from the base of the spine to the crown of the head, where the 'inner marriage' takes place. To achieve this, forced breathing techniques, known as pranayama, and visualizations of the chakras – the energy centres along the spine – are used in conjunction with the postures more commonly associated with the term hatha. The overall practice is supported with strict celibacy and a restricted, pure diet.

The sects and subdivisions of sadhus assumed their present forms through the reforming zeal of Shankara, one of India's greatest philosopher-ascetics. He lived some time in the 8th century AD, and was a monk from the age of eight until his death at 32. During his short life, he succeeded in revitalizing the entire ascetic tradition of India, and successfully restored the supremacy of Hinduism over its Jain and Buddhist rivals.

It was the example of these two religions that demonstrated to Shankara the necessity for a solid organizational base for India's ascetics, along monastic lines. Shankara himself remains India's most brilliant exponent of the advaitic, nondual philosophy of the Upanishads – his commentaries on the Upanishads and the Bhagavad Gita, completed while he was still in his teens, are classics – but he recognized the need to accommodate in his reorganization the many forms of practice, from the dual to the non-dual, which have always co-existed in India. Travelling all over the country, enthralling listeners with his inspired oratory and philosophical brilliance, he managed to divide the sadhus into ten orders – still known today as the Dasnamis, the ten names.

Each of the orders remains affiliated to one of four principal monasteries which Shankara established in the different corners of the country: Joshimath, in the Himalayas; Dwarka, to the west; Puri, in the east; and Shringeri, in the south. They also have their own monastic centres all over the country. The heads of the orders, along with their followers, would meet every three years at the Khumba Mela. Today, as ever, they still gather at the Mela to discuss monastic business and politics. Since Shankara, other gurus have followed his example and established their own maths, or monasteries.

The sadhu you meet along some pilgrim route will rarely be living in isolation. He is usually connected to one of the Dasnamis, or to one of the more recent sects. His rule of life will probably be similar to the one that Shankara laid down in the 9th century: if he is wandering, he will only stop at one place for up to three days, and will either live by begging, or will stop for food at a monastery. Walking was the usual means of travel, though today many sadhus use the bus or train. More and more sadhus now live in monasteries, since the contemporary social climate does not favour their way of life as it did. Even 30 years ago, a knock on the door by a sadhu begging for food was seen as a visitation from God which brought nothing but honour. Now the public perception is changing, in line with the shift towards Western values. Indian society no longer looks so kindly on begging. Traditionally, sadhus always travelled free on the trains. They often still do, but today, people suspect them of being criminals in hiding, or dope-smoking drop-outs who cannot or do not wish to contend with the challenges of contemporary life. Unfortunately, this perception is not altogether incorrect, and the diminishing number of genuine sadhus have to bear the consequences along with their less reputable brothers.

One genuine sadhu is an American called Charan Dass. Charan Dass has followed the sadhu way of life for 22 years. He says there are a dozen Westerners in India who have been sadhus as long as he has. He first came to India to write a book on ashrams, and never went back. After being with various gurus and sadhus, he was initiated into the Ramanandi sampradaya. His matted grey hair falls below his shoulders, his eyes laugh behind battered spectacles, his body is covered with two simple cloths. He only ever walks barefoot, and never sleeps inside. His time is given to wandering from one sacred occasion or festival to another, to scholarly study of the religious traditions of India, and to solitary meditation on the inner sound and light. The only difference between him and any other sadhu is the tiny stipend he receives monthly from a trust fund in America. When I travelled with him for a few days, people accorded him respect wherever we went – perhaps more than most sadhus receive because they are impressed by a Westerner taking on such a life. Whatever happens, Charan Dass takes it to be the will of God, and accepts it without question. Instead of resisting the flow of events, he adjusts his agenda – if indeed he has one at all. Far from being a maladjusted drop-out, he is one of the most dedicated and joyous people you could meet.

THE SHANKARACHARYA OF KANCHI

The heads of Shankara's monasteries are still called by the title 'Shankaracharya'. Bastions of orthodox Brahmin Hinduism, they represent today the religious establishment. Their monasteries are the closest Hinduism comes to the Christian ideal of enclosure. Practically all the monks are resident in the monasteries, and follow a strict monastic routine. Unlike the great majority of ascetics in India, the Shankaracharyas have considerable political influence. Shringeri, for example, resembles a small Vatican state; greatly endowed by royalty, it continues to maintain spiritual and temporal power over its own area. The Indian government has given the responsibility for resolving the problem of Ayodhya over to the Shankaracharyas. They have not, however, made much progress. The Shankaracharya of Shringeri never turns up for meetings, and the

143

head of the Puri Math holds reactionary views that the others do not subscribe to. As yet, far from offering a solution to the country, they have not even been able to agree with each other.

The Shankaracharya of Kanchi will tell you that Shankara founded a fifth monastery, his own, in the Tamil town of Kanchipuram. Shankara, he will say, came to Kanchi five years before his death, presided personally over the math he founded there, and breathed his last in the Kamakshi temple. True or false, the fact is that the Shankaracharya of the Kanchi Math has enjoyed more popular support than most monastics in recent years. The Dwarka and Puri Maths have little influence today, whereas the seat at Kanchi is esteemed all over India, owing to the exemplary saintliness of the late Shankaracharya, who died in 1994 at the age of 100. His devotees, who numbered in millions, were deeply impressed by the old man's austere observance of the ancient traditions of poverty, virtue and spiritual discipline. Even in old age, he would only ever travel by foot, wear his simple ochre robe, and eat nothing but the simplest food. Above all, his spiritual presence was evident to all who came within sight of him, and thousands attributed healings and spiritual awakenings to his influence. For most of the 20th century, he was a beacon of spiritual purity and power. When he died, the whole of India went into national mourning.

It is a hard act for Jayendra, the new Shankaracharya, to follow. He has 250 monks in his care, and thousands of lay devotees who are affiliated to the math through their family tradition. I met him while he was giving darshan in the monastery at Kanchipuram. He was sitting in front of an open doorway which was barred by a wooden railing three feet high. The room he was in was empty except for a picture of his predecessor. The 69th Pontiff of the math was sitting cross-legged on a cushion in front of the doorway. He wore a simple orange robe and a mala of rudraksha beads. His head was shaved. As devotees filed past, he gave them his blessings along with prasad, a piece of sugar or a sweet which had been empowered by mantras during the puja to the deities. His assistant had ushered me into the room with the Pontiff, and I sat a few yards from the doorway, watching the procession of devotees who had come from all over India for these few seconds of contact with their family guru. Perhaps a thousand people a day come to the monastery for Jayendra's darshan. Some, heads sunk into their chest, were too awestruck to look him in the eye; others beamed in delight; a few leant forward to whisper a request for help with some personal problem. To all of them, Jayendra offered a benign smile along with the prasad.

I asked him what was in his mind as he performed this ritual service. 'I think of God, and then I bless them,' he replied, handing me a sugar cube.

When I asked him why they came, he said that most come for darshan, to have blessings for some venture, or to have spiritual help for some personal problem. Very few ever wanted any spiritual instruction, but when asked, he would suggest some practice appropriate for the individual.

'To some, I give a mantra,' he said, without taking his eyes from the stream of faces passing before him. 'To others, I suggest the singing of bhajans, or some service done in the name of God. Very occasionally, I suggest a meditation practice. It all depends on the person's level.'

Jayendra's answer was in keeping with what I had noticed of the daily practices in his math. Though all the Shankaracharyas uphold the non-dual tradition of Shankara, in practice the math is a place of ritual and worship, like any other temple in India. During the Lakshmi puja held there in the mornings, flowers and rice are offered to a cow and to the monastery elephant. The animals are anointed with sandalwood and kum-kum, then arati is performed over them; so by the end of the puja the divine power has been firmly established in the animals. Pujas are also performed for the lingam and the Sri Cakra (a geometrical symbol of the goddess) which are installed in the shrine room of the math.

Jayendra has also added a dimension of public service.

Traditionally, the math never involved itself in secular affairs, but now it has its own home for the aged, an engineering and computer science college, and a Vedic school. In 1995, the President of India inaugurated the math's International Library for Religious Studies in Kanchipuram. Jayendra's mission to combine social action with contemplation may strike a contemporary chord, but it has met serious opposition from within the math and among its lay supporters. Many feel that the spiritual leadership of the math and its head, which was so unambiguous in the figure of the previous Shankaracharya, is being compromised by Jayendra's initiatives.

I gazed at this portly monk handing out sugar cubes, in wonder at the hand of destiny that had brought him here. Jayendra first came to the math at the age of ten, sent by his family to study Sanskrit. By the time he was thirteen, the previous Shankaracharya had chosen him for his successor. He became a monk at the age of eighteen, and has been treated as a demi-god ever since. In 1970, he went on foot to all the major holy places in north India, with people throwing flowers in his path all along the way. Now, in his early sixties, every minute of his day is regulated by tradition and protocol. People still remember – and many mistrust him for it – the time in the 1980's when he mysteriously disappeared for a few days without explanation. It would be rather like having the Pope going missing. Jayendra has never really explained what happened, preferring not to contradict the official story that he was on 'personal retreat'. Rumours still persist that he lost his nerve, and was debating whether to step out of his role.

'Don't you sometimes feel a prisoner of other people's expectations?' I asked.

'Never,' he replied without hesitation. 'I have totally surrendered to the role that God has allotted to me. That is my spiritual practice. I know that this is what I am here to do. I am an ordinary man attempting to fulfil a special duty.'

The next day I watched the ceremony in which he officially ascended the throne of the Shankaracharya. He was to be crowned, just like a king. In fact, he was a king, for in India the king was always the mediator between God and his people – precisely the role that Jayendra was officially about to assume. Hundreds of devotees and monks were pressed tightly round a dais which was heaped with flower garlands. When he entered, and sat with a diffident smile on his appointed seat, batteries of press cameras all flashed at once. Someone was pulling at my sleeve. I turned. It was a young monk, not out of his teens, wanting to stand in front of me for a better view. In a lull in the proceedings, I asked him what had made him join the monastery.

'My family sent me to study Sanskrit,' he said.

SHAIVA SIDDHANTA

In India the first known book of love songs to God was written in Tamil by Maanikkavaachakar – 'he whose utterances are rubies' – in the 3rd century AD. This poet's work is one of a dozen poetry collections, all written in Tamil between the 3rd and the 12th centuries, which are at the heart of Shaiva Siddhanta. The agamas, too, play a central role in this school. They are 28 scriptural texts given, it is said, to Parvati by Shiva when she asked him to provide a means of liberation for mortals. In highly abstruse language, they specify the appropriate forms of worship and describe a four-fold path: carya (external pujas), kriya (inner purificatory practices and yogic postures), yoga (meditation practices), and jnana (union with Shiva).

The songs of the Tamil poets are still sung in the temples of the south today, and the agamas continue to be the texts that are used in temple worship. Shaiva Siddhanta is the main school of spiritual practice in the south, and its influence is evident everywhere in the Tamil religious culture. While Shaivism in general is often described as an impersonal route to liberation which relies on the path of knowledge, it is in fact a highly composite tradition which is full of inconsistencies and exceptions. The Upanishads, and Shankara's non-dual philosophy, are only one aspect of Shaivism; Shaiva Siddhanta, and also Kashmir Shaivism in the north, contain a strong spirit of personal devotion which is not evident in the Vedas. Devotion transcends all religious differences and castes, since love is the fulfilment of all the laws. The poet-saints of the Tamil country followed the path of love, and never separated themselves from popular culture. Tamil Nadu, in particular, has always been a devotional land: their language even has a separate section of grammar devoted to the theme of love and its literature.

At the same time, Shaiva Siddhanta is founded on a highly sophisticated philosophy which has many similarities with Christianity. The soul is viewed as the Bride of the Shiva, from whom She is separated by the primordial limitation, or darkness, of individual reality. The Lord sends His grace to awaken the soul, who then comes to distinguish the true from the false. Thus the soul and the Lord gradually become united in a circle of grace and awakening. They are advaita, literally, 'not two'. Contrary to the teaching of the Upanishads, the soul is one with Shiva, but not merged in him. In Shaiva Siddhanta, the soul is part of the divine Trinity along with Shiva and His action of Grace.

One of the ways Shaiva Siddhanta differs from Christianity is in the importance it gives to the guru. The guru is crucial to the path, because he is seen to embody the divine grace which is so necessary for progress. I encountered a guru of Shaiva Siddhanta in Kanchipuram, in his monastery a few streets away from the Shankaracharya math. Sri Lasri Swamikal was officiating at a puja when I arrived. A dozen lay people were in the shrine hall, and two monks. Sri Swamikal wore crisp orange robes and a crown made of a rudraksha mala twisted into a spiral on the top of his shaven head. Hired singers were chanting the songs of a Tamil poet, and an assistant was waving a huge arati lamp in front of the lingam. When they had finished, the guru left first, and one of the monks led me through to the guru's personal quarters.

Sri Lasri Swamikal was sitting on a high chair at one end of an otherwise empty audience room. The monk prostrated full length on the floor in front of his guru, and then motioned to me to do the same. I hesitated for a second, at which the guru laughed and the monk scowled. Then I bowed with a namaskar greeting, which the guru seemed perfectly satisfied with. When I asked, he told me he had been at the math for 15 years, and that he had come to revitalize and rebuild the place. It was empty 50 years earlier, although it used to have 27 branches throughout south India. At one time, some three centuries ago, one of the main temples of Kanchipuram was under its jurisdiction. Now there are perhaps a dozen monks, and a considerable number of lay devotees, who have always played a significant role in Shaiva Siddhanta.

I asked him what spiritual disciplines were practised in the math.

'Our agamas,' he replied, 'include the astanga yoga of Patanjali, except they call it Sivayoga. Astanga (the eight-fold path) yoga includes external disciplines like non-violence and celibacy; the internal disciplines of cleanliness, contentment, scripture study; then asana, for a healthy body; and pranayama, breathing practices which activate the chakras. The last four stages are all progressive levels of meditation. But while Patanjali would have said that the goal of his yoga is mind control, one of our poet-saints, Tirumular, says that the aim is ultimately to lead you to union with Shiva. Without bhakti, we do not see much use in yoga for its own sake alone. And as you have just seen, we nourish the feeling of devotion with song and worship.'

He paused for a moment. Dispatching a monk to the kitchen to make tea, he continued in another vein.

'Have you been to Chidambaram?' he asked. When I nodded that I had, he went on to speak of Nataraja, the Dancing Lord.

'Nataraja is very important to us,' Sri Lasri explained. 'He holds the secret of our mantra. You may know that Nataraja brings the world into being through his dance of the five elements. His complete form is summed up in the word Aum, which in its expanded form contains the five syllables of the

149

Shiva mantra: Om Nama Shivaya. These five syllables are related to the five elements. We chant the mantra in this order: Ci-va-ya-na-ma. Ci represents the mystic action of Lord Shiva; Va refers to His grace; Ya is the human soul; Na is the whirl of Impurity in itself; and Ma is that Impurity operating in the soul. When you recite it this way, Va points out Ci, the Lord, to the soul, Ya, which thereby abides in bliss. Ma and Na are put at the end so that they cannot obstruct the flow of grace to the soul. This is all Nataraja's dance – the divine stream of grace given to the soul in bondage, and also in emancipation. We chant the Shiva mantra first with our lips, then in the mind, and finally in the heart. You can read the full explanation in Umapathi's 'Fruit of Divine Grace'.

Umapathi, I knew, was a 14th-century poet whose work was a core text in Shaiva Siddhanta. We chatted on for a few minutes more, but it was clear that Sri Lasri Swamikhal had said all he was going to say. He was a scholar of some standing, and had gathered a respectable library for his math in the time he had been there. There are many Siddhanta maths in south India, and, without any central organization, their spiritual direction is inevitably determined by the individual gurus who guide them. The guru of the Madurai math, I remembered, as I made a farewell namaskar to Sri Lasri Swamikhal, had cut a particularly distinctive path: he was once seen in a newspaper photograph waving a machine gun on behalf of the Tamil separatists. His reputation, it is said, has never recovered.

THE NAGA BABAS

The Naga babas are the popular model of the quintessential sadhu – they are the ones who travel naked, covered only in ashes; their hair is matted and long, their eyes are wild, and they are often hunched by the Ganga or along the roadside smoking a chillum of marijuana. They usually travel on foot in small groups, and live in the open or under a sheet of canvas. They are the warrior sadhus, who used to resist the rule of the

Muslims and more recently the British. They are still divided into six 'regiments', each of which has slightly different practices and symbols.

They have dedicated their lives to Lord Shiva – usually in his ferocious form of Bhairava – and their belongings are mostly confined to his emblems – the trident, fire tongs, a lingam, a water pot. They give unswerving obedience to a guru of the sect for twelve years, during which time they practise arduous physical disciplines. I encountered a group of Nagas by the Ganga in Banaras. On a step by their encampment were two swings hanging from the projecting roof of a building. Over one of them was slumped a young boy.

The guru of the group was called Nandsurajgiri. He was sitting on the step by the boy on the swing, a lithe man of perhaps 60 years. I asked him what the boy was doing.

'He has taken a vow to remain standing for twelve years. He can only sleep with his chest over the swing, keeping his feet on the ground. This is one of our practices, though it is only for those who the guru chooses. This boy is the youngest ever to attempt it.'

'How old is he?'

'He is eight and a half years. He has been standing since he was three. By the time he is fifteen he will be a guru.'

I stared at the boy. I had often heard of young children being taken off by the Nagas.

'How did he come to you?' I asked.

'His father came to me and asked for a child. Within three months his wife had conceived. When the child was born, he came and offered him to me. I refused, because a first born son should always be kept for the family. Later the father returned with his second child, a girl; but I only accept boys. Then he brought his third child, this boy, when he was three months old. He offered me 5,000 rupees to take him, and I accepted.'

'How did you know he would be fit for this practice at so young an age?'

'When he was three, the boy himself declared his wish to stand for God. I could see that in his previous birth he had

151

been a saint, and that this birth was an auspicious one for him to attain liberation.'

'What does he do apart from the standing?'

'He chants "Shivo'am" day and night, even in his sleep. That is the mantra we use.'

I asked Nandsurajgiri how he became a Naga himself.

'I left home as a child, chanting "Hare Krishna, Hare Ram". My life was for God alone. When I met a group of Naga babas, I knew that was the path for me to follow.'

'How old are you now?'

'Ninety-five.'

He laughed at my astonishment. 'I have been a guru since 1947,' he added.

Just then the boy woke up and saw me.

'Camera?' he asked, with the grin of any eight year old.

Nearby was a woman ascetic, whose gentle air was in marked contrast to the machismo around her. She told me that several thousand Nagas were women. She had left home in 1980, she said, to offer her life to the sanatana dharma, which she felt was in jeopardy due to the influence of modern values. Another young man – he looked young – was busy wrapping his penis round a stick and putting the stick through his legs, behind him and under his buttocks. The Nagas control the sex urge by elongating the penis, which apparently breaks the action of certain nerves.

This particular Naga, I suspected, was playing to the cameras, for there were several tourists aiming lenses at him. Posing for photos is a favourite Naga ploy for demanding money. Normally, this kind of display would be seen only at their initiation ceremony at the Kumbh Mela. There, they have been known to pull a jeep along for a kilometre with a cord attached to their penis. This seemingly impossible feat, whose secret lies in breathing techniques, has been seen by thousands, and has been photographically recorded. At the initiation ceremony in the Ganga, the guru and disciple chant mantras, the disciple offers his past life into the fire, and receives the saffron robe and a personal mantra from the guru.

He will wear his robe for the first twelve years, and travel with the guru wherever he goes. After twelve years, he receives full initiation at the Khumba Mela, and discards his robe for ashes.

He is also introduced to the general Naga community at the Mela, and assigned a responsibility within the particular regiment he is part of. Even the Nagas have their monastic hierarchy. There are seven different maths in Banaras alone, and Nandsurajgiri told me the building they were sheltering against was their 'Head Office'. Sure enough, there were more than 50 aging monks in residence, and a 'president' dressed in fine silk robes with four secretaries. The president, Sohangiri Maharaj, told me that his post is elected by general consensus for a term of six years. He himself had been 45 years on the road, but he wore the dignity of his new life well. It was difficult to picture him stretching his penis behind his buttocks.

A GORAKNATHI BABA

Devbarnath Yogi fills the room with joy and vitality. He is 72, and looks twenty years younger. What distinguishes him as a member of the Goraknath sect is the thick wooden earring which pierces each ear, not through the lobe but through the middle of the ear itself. The ear is ripped by the guru at initiation with a double-edged knife. The disciple concentrates on the guru while the operation is being performed, and for the next 41 days ingests only sugar water and milk. Then the ring is inserted, symbolizing his vow of celibacy.

Still now, Devbarnath Yogi only eats fruit and milk. The Goraknathis, whose main centres are in Rajasthan and Goraknath, practise hatha yoga, generating the power of shakti through pranayama.

'When shakti rises,' Devbarnath explained, 'the mind runs from her.' He leaned back and roared with laughter. 'But you must let her catch him. Keep the mind in front of her, so she can swallow it. Once the mind feels the electric current rising up the spine, it won't want to move. You will hear a tinkling sound in the body, too. Each of the energy channels up the spine has their own sound. When shakti is activated, you will hear the conch, the drum, and the flute inside your body. Once shakti is fully awoken, you will see no more distinctions of caste or creed, and you will know the past and the future.'

Devbarnath Yogi went on to say that the trident that the Goraknaths carry represents the three sins that must be removed before shakti can flow: thinking ill of others; speaking ill of others; and doing ill to others. Trust in the power of Shiva is the way to remove these obstacles. All drugs and alcohol are strictly avoided by dedicated Goraknaths like Devbarnath Yogi, who says that intoxicants disturb the subtle vibrational field that their practices aim to purify and energize.

Most Goraknathis, though, are not so scrupulous, and many of the sadhus to be seen by the roadsides smoking their chillums are from their sampradaya.

Devbarnath Yogi joined the Goraknathis 40 years ago. He was a householder then, and had married for love – a rare event in India, where most marriages are arranged by the families. Unfortunately, he had fallen for a woman whose family was wealthy, and from a higher caste. Her family made their lives so intolerable that eventually he left to become a sadhu. He heard later that she had died of shock some time afterwards. They had had no children, and he continued his wanderings, eventually joining the Goraknaths. He practised fanatically; many of his fellows thought he was mad, but in fact he was wild with grief. His pain gave him the energy for all his austerities, and eventually it was subsumed into an all-encompassing love. After some 20 years, he said, he finally attained full absorption into Shiva.

THE DANDISWAMIS

If the Nagas are the fighting order of swamis, the Dandiswamis are the teachers and preachers. Unlike the Nagas, who are usually from the lowest castes, the Dandiswamis are all

Brahmins. They are easily recognized by the long staff – the dandi – that they always carry in front of them. Their sampradaya runs hospitals and educational centres; seva, service, being an integral part of their practice. At their initiation, they tie their sacred Brahmin thread around their staff, and cover it with a cloth. From then on, they carry the staff with the thread at the level of the third eye. They also attach an axe head to the staff, symbolizing that all violence in them has been surrendered to God.

Sarami Swami, a Dandiswami in one of their maths in Banaras, told me that for his order, meditation was the direct path. They practised no hatha yoga, only meditation on the light of the third eye. This light is for them the formless manifestation of the Divine. The more you practise, the more the light fills the whole body, until eventually, you become the light itself. Unlike the Goraknaths, they are careful not to force the process. As soon as the third eye begins to feel hot due to the concentration, they will stop and apply camphor and sandalpaste as a coolant to the brow. They call their practice Prem Yoga, the yoga of love.

Sarami Swami had been a Senior Inspector in the Government Service. In his forties, he became deeply interested in meditation, spurred on by the inner sound he would often hear in his body (a well-known phenomenon among meditators, itself the basis of an entire meditation system, nada, or sound, yoga). He requested a transfer from the city of Allahabad to Almora, in the Himalayas, where he could practise more. Finally, when he was 50, he took early retirement, left his family for the Dandiswami sampradaya, and spent years alone in a Himalayan cave. In this, he was following the Hindu tradition of the asramas, the four stages of life which culminate in the life of the sannyasin, the renunciate. Still today, it is a common practice for a man approaching retirement to withdraw to a religious institution or to turn to charitable work. Sarami Swami came to the math a few years ago when his health began to wane. Now 70, his frail figure, like the other monks I saw in his math, had none of the vitality of

Devbarnath Yogi, who was the same age. Besides constitutional differences, their respective practices have probably influenced their physical well-being – while the body and its energies are central to hatha yoga, the prem yoga described by Sarami Swami leaves this world behind for the realm of subtle light, implying a dualism that separates the physical from the life divine.

LOVERS OF RAM AND KRISHNA

> Shiva has said that if a man dies at Kashi he wins salvation. But devotion is the root of everything, and salvation but her handmaiden who follows her. What is the worth of salvation if it means absorption, the mixing of sugar with water? Sugar, I love to eat, but I have no desire to become sugar.
>
> *Bengali Religious Lyrics, trans. E. J. Thompson. From a poem by Bengali Sakta, Ramprasad Sen*

The Vaishnavas are lovers of a personal God: they want to taste the bliss of union, not, like most Shaivites, to dissolve in a state of undifferentiated oneness. For them, love of necessity means relationship. Over the last millennium, they have developed a sophisticated philosophy of divine love which both allows for a relationship between the soul and the Supreme, and at the same time sees no inherent difference between them – just as quantum physics now sees matter to be both particle and wave at the same time. The various schools retain their own finer points of distinction on what is essentially the same teaching.

Ramanuja, the great bhakta of the 11th century in the south, encouraged the worship of Ram, Krishna, and Vishnu himself, along with their consorts. Ramanuja countered the strict monism of Shankara with a qualified dualism. His teaching spread throughout the south, assisted by his willingness to accept disciples from any caste. His commentary on the Bhagavad Gita, which honours the bhakti tone of the text, is more faithful than Shankara's to the original. The Sri Vaishnava sect in the south are the largest community to continue his direct teachings today, though Ramanuja's influence is evident in most of the later Vaishnava schools.

For some 300 years, between the 14th and the 16th centuries, a wave of enthusiasm for the path of romantic love spread all over north India. Ramananda in the 14th century, and Tulsidas in the 16th, propagated the worship of Lord Ram, using the vernacular language of the people rather than Sanskrit, and rejecting the Brahmins as intermediaries between the people and God. What need has the religion of love for caste or barriers? It asks only for an open and longing heart, willing to receive the direct communication of grace from the Lord. The Ramanandis have many maths all over north India, and comprise the majority of all Vaishnava sadhus. The Tulsidas version of the Ramayana is still the most widely read book in all India.

Vallabacharya and Caitanya, the two great lovers of Krishna, also lived and taught in the 16th century. Their descendants are widespread today, and the various schools of Gaudiya Vaishnavism, which all trace their lineage back to Caitanya, include the international Hare Krishna Movement. The Gaudiyas, especially, spread their message of love through song and dance, which remains a central feature of their worship. Following the example of Caitanya himself, ecstasy was the goal, and the signs of spiritual madness were involuntary manifestations like the hair standing on end, goose flesh, trembling, quivering, crying and loss of consciousness.

Caitanya came from Bengal, traditionally an area of intense devotion with a love of religious music and dance. He married, and when he was 22, he went to Gaya to perform his father's funeral rites. While he was there he met his guru, and returned to Navadweep, his native place, God-maddened. For a year or more he led nightly gatherings of ecstatic song and dance. Then he entered an ascetic order for a period, after which he went to live in Puri. Caitanya would often swoon in his love of Krishna, his body would turn different colours, and sometimes his joints would pop in and out like a tortoise. Most Gaudiyas today consider him an incarnation of Krishna and Radha in one body.

For the followers of both Vallabacharya and Caitanya, two main teachings are at the heart of their philosophy and practice. The first is the principle of rasa. Originally, this signified the response of someone who had a refined sensibility – who could 'taste' the hidden meanings in a dramatic performance. In the 16th century, a link was made between rasa and moksha, and a theory of rasa as a system of devotion developed. Rasa came to mean the taste of bliss, and was sometimes connected with the tantric methods by which the energy of bliss was raised up the spine to the seventh chakra at the crown of the head, which signified the union of Radha and Krishna. The primary aspiration of rasa now became the absorption of all the senses into an experience of love for Krishna.

The progressive deepening of that love is compared to the stages in the refinement of sugar. The devotee passes through different degrees of 'sweetness' in his relationship with God – from a quietistic 'waiting on God', to the role of His servant, to a friend, to parent (with Krishna as the child and the devotee as mother) and ultimately, to the lover of the beloved. The final stage of the lover, personified by Radha, is ecstatic union with God. Here, the soul is Radha in relation to Lord Krishna. In this there is no need of any outer display or form of worship, just the name of the Beloved trembling on the tongue. In this state, known as Prema Bhakti, the world and the body are forgotten, just as the gopis forgot all worldly custom and propriety at the sound of Krishna's flute. Prema Bhakti echoes the experience of Christian saints like Teresa of Avila, who called herself the Bride of Christ.

The second principle of Krishna worship is the quality of lila. Lila signifies spontaneous, unpremeditated activity. Because the gods have no desires, they are ever freely at play, in the sense of joyous, desireless action. Out of their play they create the universe. Krishna's entire life on earth was a spontaneous, desireless outpouring of natural joy and love. All the

158

events and stories surrounding him were born only of that, not from any premeditated mission or purpose. His life, then, was his lila.

More specifically, the term refers to his rasa lila, the circle dance he performed with the gopis. The entire rasa lila, according to the Bhagavata Purana, goes on forever in the forest of the heart. Whoever takes part in this lila experiences the bliss of desireless spontaneity, for Krishna's lila originates in bliss, unfolds in bliss, and dissolves in bliss. The lila, in this sense, represents the selfless participation in the eternal dance of the universe. There are echoes here of Nataraja, the dancing Lord Shiva; but the mood is different: Krishna as the divine child is more positive, feminine – he urges the flowering of ecstatic love rather than the burning away of all desires.

Krishna's devotees experience this flowering by joining his lila, which is done through meditations involving intricate visualizations of the rasa lila. The devotee must first become familiar with Krishna's world in all its details, and then enter it. He will visualize himself as inwardly female, as one of Radha's handmaidens or friends. Nothing will be omitted from the picture – the colour of the girl's sari, her family, her age, her jewellery, and so on. Some even go so far as to dress up as the woman they are visualizing.

Iskcon, popularly known as the Hare Krishna Movement, differs from the other Gaudiya sects less in the spiritual than in the worldly domain. They are the only Gaudiya sampradaya to actively seek new members through preaching and mission work. They are also the only one to have Western devotees in significant numbers, and in consequence, a source of revenue that far exceeds any of the other sampradayas. Much of their income is spent on vast temple building projects. They are in the process of building new temple complexes in Delhi and in Bangalore, and in Caitanya's birthplace of Navadweep, they are constructing what appears to be an entire city. The Delhi temple is being funded almost entirely from the local community, for the majority of Iskcon members are still Indian. When I asked the head of the Delhi centre why Iskcon felt the need to rival the Vatican, he replied that their motives were indeed the same as the medieval church builders: a large temple attracts crowds, and some of the people who come as sight-seers go away as new Iskcon members.

While Iskcon abroad has had to contend with the image of a cult, it must be acknowledged that many Iskcon members are undoubtedly serious spiritual practitioners. Members generally live in the ashrams as brahmacharis until around the age of 25, when most of them move out and get married. They will then follow the traditional four stages of Hindu life, moving soon to the vanaprasta asrama, the third stage in which they remain together as a celibate couple. As householders, they will earn their own living or be full-time assistants to the ashram. Their knowledge of the devotional scriptures is often profound, and their inner practices, which centre on rasa and lila, are as intensive as their better known outer displays. In the end, whatever public opinion may feel about a particular group, no-one is qualified to judge the spiritual life of another. A Hindu would say that it is all grace – all the play of the Lord – whatever group we join or don't join.

THE KABIR PANTH

> What is muttering, what austerity, what vows and
> worship, to him in whose heart there is another love?[2]

The work of the 16th-century poet Kabir, through modern renditions by popular figures like Robert Bly, is enjoying something of a renaissance in the Western world. Kabir's trenchant disdain of the religious orthodoxy, his emphasis on personal experience instead of received wisdom, fit well with the mood of the end of the millennium. Despite his contemporary reputation as a poet, Kabir was a spiritual leader first and a poet second: he was the founder of a renunciate tradition which continues to have monasteries all over north India.

While he shared much with the resurgent bhakti movements

of the time – he was a contemporary of Caitanya and Ramananda – Kabir is unique in several ways. First, he was brought up in the household of a Muslim weaver, and many of his teachings suggest that he was a sufi. Like them, he was never a sadhu, but married, remained as a householder and continued to work as a weaver and support his family. When he was brought before the Muslim ruler in Banaras by a Muslim sheikh, on the charge that he had made claim to divine attributes, Kabir escaped the death penalty not only by his wit, which charmed the Emperor, but also because Muslim rulers, who were normally strict in such matters, tended to overlook the inspired, and sometimes blasphemous, utterances of the sufis.

Kabir made enemies of both the Hindu and the Muslim orthodoxy. Even as a boy, his mind was immersed in the name of God, which for him was Ram, not Allah. He knew that he needed a guru to progress further, yet as a Muslim, he did not qualify. The great bhakta, Ramananda, lived in Banaras, and always used to take his morning bath at Panchaganga ghat. Kabir lay in wait for him one day on the steps, and as he passed, Kabir stuck his foot out. The guru tripped over it, and cried out 'Ram'. Kabir took this to be his initiation by Ramananda, and from then on called himself his disciple. Both Hindus and Muslims were outraged, but when they brought Kabir before Ramananda, the guru confirmed the boy's initiation.

Kabir recognized no caste distinctions, none of the asrama stages of Hindu life, and none of its six systems of philosophy. Any religion without genuine devotion was worthless to him. The one true religion was that of the heart, which recognized no national or cultural boundaries. Muslims and Hindus alike flocked to his teachings, which were orally transmitted in the vernacular through his ecstatic songs and poems. Kabir knew that one of the values of poetry was that it could easily be remembered. It also cut through the textual verbiage of the traditional teachings in Sanskrit or Arabic, which the ordinary people could not understand.

161

A man may read many books before he dies and not be
a Pandit; he is a Pandit who understands the two and a
half letters which form the word 'love'.

Guru Nanak, another contemporary of Kabir, and the founder
of the Sikh religion, often expressed his indebtedness to the
Banarsi poet, and the Adi Granth, the holy book of the Sikhs,
includes many of his couplets. Kabir continued to generate
controversy all through his life, and he even made use of his
death to illustrate the blindness of following tradition instead
of listening to the call of the heart. For Hindus, death at
Banaras leads straight to the Lord. Those who died at Maghar,
however, a town in the district of Gorakhpur, would be
reborn, according to tradition, as an ass. Despite the protesta-
tions of his disciples, Kabir, knowing his time was near, went
off to die at Maghar:

What is Kasi? What Maghar? He who dies at Maghar is
not dead when Ram has taken up his abode in his heart.
He who dies elsewhere puts Ram to shame.

At Maghar, his Moslem disciples wanted to bury his body,
while the Hindus wanted to cremate it. Kabir appeared to the
entire crowd and commanded them to lift the shroud that was
over his body. When they did so, they found nothing but a
heap of flowers. The Hindus took half of them and cremated
them at Banaras. The Moslems buried the rest at Maghar,
where his tomb is now to be found in the math that was built
around it.

The Kabir Panth – the monastic organization – has eight
maths in Banaras, the main one being the Kabir Chowra. The
Chowra was where Ghandi organized his first meetings, in
recognition of the Panth's freedom from caste distinction. It is
where Kabir actually lived, and the house of his parents is next
to the math. On the small altar there is his cap, and by the side
of it are his sandals and a huge mala of 1,000 beads said to
have been given to Kabir by Ramananda. The trident by the

altar, more of a weapon than a symbol, is much larger than the ones that sadhus carry today. It belonged to a Gorakhnathi saint who would sit on the top of it to meditate, challenging others to do the same. The story goes that Kabir levitated with his spinning wheel and called down to the sadhu to come and join him. Thereafter, the sadhu became his disciple and left his trident there.

The Panth has many more householder members than it does renunciates, and these are the source of its revenues. Both householders and monks practise seva and bhakti. They run hospitals, and distribute medicines in the villages. After eight years in the math, a few of the monks return to their villages, and preach in the rural areas. They worship no idols, and perform no pujas: their devotion is to a formless god, and to Kabir, through his representative, the Mahant of the monastery. They chant the 'Bijak' of Kabir, the main collection of his poems, for two hours a day, and do mantra japa with the mantra given to them by their Mahant. The essence of the teaching? Kabir says:

He is naturally called drunk, who is drinking the juice of Ram.

THE RAMAKRISHNA ORDER

Ramakrishna was the spiritual flame who lit up Bengal in the latter part of the 19th century. He was yet another ecstatic lover of God, a devotee of the Great Mother in her form of Kali. As the priest of the Kali temple at Dakshinewar, on the outskirts of Calcutta, he would 'climb on the altar and caress the Divine Mother, chucking her affectionately under the chin. He'd begin singing, laughing, joking and talking with her, or sometimes he'd catch hold of her hands and dance...'.[3] He became so identified with Kali that he would make offerings to his own body, draping himself in flowers and anointing himself with sandalpaste. When his communion with her seemed to wane, even for a few moments, he would feel such agony that he would throw himself to the ground in tears, rubbing his face in the earth until it bled.

Ramakrishna was the divine child in relation to the goddess and to life itself. All the psychic powers passed through him spontaneously. He would spend much of his days on the edge of samadhi, and it would need only a song to the Lord, a gesture of purity on the part of a companion, or a look of innocence, to send him into ecstatic absorption in the divine. When his parents suggested he should marry, he instantly agreed, and even told them who the girl should be, though he had never met her. Sarada Devi was to become a powerful spiritual presence by his side. Teachers came by his temple and offered to instruct him in their various techniques, in tantra, and the non-dualistic nirvikalpa samadhi, the state in which there is no distinction between the knower and the known. He accepted in complete innocence, practising and mastering all the known techniques of tantra, and astonishing his advaitin master by immediately passing into nirvikalpa samadhi for three days. His body showed no sign of life, except that his face seemed to shine; his heart and lungs were utterly still, and he only began to return to consciousness when the master began chanting at the top of his voice. Later, Ramakrishna was to enter nirvikalpa samadhi for six months, and only returned when the Mother appeared to him and said he had a mission to perform for the good of the world. The experience of nirvikalpa samadhi, that self and God are identical, helped to make Ramakrishna the universalist he was, for he saw that all religions and individual aspirations arise out of the one Godhead who lives and moves as everything.

This was the non-dual message that his disciples were to carry into the 20th century. Before his death in 1885, Ramakrishna had attracted around him a dozen young men who became the inner circle of his devotees. It was these men who later lived together as renunciates, and founded the Ramakrishna Mission, which today is active all over the world. Foremost among his disciples was Vivekenanda, whose brilliant intellect and quality of leadership not only firmly established the Mission, but gave a new dimension to Hinduism throughout India.

Vivekenanda was a voice for the new century. His own discipleship was marked by a refusal to take the words of Ramakrishna on faith alone. He had to know for himself, and find his own way to the living truth that he could see in the life of his master. He was an intellectual, and not attracted to the dualistic Mother worship of Ramakrishna; temperamentally, he was inclined to the universalist, non-sectarian view of the advaitins. Ramakrishna, however, was a living embodiment of universality, and through him, Vivekenanda did in fact come to experience and accept the worship of God with form as well as the path of inquiry.

In 1890, Vivekenanda undertook a pilgrimage through India which was to last three years. When he reached Cape Comorin, the southern tip of India, he felt a sudden desire to swim out to a rock some way from the shore. There, he had a vision of what he and his fellow brothers could do to help India. India's great strength was her spirituality, but she desperately needed the education and the science of the West in order to help herself out of her own poverty and crude superstitions. That education would have to be inspired by individuals who lived the spirit of the Upanishads, the essence of Hindu religion, and who were also trained in the new sciences. These people would be monks who had renounced all for the spirit of service, which they would undertake through an organization. The West, which was spiritually weak, could fund the organization in return for the sharing of India's spiritual heritage.

In 1893, Vivekenanda set sail for America, to speak at the World Parliament of Religions in Chicago. This was the first time that a Hindu had come to the West as a spiritual teacher. Vivekenanda caused a sensation. IIis clarity and candour struck a deep chord in the American mind. He spoke simply about the common basis of all religions, the necessity for universal tolerance, and the essential divinity of mankind. He urged self-reliance, inquiry, and individual effort, telling his audience that they should obey the scriptures only until they could do without them.

For three years he travelled across America, inspiring his audiences with his fiery oratory and simple message. It was the same when he spoke in England and France on the first leg of his journey home. When he finally landed in Calcutta, he was greeted as a national hero. Far greater than the money he had collected for what was to become the Ramakrishna Mission, far more important than the number of foreign disciples who arrived in Calcutta with him, was the psychological triumph his countrymen felt he had achieved in the West. For the first time ever, an Indian had been accepted as an equal, and their spiritual heritage had been welcomed with respect and a willingness to learn.

The Mission went into action as soon as it was established, taking part in famine and plague relief and starting its own hospitals and schools. Vivekenanda became its first General President, and another of the young renunciates, Brahmananda, became the head of the Calcutta centre. The Mission, with its colleges, schools of agriculture and industry, libraries and publishing houses, hospitals and dispensaries, includes a math which trains the monks who run the social services.

The Headquarters of the math and Mission are at Belur Math, on the outskirts of Calcutta, just across the Ganga from the Dakshineswar temple where Ramakrishna served as priest. The monks of the Order alternate their time between a life of solitude and meditation, and public service in the Mission's activities. They are sometimes known as the Jesuits of Hinduism, for their blend of scholarly contemplation and action in the world. There are over 150 centres throughout India, and around twenty in Europe and America.

Belur Math today is a serene oasis on the edge of Calcutta. Some 30 acres stretch along the Ganga, around a temple whose architecture represents the styles of the religions of the world. Vivekenanda's room is in a nearby building, containing his musical instruments and a bed which looks out onto the river. In the compound of the Dakshineswar temple – which is more alive today than it ever was – is the room where Ramakrishna used to meet with all his disciples. His two beds – one for sleeping, one for sitting on – almost fill the room, and disciples today huddle around them in a reflective silence, a relief from the press of the crowd that is always gathered at the Kali temple outside.

Vivekenanda, the man of action, would be pleased with the work of his Mission today. Ramakrishna? He is said to have always known the great destiny of his disciples' mission. Yet today, it is difficult to imagine how his ecstatic dances and visions could have produced such a cornerstone of religious establishment in India.

THE BRAHMA KUMARIS

'Celibacy is one of the great blessings in my life,' Sister Maureen assured me when I asked. 'As a woman, I feel much deeper self-respect as a celibate, because there is no call on me to relate sexually to the world. It gives me the freedom to have a more genuine engagement with both men and women, since you always get back what you put out. It also happens to give me more energy and clarity of mind.'

Sister Maureen is a married woman who has been in the 'BKs' for 20 years. She and her husband came across the organization in England when they were 21, and within a week they had committed to celibacy and a life in which the day begins at 4am with meditation. Though they now live in separate centres of the Brahma Kumaris, they are still married and acknowledge a unique bond with each other.

I met Maureen at a conference organized by the 'BKs' at Mount Abu, in Rajasthan. Abu is the home of their international headquarters, known as 'Madhuban', 'the Forest of Honey'. The conference, which was on new attitudes to learning, was filled with people from all over the world – a feature typical of most 'BK' events. This extraordinary organization,

which is affiliated to the UN as a non-governmental organization for peace, was started by a successful jewel merchant
called Brahma Baba in the 1930s, after a series of spiritual
experiences which led him to leave his business affairs and
begin teaching in what is now Pakistan. The essence of his
teaching, which he called Raja Yoga, was that the Supreme
Being, Shiva, is a being of light who contains all the divine
qualities. The human soul is also a being of light, which can be
known through meditation on the third eye. The practitioner
learns to become the light of the soul, and attune to the
greater light of the Supreme in silent communion. With practice, one comes to know both one's own inherent value and
beauty, and to recognize those same qualities in others.

The majority of his followers were women, which at the
time drew strong opposition and harassment because many of
them were of a marriageable age, and Brahma Baba advocated celibacy, along with a non-recognition of caste. Despite
many difficulties, some 300 disciples lived together and practised the teachings. With the Partition, they moved to Mount
Abu, and continued to practise in conditions of extreme
poverty. By the 1960s, a core of women disciples had become
highly proficient yogis, and had begun to teach. One night in
1969, Brahma Baba delivered the evening discourse, went
into his room, lay down on his bed and died. By then, his work
had gained a national reputation, and the Government of
India issued a stamp to commemorate him.

The women yogis he left behind continue to run the organization today. They are called the dadis, the sisters. In the last
25 years, the 'BKs' have spread into many countries, and apart
from their communities and meditation centres, they are committed to major cultural and social initiatives around the
world. They have received seven peace awards from the UN,
and are currently working on a world-wide research project
on the moral crisis of values. Their centres teach meditation to
the general public in 15 countries, though by far the largest
community is in India. Just after the conference I attended had
finished, the staff of Madhuban was preparing to receive 5,000

Indians for a week-long meditation camp!

The 'BKs' have other teachings which many find difficult to accept. They are an 'apocalypse' group, which believes the world as we know it has very little time left to run. They adhere to the Hindu teaching of the four yugas, or ages, that the universe perpetually moves through, except that they say the entire wheel of four ages turns every 5,000 years, whereas in the traditional Hindu teaching, each age lasts many thousands of years. They see the body to be the root of all evil, which is why their meditation focuses on the soul realm, and why celibacy is an aim for many married members as it is for single renunciates. Matter is dead for the 'BKs', only the realm of soul is alive. Such a radically dualistic teaching goes against the flow of many current trends in both spirituality and in science.

Whether one is distanced by such perspectives or not, the fact remains that the 'BKs' are an indisputable force for good in the world. They make no attempt to proseletize, and their world-wide programmes often make no reference to their teachings whatsoever. They never charge for any of their activities, and participants in their conferences are lodged and fed free of charge, without even the sign of a collection box. Their integrity is unquestionable.

At the conference on learning I shared a room with a prison officer called Malcolm Gillan, who had met the 'BKs' just some months before at a seminar they held for prison staff. One of the aims of the conference was to explore values. For the first time, Malcolm heard his own beliefs being vocalized – beliefs that he had never articulated to anyone before. The seminar affirmed his conviction that he was in the prison to be of service to the prisoner, and that change in the world began with change in oneself. He was encouraged to sit quietly with himself each day, to ponder his values and the nature of service. Nobody had ever spoken like this in his training sessions. The seminar increased his respect for the men in his charge, and helped him to let them see him as a person instead of a guard. What he gained from the seminar and from subsequent meetings was not so much a spiritual philosophy

169

as a set of practical life skills founded on a respect and value for others.

Of all the renunciate orders in India, the 'BKs' are probably the least corrupt and among the most spiritually vital. One reason may be that they are a relatively recent phenomenon, their founder having died only 25 years ago. Another, not insignificant factor, may be that their leaders, the dadis, are all women who have spent many arduous years in the practice of what they preach. The only qualm that is occasionally raised against them concerns their particular brand of purity. They all wear white, maintain a soft smile, and talk in somewhat sugary terms about the need for love. Since all human beings have a shadow, one wonders at times where theirs are kept.

1 Quoted in Shobita Punja, *Daughters of the Ocean*.
2 Quoted in G. H. Westcott, *Kabir and the Kabir Panth*. Munshiram Manoharlal 1986.
3 Isherwood, Christopher, *Ramakrishna and His Disciples*. Advaita Ashrama Publishers, Calcutta 1964.

GURUS AND ASHRAMS

The true form of prostration to the Guru is to remain in the Supreme
Silence where the sense of differentiation, Master-disciple, God-man,
cannot rise through the delusion of the ignorant ego.[1]

12

The word 'guru' is usually translated to mean 'the dispeller of
darkness'. It is associated with the root 'gr', from which the
Latin word gravitas comes, and the English 'gravity'. Guru,
then, also means 'heavy with wisdom'. People gravitate
towards him because he is 'heavier', more substantial than
they are. Yet his function is not to make the disciple subordinate to him, or to deprive him of his freedom. On the contrary, he exists to mirror the disciple's own essential nature –
which is freedom itself – back to him. He can only do this if he
himself is free of his own conditioned nature. Otherwise, he
will only reflect the disciple's power, lust and greed drives,
even if combined with elements of insight and clarity.

Ramakrishna's disciple, Vivekananda, was the first guru to
visit the West, at the turn of the last century. He was followed
later by Paramahansa Yogananda, whose world headquarters
is still in Los Angeles. The reputation of these early representatives of the Sanatana Dharma was spotless. Today, however,
we live in a different world. Many gurus who go abroad end
up trailing clouds of scandal. Buddhists and Hindus alike have
found it as easy as the rest of us to be seduced by Western consumerism, and the predictable cul-de-sacs of money, sex and
power. Those who feel they have suffered at their hands,
however, would do well to bear in mind the story of Rakhal,

one of Ramakrishna's closest disciples.

Ramakrishna, a strict celibate, used to share his room with his closest male disciples, while his wife, Sarada Devi, slept in another room across the temple compound at Dakshineswar. Rakhal began to wonder why the master frequently left the room at night, and began to suspect that Ramakrishna was having a secret sexual relationship with his wife. One night he followed his master out, and, with one thought in his mind, went straight to Sarada Devi's door. There was only silence, and it seemed Ramakrishna had gone somewhere else. As Rakhul was returning to their room, he heard a sound in the bushes, and there was Ramakrishna, who had been relieving himself. When Ramakrishna saw Rakhul, he laughed, and said, 'You have done well. It is a disciple's duty to watch his guru day and night.'

The Dalai Lama has criticized Western seekers for their lack of discrimination in their quest for a guru. In Tibet, the disciple is expected to doubt the guru until he is certain of his integrity and aptness for his own particular temperament. Genuine gurus have always been rare, yet the guru is a fundamental part of Hindu life, and over the millennia a whole set of standards and means of evaluation have developed to enable the would-be disciple to use his discernment in looking for a master. One of the reasons that the disciple will live with a guru in his ashram is so that he can see him under all circumstances. We in the West have no such guru culture. We have little understanding or precedent for the guru-disciple relationship, so we tend to project upon it the only relationships we are familiar with – those of father/mother, lover, or saviour; and more recently, of the therapist.

In reality, a guru is rarely a psychotherapist. Once, when a woman came to Ramana Maharshi with a litany of family troubles, he turned to someone present and asked, 'What does she want me to tell her? She needs to seek professional help.'

The realm of the psyche was not Ramana's province. For him, and for any guru who has realized the truth of his own nature, the psyche is not to be taken seriously. He cannot

H. W. L. Poonja. The non-dual master from Lucknow.
Photo: Courtesy of Gangaji Foundation.

Nanagaru, the guru from Andhra Pradesh.
Photo: Roger Housden.

Mata Amritanandamayi, from Kerala.
Photo: Courtesy of Amritanandamayi Mission Trust, Kerala.

Satya Sai Baba, the best known guru of all time.
Photo: Courtesy of Shanti Nilayom.

Chandra Swami, man of silence.
Photo: Roger Housden.

Carved rock statue of Ganga. Ellora cave sanctuaries. 8th century.
Photo: Richard Lannoy.

Shiva Nataraja with musicians. Ellora cave sanctuaries. 8th century.
Photo: Richard Lannoy.

A Rabari woman from Kutch.
Photo: Roger Housden.

A boy as Krishna in a village festival. Andhra Pradesh.
Photo: Roger Housden.

Above Group of yoni-linga with naga snakes round the principal image. By the Ganges at the Banaras ghats.
Photo: Richard Lannoy.

Top right Arunachaleswarar Temple, with the town of Tiruvannamalai in the background. View from Arunachala Hill.
Photo: Roger Housden.
Below right The gopuram of Thanjavur Temple. 11th century.
Photo: Richard Lannoy.

Devbarnath Yogi, a Goraknathi sadhu.
Photo: Roger Housden.

Charan Dass, an American, has been a sadhu for more than
20 years.
Photo: Roger Housden.

A Naga Baba in Banaras.
Photo: Roger Housden.

A darshan – even through the medium of a photograph – can turn into a lasting guru-disciple relationship if it is your destiny, and if you recognize each other in the inner heart, hri-dayam. This is the pre-requisite: it is not a relationship to be decided by the rational mind. You cannot seek it in the way you would select a therapist. It happens; and whatever prac-tices the guru may prescribe – devotion, inquiry, or tantra – the relationship itself remains central.

Yet it is just when you think it is 'happening', that you are most prone to projection and delusion. Then is the moment to use both common sense and discernment. We all want to fall in love, and most of us want someone to come along and save us. Our own needs easily cloud our judgement. Is there any hint of manipulative behaviour; of compromising your free-will; of requests from you for money or goods? Is there any suggestion that this is the only way to the truth? Does this guru draw attention to himself or to the divine who lives in you? What is it that has impressed you: charisma, demonstra-tions of siddhis, promises of spiritual or worldly attainments if you follow the guru or his programme; or an awakening of a dimension of peace and joy in your own being? As in any pro-found relationship, you can never know for sure what you are embarking upon, however exalted you may feel; so you begin with a mixture of trust and doubt. If you enter a relationship and you see elements later that go against your own integrity, what do you do? To rationalize away what is before your eyes, for the sake of maintaining the status quo; or to succumb to the fear of reprisals, is to lose yourself in an all too familiar game of power. The best protection we can ever have is to act according to our own inner conscience, whatever the apparent consequences.

A genuine guru will never actively seek disciples or even try to build an organization – why should he, if he has no needs of his own? He will not even necessarily call himself guru – he is called such because others call him so. While they are drawn to him by the power of his inner realization, he is not actively trying to attract people. It is in this passive sense that the

An 8 year old Naga Baba who has taken a vow to stay standing for 12 years. He sleeps with his head on the swing.
Photo: Roger Housden.

A series of dancing figures showing poses from the Natya Shastra,
the classical dance text.
Chidambaram Temple. 10th century. Photo: Roger Housden.

pretend to believe in it, nor in its dilemmas. All h
bless the individual and inspire faith in them. His
tion is to point to the unchanging Self that lies b
moods and anxieties. There are psychotherapist:
who have genuine spiritual knowledge and exp
yet do not live permanently in the silence beyon
Such guides are better suited to most people th
tional guru, who either just gives his blessing, or
speaks at all – in uncompromising language tha
too radical. We need to have developed a healt
ever thinking of giving it away.

Neither is a guru the same as a spiritual lea
come out on a stage for an hour, inspire 5,00
climb back into his neuroses as soon as he has
hotel room. The spiritual leader performs a gen
pointing people in a direction, and inspiring the
first steps. But he is not in intimate contact w
who see him both on and off stage, and to whor
inner guidance over a long period of time. Th
the figure is, the more his audience can build
of him, and not be obliged to deal with their o
material. Time and proximity are usually – the
– as necessary in this relationship as in any oth
ed on love. A guru will sit through the shado
ciples and continue to point them silently to v
beneath their own projections. He is as like
dozen disciples as ten thousand. In any eve
following is no indication of his inner statur

If we want wise counsel, or spiritual ins†
many people to choose from. If we want the
saint or guru, there are some, including a
mentioned in this chapter, who can be foun
in the West. We can receive the grace of the
ing to our capacity, and walk away. The
saint can be life-transforming. All the Hind
size the importance of seeking the compa
and spending regular time in their atmos

174

guru is said to find the disciple. He simply responds to the needs of others. He will be all things to all people, depending on their perception of him. The guru in India rarely just concerns himself with mature souls whose interest is self-realization. In Bodh Gaya, I watched Sarath Babuji of Shirdi sit for hours in his hotel room receiving all the hotel workers who had come to hear of his stay. They wanted his grace to receive a boy child, to settle some marital problems, a dispute at work, an illness, or to find the funds to send their children to an English Medium school. To each of them he gave his blessing, and a picture of his own guru, Shirdi Sai Baba. The guru does not distinguish between so-called mature souls and anyone else. Everyone is equally worthy of his attention in his eyes, since we are all a unique expression of the Divine.

If he is a householder, the guru may receive a few people at a time into his own home, as does Ramesh Balsekar, the jnani in Bombay who was the disciple of Nisargadatta Maharaj. He may, like Nanagaru, be often on the move, going from one disciple's house or public commitment to another. He may live in a cave underground, like the remarkable Nitai Baba, outside Vrindavan. It will depend on his role in life. While some gurus are renunciate sadhus, others have families. Spiritual realization does not seem to confine itself to a particular lifestyle.

Most often, the guru will live in an ashram. Ashram means a 'place of striving'. Since they divide the whole of life into four asramas, Hindus recognize that life is one endless struggle. What changes is the goal in view. The first asrama, the brahmachari stage, aims for right action, dharma. The young man is schooled in ethics and the spiritual principles that will help him lead an honourable life. The second asrama is the householder stage, where the goal is wealth and its enjoyment. The third, the vanaprasta, or forest dweller, aims for self-knowledge, while the fourth, the sannyasin, aims for moksha, liberation. The last two can happen in the context of the guru's ashram, the place of spiritual striving.

An ashram forms when a guru stays in one place and his disciples congregate around him. In due course, the disciples buy land, build facilities and make endowments. Most ashrams in India today are the husks left by gurus who are no longer alive. Over the centuries, thousands of gurus have come and gone, and have left their relics in the ashrams which grew up around them during their lifetime. A few of these, such as the ashram at Haridwar which houses the mahasamadhi of Ananda Mayi Ma, and the Sivananda ashram at Rishikesh, remain places of powerful spiritual influence. The Sivananda ashram enjoys the presence of three living gurus – Chidananda, Brahmananda, and Krishnananda – all of whom are direct disciples of the great master, and who have their own significant spiritual authority. Neem Karoli Baba died in 1973; but his ashram, at Kainchi, in Uttar Pradesh, is still a place of great spiritual power. Many of the ashrams of past gurus, however, are more like memorial halls with residential facilities attached. They can be good places to stay for their tranquillity and policy of payment by donation, but not necessarily for spiritual sustenance.

The ashrams of living gurus naturally reflect the disposition of the founder, and their perception of the needs of the disciples. If you stay at Ma Amritanandamayi's ashram, you will be put to work. If you stay with Chandra Swami, you must be prepared to meditate at least four hours a day. Yet both these masters point to the same truth, that the guru is none other than who we are. Ultimately, they can lead us to nothing but this realization. While this is a truism that we in the West like to hear, we usually prefer to accept it from the safe position of the intellect. Gurus of this stature, however, will – if we allow it – lead us to the actual experience. That, in the end, is their only function.

POONJAJI

It becomes overwhelmingly important for us to become detached from our everyday conception of ourselves as potential subjects for special and unique attainment and

fulfillment ... a spiritual guide worth his salt will conduct
a ruthless campaign against all forms of delusion arising
out of a spiritual ambition and self-complacency which
aim to establish the ego in spiritual glory.[2]

Chloe Goodchild and I first met Poonjaji in the first week of
1990. It was a week we shall never forget. We had heard for
some time of an enigmatic man based in Lucknow whose self-
realization had occurred through the agency of Ramana
Maharshi, the great sage of Arunachala. We had read about
him in books by the French Christian sadhu, Swami
Abishikhtananda, who spoke of the profound impression
made upon him by a man he called Harilal. We knew from a
French friend who had spent much of the 1970s in India that
Harilal was Poonja. Our friend himself had had several
encounters with him at that time, and was as impressed as
Abishiktananda had been, though rather more cautious. He
spoke of the energy that poured so intensely from Poonja's
eyes that he had to wear a light cloth over his face whenever
he went through the streets, in order not to draw attention to
himself.

Poonja, we were told, did not consider himself to be a guru
in the ordinary sense, because he was of the 'already enlightened school', whose supreme exponent is Ramana Maharshi.
This school follows the advaitic teaching of the Upanishads to
its logical conclusion: if there is already nothing but the divine
that exists, then what is there to achieve, and what path can
you follow? You are already that which you seek. Seeking
itself takes you away from who you already are. The only
thing to be realized is this, that you are already where and
who you need to be. Such a view naturally excludes the concepts of guru, disciple, and a method to be followed. These
presuppose ignorance and a path to be trodden towards freedom. For Poonja, there was nothing to be done: no meditation, no sadhana of any kind. All effort only takes you further
away from who you are looking for. Poonja did not accept disciples, but he was willing to engage with people in temporary

177

encounters to help them see that they needed neither him nor anyone else to lead them where they wanted to be.

Such a teaching is music to the ears of a Westerner. No need to leave one's life in the world to become a monk; no need for rigorous spiritual disciplines before breakfast, no need for the messy business of 'surrender' to a guru; and above all, the fruit is there for the eating now. Instant enlightenment available at last. Who needs to slog around in the heat and grime of India in search of the ultimate guru when you can sit in your favourite chair eating a mango and know you are already It?

We were as seduced by the idea as anyone would be – though it must be emphasized that it was our own admixture of conditioning and genuine search that was leading us on, not any ploy of Poonja's. The rumour that an American, one Andrew Cohen, had recently returned enlightened from his own encounter with Poonja to begin teaching in the West, only spurred us on. Poonja, however, was not easy to find. He had spent much of his life on the move, though his family and children lived in Lucknow, and that remained his base. He had supported them through his work as a mining engineer, and had then taken early retirement to follow his spiritual wanderings. When we managed to reach him in Lucknow on the phone, he said he may be about to leave for Goa, and that we should ring again in a few days. When we rang again, he said he may be going to Haridwar, and to ring again a few days later.

A week later, he asked us to meet him in his house in the old part of the city. The room we were ushered into was small, simple, with a single picture of Ramana Maharshi on the wall. Three Americans were already there. One, Anna Douglas, was a Buddhist teacher from California; Andrew Getz had just spent three years as a monk in a Thai Buddhist monastery, and the third was Eli Jaxon-Bear, a therapist from the West Coast. Under the picture of Ramana was sitting a large Indian in plain white. He was a handsome man of about 80, with an air of great physical strength and nobility. Those eyes that had once had to be covered with a cloth were now both grandfatherly and authoritative. They seemed to demand an answer without asking a question. There was no air of reverence in the room, no deep silence, or any hint of the notion of guru and disciples. It was an ordinary gathering of people, it seemed, assembled to pass the time of day.

Poonja asked us what train we had taken to arrive in Lucknow, and then gossiped casually for several minutes about the best and worst trains to Lucknow, asking the others which ones they had come on. Suddenly he turned to me and said, 'What can I do for you?'

I faltered. All my projections and expectations swum before me. One answer was that I wanted a bolt from the blue that could solve my questioning and searching once and for all. Another, closer to the truth, was that I wanted to be helped to see more clearly how I got in my own way. Still another was that I would simply have liked to sit in silence with him.

'I have always been attracted intuitively to advaita,' I replied at last, 'but I find it difficult to reconcile with my own experience of devotion and love. If there is only one reality, how are we to account for the existence of love, since love requires a relationship?'

Poonja roared with laughter. 'Now who is asking that question?' he replied. 'Is it the question of a philosopher or of a lover? Either way, you are missing the point. What is the point? You are the point. Who are you? That is where you will find your answer. Tell me, Mr Roger [he insisted on calling me this way from the moment I walked into his room], tell me, who is it that has come to India in the disguise of this body I see before me? If you can speak as that, you will know all about love.'

'I suppose I can only say I don't know who I am. I am beyond my own thoughts and words.'

'But who is saying this to me at this very moment? What is the source of these words and this talk about love?'

I sat there in silence. I was tempted to leap up and clap my hands, like a practitioner in Zen might do when confronted with a koan by his master. It would have been a contrivance, and I sat there feeling uncomfortable under the gaze of everyone else in the room.

Poonja smiled. 'When I first went to see Ramana,' he said, taking the heat off me, 'I asked him to grant me the vision of Lord Krishna. At that time, I was mad with bhakti for Krishna. I had been a lover of his form since childhood, and had always longed for his direct darshan. "Go and meditate on Arunachala," Ramana said to me. So I did, and sure enough, Krishna came to me in person. He was really there, in front of me, and I played with him like a child. When I returned to Ramana and told him about my vision, he asked me, "Where is your Krishna now?" "He is not here now," I replied. "Then rest alone with that which never comes and never goes away," said Ramana. In that moment, I knew the unchanging truth of my own existence, and who I thought I was died for ever.'

He turned to Chloe, and began to question her in a similar way. Then he asked the others if they had anything to say. When one of them spoke, he immediately turned their question or their statements back upon themselves. For a couple of hours this Socratic dialogue continued, until Poonja suddenly got up and said he would see us the next morning.

The next day, Poonja's questioning did push me beyond my own words. He was asking Chloe what she saw in front of her. She said she saw a yellow wall. 'No,' Poonja roared. 'The yellow wall was here yesterday. It is of the past, and only the eyes see the past. But what does the I, the Self, see?'

Then it hit me from the inside, and the words burst out of my mouth: 'The I is not in time or space,' I blurted out. 'It is nowhere, everywhere. So the world disappears when "I" emerges – because the "I" is the world. If the Self is the world, there is nothing to be seen because there is no separate seer. The Self can only see Its Self everywhere. My God, I see!'

My body was alive with a sensation of lightness, clarity, and a kind of joy.

'Ah, there you are!' Poonja exclaimed in delight. 'Now who is Mr Roger now?' The whole room, including myself, collapsed in laughter. 'Do you know the story of the tiger and the donkeys?' he asked. 'A tiger cub lost its mother and was found by a family of donkeys. They took him with them and brought him up to bray like themselves and to eat hay. The tiger cub became convinced he was a donkey until one day an adult tiger saw him in the field with the other donkeys and caught him before he could run away. "Who do you think you are?" the tiger asked the cub, disgusted that one of his kind could act in such a lowly manner. "I am a donkey," the cub replied. The tiger took him off to the river by the scruff of his neck and showed the cub his reflection. "Now tell me who you are," the tiger exclaimed. "I am a tiger, I am a tiger," the cub shouted in delight. "Then roar," the tiger said. And the tiger cub roared. Now, Mr Roger, I can hear you!'

We all fell about the floor roaring with laughter.

That night Chloe couldn't sleep. Her body felt as if it were on fire, and at one point she had a vision of Shiva who came towards her as if she were his consort, Shakti. She kept gazing at him, and as he dissolved, she was aware of her own thoughts and feelings dissolving as well. By morning there was something tangibly different about her. She seemed to be in a state of deep relaxation. She said it was as if her mind had been taken away. There was no thinker present, no doer as such, though she was more awake and alive than ever. When she told Poonja what had happened the previous night, he looked at her and said he already knew about it, and that he was very happy for her. She was ready for 'the final assault', and should come to see him alone the following morning. When she did so, half-expecting some revelatory teaching or event, Poonja asked her to accompany him to the doctor, who had to give him some more medication for his diabetes. On the way, they walked through Lucknow's zoo. 'The final assault', it seemed, was to be nothing more spectacular than a stroll through the town with an elderly man. He told her she should just relax in the knowledge that there was nothing more to do, and that her name from then on would be Shakti.

We left Lucknow for England at the end of the week. Eli Jaxon-Bear said how lucky I was, that my partner should have become enlightened. He would like nothing more, he said, than for the same to happen to his own wife. Neither Chloe nor I would have used a word like enlightenment to describe her condition; rather she was in a state of samadhi that was to last for several months, during which time the normal concerns and worries of the world never touched her. Far from being a mental stance, or an adopted attitude, hers was a state of awakened energy, and Poonja was right to call her Shakti. Eventually, however, just as my own 'experience' had faded in a much quicker time, Chloe's conditioned mind gradually returned to the foreground – although the alteration in her energy pattern has left a lasting trace.[3]

That one week raised as many questions as it answered, and we returned three months later to find 20 people now with Poonja. Among them was Eli, who had returned with his wife, Tony. For us, this visit was low key; Poonja wanted to know why we had come back, since we had 'got' his message on our first visit. We, however, were not sure what we had 'got'. In our different ways, we had both had a profound experience; but there was still an experiencer who could talk about it. This was not the permanent, non-dual reality of Ramana, however much we might have wished to convince ourselves to the contrary. Soon after we left we heard that Poonja had confirmed the enlightenment of Eli's wife, Tony, and given her the name Gangaji. He had also endorsed her to teach on his behalf in the West. Gangaji now commands audiences of hundreds in different parts of the world. Most people say nothing but good of her, and seem unanimous that she is a genuine voice of the heart.

Her message is the same as Poonja's, and people are encouraged to affirm their true nature in the realization, 'I am That'. But who is the I that is making the statement? Is it the I who is indeed That Totality, or is it the more familiar I who thinks it would like to be That, and adopts what it imagines to be the appropriate posture of ecstatic aliveness? We are all so susceptible to the power of self-hypnosis (self-hypnosis – nobody is doing it to us) that it is often difficult to distinguish our authenticity from our own delusions. Perhaps teachers are even more prone to their own delusions than most of us.

Poonja's own fortunes have changed dramatically since 1990. After spending 40 years avoiding the guru-disciple relationship, he has now moved into new quarters offered to him by a recent disciple in the suburbs of Lucknow, and is surrounded by three to four hundred disciples daily, practically all of them Westerners. His followers have started a bookshop, and many of them earn a living sub-letting houses to incoming devotees. One reason for his change in circumstance is that his diabetes is now sufficiently advanced to prevent him moving about as he used to. Another is that he was 'discovered' in the early 1990s by the Osho community, many of whose members decamped to Lucknow. Osho was the other Indian guru who promised instant enlightenment to an eager Western following, so, with Osho's death in 1990, the move to Lucknow was a natural one for those who had not managed to 'get it' at Osho's hands. The Osho people now form the larger part of Poonja's inner circle, who look after him and administer the satsangs. The titles of a recent video on Poonja, *Call off the Search*, and a book, *Wake Up and Roar*, aptly convey his message. A biography by David Godman, who wrote *Be As You Are: The Teachings of Ramana Maharshi*, is due to appear in 1996. All the satsangs are recorded, and the tapes are available on sale in the community bookshop, as are videos of Poonja and interviews with his disciples.

The satsangs are an entirely different affair to the mornings we spent with Poonja in 1990. Poonja still occasionally engages with a particular individual in the way he did me, but usually, the time is now given to reading out the letters that pour in from all over the world declaring the new insights and realizations that the writers have received through the grace of Poonja. (Both Chloe and I wrote similar letters to him on our first return to England.) The mood now, though, is often loudly devotional, as might be expected from the former disciples of Osho – in sharp contrast to the clarity and simplicity of Poonja himself. I can only suppose that Poonja has submitted

183

to the inevitability of the process, seeing that whether he wishes it or not, people will project their needs for a divine father onto him and worship him accordingly.

He has rather laid himself open to such ardent attention by suggesting that the ultimate boon is so easily available. The story goes that the Lucknow mantra is 'I had it, but I lost it'. Some, it appears, have been driven to the edge of despair, even suicide, by the realization that what they thought was final enlightenment was another passing stage. Then, in 1994, Poonja stated in a Lucknow newspaper that nobody had ever been enlightened through his agency, implying that Andrew Cohen and Gangaji were simply building a career for themselves at the expense of his name. He used to tell people they were free, he said, in an aside to one of his close disciples, so that they would go away! Nowadays, having perhaps heeded the warning signals, he is encouraging disciples to stay with him for longer periods.

The story of Poonja is significant because it raises so many of the issues involved in the notions of guru and moksha. Poonja is unquestionably a man of extraordinary power. He certainly has the capacity to awaken people to their own nature through the agency of his presence. In the Hindu tantric tradition, this is known as the power of shaktipat. It was a central feature in the teaching of Muktananda, another figure who caught the imagination of the West in the 1970s and 1980s. To my knowledge, Poonja makes no mention of shaktipat. It is, after all, a term from another tradition to advaita, in which there can be no transmission as such, since there is only one Self who can recognize Its Self. The fact remains that in his presence people continue to experience the kinds of states that Chloe and I knew. There are many accounts now of people lying awake all night burning, and samadhis that last for weeks.

The events around Poonja inevitably raise the question of responsibility. Is it the guru's responsibility if individuals accept his affirmation, mistakenly assume they are liberated beings, and then collapse when they realize their misapprehension? Or is it their own pride and ignorance that is being revealed to them? Likewise, are individuals at fault when they take the pronouncements of their guru to heart and begin teaching from the standpoint of an enlightened being? The traditional answer is that all is the guru's play, his lila, and that in a life of spontaneous, unpremeditated activity such as the guru's, the question of responsibility is irrelevant. Being a liberated being, he is beyond all ethical and moral obligations. Then, from a strict advaitic point of view, everything that happens is the natural unfolding of the larger divine play, so whatever occurs, however unsavoury, is all within the divine, and has its part in the overall process of creation and dissolution. When responses like this, which are so deeply ingrained in the Indian view, come into contact with the democratic, person-centred values of the West, there is bound to be misunderstanding at best, and suffering at worst. The worst has already happened frequently enough in the case of many Buddhist and Hindu teachers in America.

The issue of responsibility also arises when a guru's teaching appears incomplete. The Buddhist traditions offer multi-layered definitions of enlightenment that point to how subtle the whole matter is; and which make Poonja's teaching seem, if not misinformed, then certainly simplistic. Poonjaji can and does point out the true nature of a person; but in the Buddhist understanding, this is only the first in a series of stages of enlightenment. This first step, called 'entering the stream', confirms the cutting of the three fetters: the belief in a separate identity; the belief in the necessity for rites and rituals; and the removal of all doubt about Who I Am. This, in the Zen tradition, is satori, without the experience of which a practitioner has not even begun on the path. Poonja seems to catalyze this awakening in people.

As far as it goes, this is an invaluable and uncommon service. But as the Zen master Amo Samy says,

Awakening can be partial or full, one-dimensional or many dimensional. Many a Zen master is stuck up with the first levels of withdrawal of objectifications or with emptiness or with oneness. Some get caught up with "no thought, no Buddha, no God." Some get stuck up with spontaneity, freedom, and no-consciousness; they don't know the self which inhabits all the realms. Some talk of nonduality, but they don't know that the dual is an inner moment of the non-dual. Some shout that there is no self, "there is nothing at all"; such people have not tasted the true self of no-self, and are only playing with concepts ...'[4]

It may be covered in an instant, but the road is long, even so.

It seems there is a danger in Lucknow of confusing a stage on the way for the journey. Yet wherever we go, if there is not that danger, there will be another one. There would be no journey without apparent wrong turns, and the troughs and hills of hope and despair. My personal contact with Poonja was one for which I remain lastingly grateful. Yet, in the end, I can only look upon him and the drama around him as a play of mystery. This is the case for every guru discussed here, whatever my personal inclinations. Ultimately, opinions are worth little: the seeker himself is responsible for his own story, and can only stay as awake as he can in the situations he dreams up on the way.

NANAGARU

There could hardly be two people more different than Poonja and Nanagaru, though both of them ascribe their awakening to the grace of Ramana Maharshi. Nanagaru has spent much of his life as a farmer in a village of Andhra Pradesh, in the region of the Godavari river. Some 20 years ago, a saint came to him in a dream and kissed him on the cheek. Some time later, he saw an advertisement in the newspaper for a book on spirituality. The advert caught his eye, and he sent off for the book. When he opened it, he found the photo of the same saint who had kissed him. It was Ramana Maharshi, whom he had never heard of before. He made a pilgrimage to Ramana's ashram at Arunachala, and returned frequently over the ensuing years, though Ramana had died some 15 years previously. His whole life began to turn on Ramana's teachings, and he began to preach Ramana's message in his neighbourhood. Then, some years later, he was in Ramanashram when, in the morning, between sleeping and waking, he – as he put it to me – felt his mind falling once and for all into his heart. From then on he was a changed man. It was as if he was living by a force other than the ordinary personality, which had gone into abeyance. People began to see him as their guru instead of a preacher, and his name quickly spread throughout Andhra Pradesh.

Today, he travels throughout south India, staying at the home of one or another of his disciples for a few days, then moving on. Whenever he arrives somewhere, people from that area come all day long with their problems and pleas for help. He listens to them all with deep attention, blesses them, sits in silence with them, gives a talk sometimes to the gathered assembly. He is the archetype of the traditional Indian guru – a soul doctor, a counsellor, a friend, a wise guide in the affairs of life, and for those few who want it, a spiritual presence and teacher.

I first came across Nanagaru in Ramanashram, at Tiruvannamalai, in the last days of 1993. A friend had told me that a guru was giving darshan near the library that evening. Arunachala and Ramana's cave were sufficient for me, I thought; I felt no particular attraction for the darshan of yet another guru. It happened that the library was next to my room, however, and as I returned from the cave that evening I saw a crowd of Westerners outside sitting in silence before a man in his early 60s who was sitting on a chair. At his feet were a bevy of well-dressed Indian women. They were all gazing at the man intently. The man's eyes were drifting slowly from one person to another. I couldn't help feeling that he looked like the cornershop grocer. Every now and then he let out a prolonged belch, and rubbed his stomach.

I sat down, intending to stay until the first mosquito arrived. In moments I was aware of the depth of the silence in the group around me. Nanagaru kept gazing at one individual after another, sometimes resting his eyes on a person for minutes on end. At the same time he would raise his right hand in an open palm blessing. My body became as still as a stone. All thought of going anywhere vanished. All thoughts of any kind vanished. His look was one of the most tender compassion, of a lover to his beloved; yet there was no sense of anybody doing anything, wanting anything, trying to create some effect; just the innocent and empty gaze of love, available to all, and yet intensely personal, it seemed, with each individual. His body seemed to carry no tension at all; his whole being flowed unobstructed out of his eyes. After half an hour or so, he silently bowed, and got up to go to his room. Nobody moved, and the silence continued for several more minutes.

When I did finally move, I made my way without forethought to Nanagaru's door. It was half open, and one of his disciples was standing in the entrance. I asked if I could see Nanagaru, and the disciple ushered me in. Nanagaru was sitting on his bed. He had just picked up a newspaper.

'Which country?' he asked. When I told him, he asked me if I read *The Times*. When I told him I didn't, he asked me about the other good newspapers in England. I responded briefly and then came to my point: 'I was deeply touched by the silence you led us into just now,' I said. 'But what I really want is to be that silence myself, wherever I am. I cannot always be in India with someone like you.'

'You like the silence?' he asked, leaning forward like a delighted child. 'Come to Veerupaksha Cave with me tomorrow, and I shall answer your question.'

I agreed to meet him at 3pm the next afternoon, when he would take me to the cave in his car.

The next day at the appointed time, I piled into an Ambassador car along with half a dozen of Nanagaru's Indian devotees. Nanagaru himself led the way in another car. We drove into town and climbed the short path up to the cave, whose entrance was already packed with expectant faces. Nanagaru went into the cave, paid his respects to the place, and returned to sit under the tree outside. He then proceeded to speak to his Indian audience in his native Telegu for the next half hour, while I and the other Westerners sat in the silence. The silence was tangible, even when he was speaking, and it didn't matter that he never returned to my question. That evening he sat on the floor in the ashram dining hall along with everyone else, quite inconspicuous, in an ordinary dhoti, without any special attentions or favours. The man seemed to glide rather than walk through the day.

That evening, when I arrived for his darshan, he motioned me to come and sit by his side. Every few minutes, he would look down with an innocent tenderness, and stroke my head. To begin with, I felt a certain self-consciousness at receiving such undivided attention in public; but my awkwardness soon gave way to a tranquillity and ease that was to remain with me for weeks afterwards. The next day, Nanagaru was leaving. I was among the crowd that had gathered to see him off, and as he made his way to his car he came over to me and held me in his arms. 'Roger,' he smiled, 'Roger'; like some lover taking his leave. I have since witnessed him act in the same way with many people, treating each one as if they were the only person in the world. I have never seen such a living example of the way Krishna must have acted with the gopis.

Some months later, I went to stay with Nanagaru at his village, and accompany him for a few days on his rounds through Andhra Pradesh. It was a journey into the heart of rural India. The village was built in traditional style. The houses were not unlike Spanish haciendas, with verandahs supported by carved wooden posts and red-tiled roofs. Nanagaru would sit on his verandah, read the newspaper, and receive the trickle of people who came to see him. His family disapproved of the public attention they were getting, and discouraged Nanagaru from using their house as an open forum. This was one reason he now travelled so much. He put me up in a house next door which belonged to a devotee who had gone away on business. On my first morning, there was a knock at the door, and I opened it to find Nanagaru there with a cup of coffee. In the evening, he brought me into the kitchen of his house and stood over me as I made my way through the food his wife had prepared for me.

'Nice food?' he enquired in his rudimentary English. 'Very nice food?'

When I confirmed my pleasure, he beamed, insisting on offering me more. 'Very nice food,' he repeated. 'Very nice food.'

Over the next week or so we went to several different homes over an area of perhaps 100 miles, accompanied by one of his few male devotees who took charge of all the arrangements. At each stop, he and I were ushered to the table first, while the women hovered around watching us eat, as he had watched me. Then the men of the family ate, and finally the women and children sat down. During the day dozens of people would come and sit at his feet while he would give them a talk on some aspect of Ramana's teaching, respond to their problems, or occasionally sit in silence. We went to three weddings, blessed the foundations of a new house, visited a paper factory, and a temple that someone had recently built in his honour. Nanagaru was the same still presence wherever we went. He flowed at the same slow pace, and never showed any trace of a reactive mind. In the car, as we went from one place to the next, he would gaze at a tiny picture of Ramana that he held in his lap, apparently lost to us and the journey we were on. Yet as soon as we stopped, he would be totally present to whatever situation we walked into.

A number of Westerners have now accompanied him in this way, some for much longer periods than I. Everyone that I have met confirms the same experience of prolonged inner silence in his presence, and nothing but an undemanding simplicity on his part. One, a 70-year-old man from New York, told me that he had watched Nanagaru weep for an hour while an old woman told him her story. He himself had not been aware of anything special happening to him while he was with Nanagaru, although it was a warm, if uneventful time. Then, a few days after his departure, he realized that a sadness which had been with him all his life had completely vanished.

Since his own awakening was not the result of any specific sadhana, other than a spontaneous love for Ramana Maharshi, it is not surprising that Nanagaru recommends no particular method or technique himself. His own way of working with people is clearly to have them in his presence while going about the business of everyday life. Being a householder himself, he does not separate the spiritual from the secular. Much of his day is spent dealing with people's everyday concerns, and playing his part in the life of his community. He will talk for hours to his Indian devotees on various aspects of advaita teaching, but with Westerners, he is invariably silent – except when he asks about their country and their national press. His economy with words is partly because of his poor English, but also because he knows that many Westerners, unlike most of the Indians around him, seem to value his silence more. Westerners are already full of concepts and theories, and are usually grateful to experience what lies beyond them.

People come and go from him without any mention of a relationship of guru and disciple. He responds spontaneously to a person's openness, but his response carries no weight or demand. He seems to represent an invitation to fall into the inner heart, where all differences, formal relations and emotional needs dissolve. Silence was also the teaching method of Ramana Maharshi, who considered it the only real form of communication. Yet Nanagaru's presence naturally draws people, and his Indian followers, being culturally attuned to the guru-disciple relationship, treat him accordingly.

Nanagaru's followers have recently built a small retreat centre near Ramanashram, in Tiruvannamalai, which they have called Andhra Ashram. Nanagaru plans to be resident there some months of each year, so he seems certain to become far more widely known than he is at present.

MATA AMRITANANDAMAYI

The village of Parayakadavu sits on a spur of white sand with the Arabian Sea on one side and an inland waterway on the other. Coconut palms stretch along the empty beach as far as the eye can see. Other than the occasional bus and the old fashioned steamers which chug sometimes up the waterway on their way from Quilon to Aleppey, the village is as sleepy as it must have been 100 years ago. Men sit under the palms playing cards. Others put out to sea in long wooden dug-outs which need a dozen men to push them into the waves. They don't have far to go for a catch: three or four boats put out at once, dragging a trawl net between them, no more than 500 metres from the shore.

To the outside eye, it seems a perfect idyll along this stretch of Kerala coastline. Here, as anywhere else, village India hides her suffering well. It was in this village, in 1953, that the girl Sudhamani was born in a hut of woven palm leaves into a family of fisherfolk.[5] Her mother had already given birth three times, and being a girl, Sudhamani was not a cause for especial joy. During her pregnancy, her mother had had several visions and dreams of Lord Krishna, but gave no particular significance to them. Strangely, Sudhamani was born a blue-black colour (the colour of Krishna), whereas both her parents were light-skinned. They called the doctor, thinking the child may have some illness, but nothing was diagnosed. It was strange, too, that the infant would always lie in padmasana, the lotus posture, and would have her hands in the chinmudra, with the tip of her thumb and her forefinger touching to form a circle. The chinmudra represents the unity of the individual self with the Supreme.

As soon as she could speak, which was from six months old, Sudhamani began to sing the Divine Names of God, and by the time she was two, without instruction from anyone, she was singing prayers to Lord Krishna. By the time she was five, her songs to Krishna were known throughout the village. Her family assumed these were just the play of an innocent and joyful child.

By the time she was 10, Sudhamani's mother had had five more children, and was becoming permanently ill. Sudhamani had to leave school and run the household. She would be working from 4am until night, caring for her brothers and sisters, feeding the cows, doing the household chores. Her family laughed at her singing and pining for God, and made fun of her dark skin. Her mother and elder brother, especially, became cruel towards her, tormenting her at every opportunity, and piling ever more chores on her shoulders. Sudhamani would refuse to react to their taunts, and would constantly be calling for the vision of her Lord, Krishna. Everything she did in the day, she did for Him. The great pain in her life was due, not to her hardships, but to the anguish of her separation from Krishna.

It would be difficult to imagine such a story being told – and this is just the beginning – anywhere other than in India. But souls like Amritanandamayi still seem to have a preference for incarnating in this land. Two other great saints of this century, Ananda Mayi Ma, and Ramakrishna, both of Bengal, had similar childhood experiences. Ammaji, as she is now known, has even implied that she is the reincarnation of Ramakrishna. In her teens, Ammaji went on to have regular visions of Krishna, and eventually, to take on the mood, bhav, of Krishna for her own – as did Ramakrishna himself.

Through the ardour of her devotion, Ammaji reached the state of non-difference with God, the advaitic vision of the jnani. As she began to take on the attributes of Krishna, the villagers began to worship her as an incarnation of the Lord – though her parents still treated her harshly. They thought her behaviour was due to some mental imbalance, and for years Ammaji had to suffer ostracism and beatings.

Early on, some of the villagers challenged Ammaji to produce miracles, since she was supposed to be an incarnation of Krishna. She replied that her goal was to inspire people with a desire for liberation, whereas miracles only create the desire to witness more miracles. They continued to press her, and eventually she said that she would show them a miracle just once to strengthen their faith. The following week over a thousand people, having heard of Ammaji's promise, gathered around her on the beach. She asked one of her challengers to bring her a pitcher of water. As usual, she sprinkled the crowd with it, in blessing. Then she asked the same man to dip his fingers in the water that was left in the pot. He discovered the water had turned to milk! The milk was then distributed among the crowd as an offering from God. Ammaji called another sceptic, and asked him to dip his hand in the pitcher. The milk had turned into a fragrant pudding (known as pan-chamritam), made of milk, bananas, sugar and raisins. The crowd began singing praises to God, and the pudding was distributed among them. Yet the pitcher remained full! Christians will recognize the story – except that this one happened only 20 years ago, and hundreds of eye-witnesses are still alive to confirm it.

Today, her parents' house is within the compound of what has become her ashram. That same little fishing village now sees devotees stepping off at the landing stage from all over the world. When I arrived at the ashram gate the man there told me Ammaji had gone to Trivandrum, a couple of hours away. This was the start of one of her pan-India tours. I asked him how long he had been in the ashram.

'Three or four years now,' he said. 'I took early retirement from government service to come here. When I first came, a few years ago, I knew it was where I wanted to spend the rest of my life. Why live in idleness and the pettiness of family concerns when you can live in the company of a saint?'

'How did your family respond to your decision?'

'They came with me,' he smiled. 'We all live here now.'

Leaving my bags with the gatekeeper, I walked into the meditation and shrine hall. At one end a team of women were folding the pages for the new issue of the ashram magazine. As I made my way upstairs to the offices, an American woman in white came hurriedly down the other way. When I tried to ask her about Ammaji's whereabouts, she impatiently brushed me aside and pointed upstairs. A few seconds later, when I had reached the landing and was not sure which way to go, she returned back up the stairs again.

'I'm sorry,' she said. 'We're all pretty stressed out here right now. Mother's been here all winter, so thousands of visitors have been coming non-stop. And when she's here, you know, it's so intense that you end up hardly sleeping. She barely eats or sleeps herself, and is busy all the time, so those of us who are here permanently end up adapting to her rhythm. Quite honestly, it's a relief to have her gone for a few days.'

Now, in the middle of this fishing village that in every other way has hardly changed since Ammaji's childhood, stands one of the better known ashrams in India. There are accommodation blocks, two dining halls, an ayurvedic medicine centre, and all the usual, probably inevitable, ashram politics and jostling to be nearest to the guru. When Ammaji takes her evening walk down to the beach, the devotees, mostly women, have been known to almost come to blows for the honour of holding the flashlight for her. Ammaji was wary of having an ashram from the very beginning, seeing it to be a prison that would constrain her spontaneous freedom. Once, after an administrative meeting with some devotees, she crashed through the ashram fence, breaking it to bits, and went off to walk on the shore by herself.

After a morning in the ashram and watching the fishermen put out to sea, I made my way to Trivandrum on one of the battered buses that ply their way up the coast road. Posters advertized Ammaji's visit all over the town. Banners proclaimed the good news across the street which led to her satsang. Makeshift teashops and bookshops lined the path to the ashram that had been constructed by her Trivandrum devotees. I felt like I was going to a fair.

At the end of the lane, perhaps 1,500 people were sitting on the ground under a canvas roof, singing bhajans led by a group of musicians on the stage. The great majority were women. After half an hour or so, the music stopped and one of the men on the stage began to give what appeared to be a spiritual discourse. While he was getting into his stride, I went round to the ashram building behind the stage. Here there were a number of Westerners, one of whom was laying a carpet of rose petals up the middle of the stairs to the first floor. Ammaji was about to come down and begin her evening's work.

At the bottom of the stairs I met an American called Tom, who was travelling around India with Ammaji on her six-month tour.

'I've never lived like this in my life before,' he said. 'We get to sleep only three hours a night, because Amma is up and ready to go by then. Her darshans last 'til two or three in the morning, we lie down on the roof for an hour or two, then we get ready for the morning darshan. But I've never had so much energy. You get used to it, especially being in her presence all the time. It's like being plugged into a generator. The whole point of spiritual practice, as she sees it, is service to others, and that's what we do. We are here to make the whole thing run, so those people out there can get what they came for.'

'What have they come for?'

'The Mother's grace. She hugs every single person in the hall, and listens to whatever each one wants to unburden on her. She won't leave 'til she has met every one, no matter how many people there are. That's why the darshans go on for so long.'

Just then the Mother herself appeared. A small, compact woman in white with a radiant smile, she came down those stairs like someone with an appointment. She seemed to exude an air of both joy and efficiency. People had appeared from nowhere and lined her path, which was now marked out with rose petals the whole way to the stage.

She took her seat at the front, and with her musicians, immediately launched into a stirring bhajan. The crowd joined in, and soon everyone was swaying and clapping, not unlike some revivalist meeting.

Within a few moments, Ammaji was raising her hands in the air like one possessed of some ecstatic spirit; her eyes were turned towards her forehead, her expression was rapturous. I turned to Tom, who had followed me out to the side of the stage.

'What happened to her Krishna bhavs?' I asked. 'Does she still take on the appearance of Krishna?'

'Those were replaced by Devi bhavs,' he answered. 'Now she dresses up as Kali every week and takes on the mood of that goddess, just as Anandamayi Ma used to do. People often think she is possessed by an external divine force, but she says all the gods are within, and that a Divine Incarnation like herself can manifest any of them at will.'

'Why does she do it?'

'For the benefit of her devotees. It helps many of these people deepen their devotion to God. It gives them faith. Most people are not ready to be awakened by hearing, say, the spiritual wisdom of the Upanishads.'

The tempo on the stage was slowing down, and people were already beginning to queue up in the rope corridors that had been made for the next act in the proceedings. When the music stopped, Ammaji sat for a few moments in silence. Two American attendants appeared, and then the hugging marathon began. People filed up in front of the stage, Ammaji greeted them with a broad smile, and then leant forward to hold them in her arms. Sometimes she would whisper something in their ear, sometimes they would say something to her, often she would kiss them all over their cheeks. There were young men who leant forward awkwardly, rarely looking her in the eye; old women who cried as they came up; grand ladies who were delighted to be doing the done thing; babies by the hundred who were thrust forward by mothers anxious for their child to get a good start in life; loving devotees longing for the embrace of their spiritual mother; the blind and the infirm, there for healing, who were guided into position by the attendants. These, after an hour, were pushing and shoving people around as if they were on a factory assembly line.

Ammaji herself never ceased to be utterly present for every person in the queue. She held each one of them as if they were her only child. Her eyes shone, her sweat ran, she paused neither for water nor for breath. Her right shoulder was black from the run of eye make-up, tears, and sweat from more than 100 people already. Even so, I wasn't sure I needed to be part of this assembly line. I mean, it's all right for village Hindus, but...

'Haven't you had darshan yet?' It was Tom, back at my side again. 'You can go up now, no need to join the queue. She lets the few Westerners who are here come up when they like. In London you would have to wait all day. Go on, there's a space.'

Before I could give it a second thought, I was two hugs away from the front. A warmth began to spread through my body, and I found myself smiling. When I took my place in front of her she opened her eyes wider than ever and enveloped me in her sturdy arms. I melted. She was already melted. We clasped each other for minutes on end, the lightness and warmth in my body returned by hers. Eventually, she leant back, gazed at me, and we beamed in delight. We had met behind my veils.

I stood to one side, watching her continue with one person after another. Every now and then she would look over at me and give an ecstatic smile. I wandered off around the grounds, looking at the bookstalls, buying a drink, stopping to talk. All the while, I thought, Ammaji is there doing what she is here for. I went back to watch her again, in awe at how she treated every single soul as a special person, whatever their motives for coming to her. It was one of the most compassionate examples I had witnessed of the teaching of non-difference. That night, I woke up at two in the morning, and realized that she was still on that stage.

SATYA SAI BABA

Sai Baba says that his only real miracle is love, and doubtless most of his devotees would agree; but his lesser miracles continue to draw ever-larger crowds, and millions all over the world have heard of the man in orange with a fuzzy hairdo who produces sacred ash from the end of his fingertips. The only person anywhere in the world who draws larger crowds is the Pope, and even then, only in southern Europe and South America. The most recent country to be hit by the Sai phenomenon is Japan. Since a recent television documentary on Sai Baba there, planeloads of Japanese have been arriving every week at Puttaparthi, the main ashram of the saint. What used to be a tiny village five hours from Bangalore now has a runway capable of taking international charters. On the occasion of Sai Baba's 60th birthday, over a million people were received there and fed for seven days free of charge.

Satya Sai Baba has been performing miracles since he was a child. At the age of 14, he threw away his school books and proclaimed himself to be a reincarnation of the Muslim saint, Shirdi Sai Baba, who died in 1918, eight years before his own birth. In the village where he grew up, near by the present ashram, was a tree that he named The Wish-Fulfilling Tree. From it, he would pick any fruit that his friends asked to eat. The ash that he produces from his fingers at the daily darshan in Puttaparthi now also collects daily round a photograph of him in London. It is distributed among the English Sai Baba community. Every day, in Puttaparthi, some of those fortunate enough to be called for a collective interview – in which twenty or so people see Sai Baba in a room apart from the thousands outside – come out with gold rings, watches and other paraphernalia that the miracle man has produced for them personally as a special token of his love. The sick sometimes come out cured, the lame walk, even the dead have been known to rise.

There have been just too many examples, witnessed at close quarters by too many people – and over a period of 50 years – to sustain any charge of trickery. In any case, what are normally called miracles are well authenticated all over the world. There is a man in Glastonbury, England, who also produces sacred ash from his fingers. Geoff Boltwood is a healer and something of a prophet who produces not only ash but sweet-smelling oils from his hands during his healings. The fragrance remains on the patient's body for hours afterwards.

There is a psi-research unit in England which has collected many examples of such occurrences.[6] In the case of manifested objects, its studies seem to show that they are always teleported from somewhere else, never manufactured out of nothing. It seems that spirits of the astral world – the dimension of subtle existence – are enlisted to help the miracle worker produce his results.

All the traditional teachings in India strongly condemn the practice of siddhis, the spiritual powers, because it can be a side road in which the practitioner can delude himself for lifetimes, and miss the true goal of liberation. The recent example of Premananda serves to bear out their warnings. Premananda is from Sri Lanka, and like Sai Baba, began to manifest objects at an early age. As he developed a following, he began to imitate Sai Baba's style right down to his dress and his Afro hairdo. He moved to Tamil Nadu, near the town of Trichy, and his ashram grew steadily. He would produce sacred ash daily, and on two occasions a year, just like Sai Baba, he would produce a large stone lingam out of his mouth. He had a substantial foreign following, and the ashram ran orphanages and did other charitable work, again like Sai Baba. The last I heard of him, in January 1995, he was in jail awaiting trial for rape and embezzlement, on the evidence of both foreign and Indian ashram residents.

I am not suggesting that Sai Baba is another Premananda, although there have been periodic charges against him of sexual misconduct with young men. A book was published in the 1970s by one of his closest disciples of the time which spares no detail of Sai Baba's sexual proclivities.[7] People have been murdered at Puttaparthi too – three of them in 1994 – in circumstances which have never been properly investigated. Yet, in a community in which there is a constant shifting population of tens of thousands of people, it is surprising that more unsavoury incidents and stories are not reported. The point is that miracles do not prove a person's saintliness, much less their divinity. For that, we must return to Sai Baba's insistence that love is his greatest miracle. How do his devotees experience that love, and what happens to them as a result of it?

Nearly all the stories in the voluminous Sai literature connect a person's spiritual awakening either with the experience of a miracle, or with an unbidden visitation or intervention from Sai Baba into their personal lives. The former will invariably confirm that the miracle awoke or strengthened their faith. This, says Sai Baba, is why he performs them. He has always emphasized that he is a guru for the masses, not for the few. Most people are not ready to hear deep spiritual teachings, whereas few will remain unaffected by an event that challenges the status quo of their habitual belief systems. Those who baulk at this explanation may remember that Christ used miracles for the same purpose. Sai identifies himself with the words of Krishna in the Bhagavad Gita, where the Lord tells Arjuna that He returns to earth periodically in human form whenever righteousness fails and evil holds sway. Krishna's mission, which Sai Baba takes for his own, is to restore the dharma across the world. Sai has often said to his older devotees that there would come a time soon when so many people would come to Puttaparthi that they would not be able to glimpse him over the multitude of faces. That time has already arrived.

People everywhere have had visions of Sai Baba, often only realizing his identity later. He will appear in a dream, in a daylight vision, even in the eyes of someone else. A friend of mine was lying on a table where she was receiving treatment from a healer. When his head bent over hers, she was astounded to see in the pupils of both his eyes, as clea as a photograph, the image of Sai Baba, whom she had never heard of. She thought she was imagining things, until a few days later she saw the same picture in the house of a friend. Within months, she was on a plane to Puttaparthi. People all over the world have been 'called' to Sai Baba in this way, and naturally, such a personal invitation awakens devotion and, often, a reorientation of life towards spiritual values.

Faith and action are what Sai Baba stimulates in his

devotees. Spiritual practices like meditation are not in the foreground of his teaching. While he suggests to those who ask that they meditate on their chosen form of God in the heart, there is no meditation hall as such in Puttaparthi. The main activities there are bhajan singing, and the daily darshan with the guru. There is a museum of the world's religions, and in a series of huge statues a hundred feet high, the different forms of God from around the world are celebrated. The message is that it doesn't matter who your devotion is for, as long as that flame is alive in your heart.

Sai Baba has said many times that what he wants are worker bees who will go out and put his message into action. His message? You can see it written over the counter in any Hard Rock Cafe around the world: 'Love All, Serve All'. The founder of the well-known Hard Rock chain, Isaac Tigrett, was travelling in India soon after starting his first restaurant in England in the early 1970s. He saw a large poster of Sai Baba in a hotel and knew that this was his guru. He went straight to Puttaparthi, and stood at the back of the crowd which was gathered for darshan. Sai Baba walked through the crowd to him, gave him some vibhuti and told him to eat it. Though Tigrett came back to Puttaparthi from then on at least once a year for several weeks, Sai Baba was never to look at him again for seventeen years. He became something of an ashram joke, for most people at least get to have an interview after returning to Puttaparthi a few times.

Tigrett kept coming though, and his faith in Sai Baba never faltered. It was assisted by a couple of extraordinary scrapes with death in America. Tigrett was a high flyer who was living the life of success to the full. Driving down Highway One in Big Sur one night, blind drunk, he missed a bend and sailed over the cliff. His Porsche spun over a dozen times as it fell. Before it reached the bottom, Tigrett realized that Sai Baba was sitting in the passenger seat with his arm around him. When the car hit the ground it was shattered to pieces. Not even the engine was left under the hood. Tigrett stepped out without a scratch. He flew immediately to Puttaparthi to thank

Sai Baba but, as usual, Sai never gave him a glance.

A few years later, Tigrett was lying on the floor of a hotel room in Oklahoma. He had taken an overdose of cocaine. In an ensuing epileptic fit, he had swallowed his tongue. He was on the edge of death when Sai Baba appeared, pulled his tongue out of his throat, and began beating his chest to restart his lungs. When he began to breathe again, Sai Baba disappeared. He went to Puttaparthi to give thanks but, as usual, Sai Baba never looked at him.

In the early 1990s, Tigrett felt the time had come to sell his interest in the Hard Rock Cafe. He had always sensed that Sai Baba had had a direct hand in the success of the business, and that the profits were to serve some humanitarian cause of Sai's. (Sai Baba has founded many schools, universities, hospitals and charitable institutions.) Tigrett received the sum of $108 million for the chain, the exact number of beads on a Hindu mala, and the number of the Hindu names for God. He went to Puttaparthi with a cheque for $54 million. This time, as he stood in the darshan, Sai Baba waved to him to join that day's interview group. Tigrett was so astonished that he looked behind him, presuming that the saint was motioning to someone else. In the interview room, he told Sai Baba about the cheque, which Sai already knew about.

Sai was silent for a few moments, then he said, 'We shall build a hospital. The largest specialist hospital in South Asia. It shall be ready one year from today.'

It was a miracle as remarkable as any that this hospital was indeed opened by the President of India a year later, and the first heart operation was carried out there on that day. Its services are free. An international team of architects worked day and night on the plans for three months, and the entire complex was constructed on some waste ground near the ashram in the remaining nine. It would have been an extraordinary feat in a Western capital, but this was in rural India, five hours from the nearest city.

Most of Sai's foreign devotees come to India for a couple of weeks, and then return inspired to put their renewed energy into their daily lives. Some, however, stay on at Puttaparthi for years. There are many women there who consider themselves the gopis of their teacher. One woman I met had spent eleven years running wherever Sai Baba went in India (he has never gone abroad.) Her one desire was to be in his presence, and receive a look or a touch of the foot from him. In all that time she never had an interview, but that was of small concern to her. What mattered was to be in the presence of her beloved. When she or the others like her did not see him for a few days, they went through all the pangs of an abandoned lover. Eventually, she started having dreams of Arunachala mountain, and felt that Sai Baba was directing her to go there, so she could wean herself from her dependency on him. Then she had a dream in which Sai Baba dissolved into Ramana Maharshi, which she took to be an indication that she should practise the more solitary path of inquiry, 'Who am I?' advocated by Ramana. She also knew that Sai's fundamental teaching was the advaitin view of the divinity of each individual. (Once when a young man came up to him in the darshan and boldly asked, 'Are you God?' Sai Baba pointed back at the boy and replied, 'You are God!') She, along with several other long-term Sai devotees, have since moved to Arunachala, where they now feel as close to Sai as they did at Puttaparthi, which has become so overcrowded. One of Sai Baba's first bhajans, she remembered, written when he was fourteen, sings the praises of Arunachala Shiva.

Sai Baba sometimes intervenes directly in the course of his devotees' lives. Two other long-term devotees are Cass and Sharma Smith, from California. Sharma had already been coming to Puttaparthi for ten years when, in 1988, Sai said to her in an interview that he was going to find her a good husband. She had been sitting there feeling miserable on the eve of her departure, knowing that she was going to have to resolve an unsatisfactory relationship back home with someone who shared none of her spiritual aspirations. Sai had read the troubles in her mind. When she arrived at the airport hotel that night, she had a dream in which Sai Baba appeared and told her to stay. When she asked for how long, he showed her a calendar with a date circled on it. The next day, she changed her ticket for that date, and returned to the ashram. She went first to the cold drinks stand, where a friend of hers was standing with a man. It was the same man she had seen for years in dreams. Five days later, they had agreed to get married. It happened that his ticket was for the same day on the same plane back to California. They have been inseparable ever since.

Cass Smith returned to Puttaparthi for a year in 1991, during which time his main practice was to serve in the ashram and to chant the Gayatri mantra. During that year he was asked by Sai Baba in an interview what he wanted.

'I want liberation,' was his reply.

Almost immediately, he contracted hepatitis, which he suffered for five months. Then he caught typhoid, and finally he had to bear an inflammation of the legs which caused him excruciating pain. For most of that year, he was on the edge of death. Sai Baba's purifying grace does not always come in the form one might expect.

Satya means truth, and Sai Baba in his present form has not come to mince words. Faced with such an extraordinary phenomenon, the individual can only make up his own mind, or rather follow his own heart. He may be for the multitude, but Sai is not for everyone. His miracles put off many, even as they attract others. The crowds are another deterrent for those who prefer a more personal relationship. Bhajans are not to everyone's taste. Whatever one's personal prejudices, one can only have a deep respect for the faith that Sai Baba has undoubtedly awoken in the hearts of his devotees, and for the actions that have sprung from that faith. He says he will live until the age of 96 – until 2022. If you are young enough, you will even have a chance to meet him after that, since he has vowed to take another birth in Mysore eight years after the death of his present body. He will then be known as Prem Sai Baba. Prem means pure love, and the next century, Sai Baba has said, will be full of it.

OSHO COMMUNE INTERNATIONAL

The Indian on the black gates – the kind that protect mansions in Mill Valley or Hampstead Heath – looked just like the rogue guru himself: long, flowing beard, large doe eyes, a woolly hat on his balding head. He directed me round to the side entrance where, he said, I would have to take an Aids test before being allowed in. That would be 200 rupees, plus 20 rupees standard entrance ticket. Though there were plenty of Indians outside the gates, watching the foreign girls, there were none to speak of inside – £4 is more than most of them earn in three days.

My Aids negative confirmation in my hand, I was finally greeted by one of the team of twelve who manage this most Western and opulent of all ashrams in India. I mentioned the uncanny resemblance of the man at the gate to Osho himself.

'That's his brother,' she explained. 'His family are very involved here.'

There is nothing remotely Indian, however, to be found in this exquisitely designed and landscaped 'Buddhafield', as Osho called it. Not even Indian currency is allowed, since it is a common way for diseases to spread – you buy coupons to use in the various facilities. The ashram at Poona which repeatedly captured the world's headlines in the 1970s and 1980s has undergone an extraordinary rebirth since Osho's death in 1990. Japanese gardens, swimming pools, a health club ('Club Med' – get it?) and Western restaurants, have been added to the existing alternative university, and the tent-like structure in steel and glass known as 'The Buddha Hall'. The university has many more courses available, the restaurants have their own organic vegetable gardens, the ashram has its own wells and rigorous hygiene testing systems. Most of the buildings are in black and white, and – appropriately – have an air of the post-modern look of corporate architecture. These people mean business. As a mid-1980s bumper sticker said, 'Moses invests, Jesus Saves, Bhagwan Spends'.

Now Bhagwan is dead: long live Osho. With the troubles of Rajneeshpuram, Oregon, far behind them, Osho Commune

International in Poona can only be delighted at the way business has gone over the last five years. Far from dying along with the guru, the Osho Commune is receiving more visitors than ever before. (Though it is called a Commune, hardly anybody actually lives on the premises.) Since 1990, the number of new disciples, sannyasis, has been increasing four-fold each year. Osho's books are going through a worldwide publishing explosion. In 1993, over 640,000 Osho books in English were sold worldwide. In the same year, 120,000 were sold in Russia, and over 300,000 in India in six languages. Two of Germany's largest health insurance companies are buying hundreds of Osho's meditation CDs for use in their health care programmes, and in Asia, a satellite channel covering 38 countries now regularly beams Osho's discourses in English.

Why? One can only presume that the cliche has been confirmed yet again: the more someone – especially in religion – achieves notoriety in his lifetime, the more he will be revered as a prophet after his death. Osho was risky territory while he was alive. Many who may have been sympathetic to his teaching would never have wanted to associate themselves with a cultish following whose antics and scandals were railed against the world over. Now he is dead, people are free to use his teachings as they wish without the stigma attached to them in the 1980s, and without the need to belong to a group. You just buy the courses you want at the Commune, watch a video of Osho at your leisure, and get on with your life.

This, perhaps, is the other main reason for Osho's success in the 1990s. He appeals to the instant gratification mentality. He used to say that his disciples wanted instant enlightenment, so that is what he offered. Cynics might quip that an instant high may have been a more accurate description. His Dynamic and Kundalini meditations are aimed at rapidly stimulating the psychophysical organism and to provide the kind of relaxation that comes after any strenuous physical effort. Businessmen can practise them before work and get through their day with more ease and vitality than otherwise. His techniques, introduced by Osho trainers, are used in corporate management throughout the world. Bus drivers in Stockholm have regular Osho meditation courses financed by the local government. As stress management tools, these methods are undoubtedly effective. A large proportion of the visitors to Poona are people with a busy and successful schedule. What could be better than to come to a beautiful, pollution- and disease-free zone in India – the only one in the subcontinent – and cool out with friends in a warm and meditative atmosphere while imbibing the spiritual ideas of a brilliant orator? Osho always said that while Jesus spoke to the poor, his audience was the rich. The affluent West has time on its hands to attend to spiritual matters. The poor, East and West, can only think of survival. Osho's point was, you do not have to change your life to practise his methods and subscribe to his ideas; you do not have to give up your wealth, you have to learn how to enjoy it and lighten up. Nowadays, this is truer than ever – no mandatory orange clothes, such as were commonly seen in the 1980s; no group to lean on the individual, not even a guru to tell you to drop this or take up that. Just a message of pleasure, meditation and self-loving. Few people would argue with it, not even in India, where Osho's books are now to be found on every newsstand.

Yet Osho Commune International is not the place of free love it was in the seventies. On the contrary, since the Aids scare, sexuality is now seen as an energy to transmute into personal aliveness, not to waste in gratuitous licence. There is plenty of affectionate hugging, but that is as far as it goes. The whole way of life in the Commune is in fact highly structured to maintain the atmosphere of a sacred space – to preserve the 'Buddhafield', as Osho put it. All visitors wear a statutory maroon robe while in the Commune; at certain times during the day, everyone will stop what they are doing for fifteen minutes and dance to loud music, or stand like statues in silence. As in Aldous Huxley's *Island*, a cock crows on the hour to remind people to recollect themselves. There are meditation sessions throughout the day for people to choose from.

One evening I went to the meeting of the Osho White

Brotherhood, the main event of the day. Everyone had changed from maroon to white. Fifteen minutes before the meeting started, people were walking along the paths to the Buddha Hall in silence. There must have been almost 1,000 people sitting on the marble floor in front of a stage. Two men appeared from the wings, carrying a white armchair, which they set down in the middle of the stage. This was the chair from which Osho used to give his discourses. Music started up on the loudspeaker system, and more and more of the meditators began to sway and dance on the spot. Suddenly, after fifteen minutes or so, everything stopped and the entire crowd let out a yell of 'Osho!' with their arms in the air, as if his presence were still among them. The same routine was repeated four times, and then a giant video screen was let down over the stage. For the next hour, everyone sat in rapt attention as Osho, in top quality close-up, gave one of the discourses he first offered ten years before. At the end, still in silence, everyone filed outside, collected their shoes, and went off into the night.

The event was stage-managed to perfection. Osho Commune International offers a haven for those who have time to review their values and the way they are using their lives. It offers skills and techniques to enhance the quality of life and to be a more open and loving person. As such, it is performing a valuable service for a pressed and anxious world. Osho must have known that the revolution in consciousness implied by a spiritual path is neither to be confused with personal development nor to be won lightly. Yet he gave people what they wanted, and spoke to the values of his time in the way he was able. Poona is his living testimony.

CHANDRA SWAMI

When I arrived at Sadhana Kendra Ashram, Chandra Swami was playing badminton. His 65 years were pitted against a 20 year old. In a fold of his dhoti there were some rupee notes.

Chandra Swami was taking bets on the game. A couple of French disciples were cheering his opponent on. Whenever the boy was about to serve, Chandra Swami would make noises or jump about to distract him.

To no avail. When he had lost the match, he went off to the meditation room to lead the evening meditation. Chandra Swami has been in silence for decades, but he speaks volumes with a constant flow of smiles and laughter. He is the archetypal guru figure – flowing white hair and beard, eyes that would melt a rock, a face radiant with strength and beauty. He was born in 1930 in a village in Pakistan named after one of the great saints of northern India, Baba Bhuman Shah. Bhuman Shah lived in the 18th century, and his shrine in the village was a major pilgrimage centre until the Partition in 1947. From an early age Chandra Swami had visions and dreams of the saint, who claimed him for his own.

When the boy had completed his degree in sciences, and had migrated to India after the Partition, he broke off his MSc studies to live the life of a spiritual recluse. He first lived in a cave in Jammu Kashmir, and then retired to an uninhabited island in the Ganga near Haridwar, where he lived for many years. Throughout this time Bhuman Shah acted as his guru from the higher planes. It was on this island, some 25 years ago that Yvan Amar, a young Frenchman, first discovered the recluse, who took him as his disciple. Gradually, others came, and they eventually persuaded Chandra Swami to move to the mainland, so that his disciples could visit him without the constant fear of snakes and wild animals. His first ashram was outside Haridwar, and in 1992 he finally moved to his present, more remote ashram of Sadhana Kendra.

Sadhana Kendra is on a bend of the Yamuna facing the mountains of Himachel Pradesh. The nearest small town is ten kilometres away. You have to want to get there: the journey from Dehra Dun involves a two-hour bus trip, a walk through the town of Vikas Nagar, a ride in a tempo, and a kilometre walk up a track. It is the perfect location for a place which is dedicated to serious meditation and spiritual practice. There are four compulsory one-hour meditations a day, beginning at 4am, preceded by a brief session of bhajans. Two French women have been living there for some years, along with four or five Indians. Others come and go daily. Chandra Swami has a large following, especially in Kashmir, where the many devotees of Bhuman Shah regard him as his spiritual successor.

For six months of the year Chandra Swami holds morning satsangs in which he will answer questions on his notepad. During one satsang, someone said they despaired of ever being free of the veil of ignorance.

'The veil of ignorance is voluntary,' came the written reply, which is read out aloud. 'You have vested interest in ignorance. That is why you find it difficult to remove it. It is like attachment. You have vested interest in being attached. That is why you cannot give up attachment, even if it gives suffering to you.'

I asked him a question about meditation, and the balance between effort and non-effort.

'Most people need the support of an object of meditation, a name or a form of God,' he wrote. 'We must start where we are, in duality, even though the ultimate truth is non-dual. Some prefer to sit without any form, and gently fall into the silence with an ever-increasing awareness. It is according to your nature. Both need a certain effort to begin with, but both lead beyond effort to progressively deeper levels of relaxation. When you are being meditated, instead of being the meditator, you have fallen from the dual to the non-dual.'

I followed with the same question I had asked Nanagaru – how can this silence I know in his presence remain ever-present?

'The permanent silence can only be known by one who has realized the truth of his own nature. In the meantime, a sadhaka must continue to meditate, live a spiritual life in his relations with others, and strive not to follow the dictates of his instincts. Above all, he must have faith since, even though he must make efforts, it is not in his hands anyway. The spiritual path is a journey of lifetimes. Give up all arguments and "roast your heart in the fire of love", Lalashori, the Kashmiri woman yogi used to say.'

When he answers someone, Chandra Swami gives them only the briefest of looks in the eye. It is as if there is nothing in him to engage with the personal. Yet he is utterly present to whoever he is with; he exudes a strong, tender warmth and a rigorous clarity. His charisma does not overwhelm others with emotion and draw them towards his personal form; it encourages them to open out into the larger space he inhabits. The same warmth is there all the time, whatever he seems to be doing. It was there in the badminton match, it is there when he eats, or walks down the corridor. He is the same compassionate and immensely joyful presence wherever he is.

Though he will draw on all the different spiritual streams in answer to people's questions, it is evident that his real teaching is the way he leads his life. In the end, Chandra Swami doesn't do anything; he is utterly unself-conscious. Yet his ashram functions with unusual efficiency; he is always giving time to people, overseeing the new building works, signing cheques, answering the mail, living a life – but, it seems, with not a single gesture out of place. He has died into the stream of life.

1   Muruganar, Sri, *The Garland of Guru's Sayings*, verse 310.
    Ramanasram, Tiruvannamalai 1990.

2   Merton, Thomas, in an essay called 'Transcendent Experience',
    quoted in Edward Rice, *The Man in the Sycamore Tree*. Image Books,
    New York 1992.

3   For a full description of Chloe Goodchild's experience with Poonjaji,
    see her book, *The Naked Voice*, Rider, London 1992. Out of print,
    available only through the author. Cheques for £11 inc. p&p payable
    to The Naked Voice, P. O. Box 1892, Bath BA1 9YY, UK.

4   From an unpublished manuscript by Amo Samy.

5   For a full biography of Ammaji, see *Mata Amritanandamayi: a
    Biography* by Amritaswamipananda. Amritanandamayi Mission Press,
    Kerala 1988.

6   The Society for Psychical Research, 49 Marloes Rd, London W8 6LA.

7   Brooke, Tal, *Avatar of the Night: The Hidden Side of Sai Baba*. Tarana
    Publications, New Delhi 1982.

PART FOUR

THE OTHER TRADITIONS

SIKHS AND JAINS

13

THE GOLDEN TEMPLE OF THE SIKHS

As you approach The Golden Temple the first building you see is a long white terrace with a clock tower in the middle, under which an arch leads to the temple precinct. A marble court-yard and high, ornate railings separate the white building from the bustle of the town outside. Already, there is the sensation of drawing near to a temenos, a sacred space which has been marked off from the attitudes and activities of secular life. There are shops along the outside of the long white row, mostly selling books and flowers; but no-one calls out for your attention; no-one tugs at your sleeve to sell you postcards. I got all the way to the entrance before it dawned on me that there was not a beggar in sight. Begging is against the tenets of the Sikh religion. There is consequently a community of some 13 million people in India who do not have a beggar among their number. I could not deny the logic that begging must, then, be determined by conditioning and frame of mind as much as by circumstance.

Under the clock tower is a water stand, a large circular counter of white marble round a marble tub. Blocks of ice dripped their way into the tub, and servers dispensed free sherbert water to all. A large shoe stand took everyone's shoes

blue turban frames a face which has all the qualities of an eagle. Instantly welcoming, he reminded me that the word 'Sikh' comes from the Sanskrit, shishya, meaning disciple.

'A Sikh's true calling,' he said, 'is to study at the feet of a teacher. After all, we are Indians. We grew out of the Hindu tradition. The concept of the guru is fundamental to us. The religion of the Sikhs did not begin and end with Guru Nanak: it was a development that took place under the guidance of all ten Gurus. For us, they are all incarnations of Guru Nanak, and each one was responsible for adding a further dimension to the tradition. The last Guru, Gobind Singh – he died in 1708 – breathed new life into the Sikh community, and ended the Guru line. He instituted our Holy Book, the Granth Sahib, as the final Guru, and he placed it on a seat in the Temple higher than his own. The Granth Sahib is the collection of poetry and songs written by the Gurus to convey their wisdom, as well as other songs by saints like Kabir. Listen, you can hear it now, being sung in the Temple.'

From the moment I had entered the precinct I had been aware of a background of devotional chanting, kirtan, which was being relayed around the pool. It was unobtrusive, with none of the emotional excitement of the qawwali music of the sufis, which is so well known in the Punjab, and in Amritsar itself. Two or three male voices, accompanied by a sitar and harmonium, rippled across the water in soft, devotional waves. I had thought it was recorded music, as is often the case in Hindu temples, but Devinder Singh said that recordings were not allowed:

'If we are to praise God,' he said, 'then we have to do it in person. We cannot expect a machine to do it for us.'

The Granth Sahib was not only being sung continuously 24 hours a day in the Golden Temple, Govinder Singh went on; it was also being read aloud in the four quarters of the precinct by a roster of Temple officials.

No wonder this place had such a tangible spiritual intensity. Day and night people came here to sing and pray. The Sikhs have no regular congregations and no pujas. Each is

217

answerable to his own soul and praises God in his own time as much as he is able. The priests do not mediate for others; they sing the kirtans and take the readings of the Holy Book.

As I gazed on it that evening in the light of a full moon, I saw that The Golden Temple floats on the water. It took on the likeness for me of the Primordial Ark, the original Ship of God. Pilgrims were filing towards it across the lantern-lit causeway known as 'The Guru's Bridge' – for there is no other way to Him, say the Sikhs, than the bridge of grace, which is the Guru himself. The Temple itself is a small golden square, two stories high, with a dome. The gold leaf was applied in the 19th century, the Temple having been destroyed and rebuilt many times. On the ground floor, the original copy of The Granth Sahib rests under gold cloths. To one side sit the singers. Four doorways open the Holy of Holies onto all directions, symbolizing its welcome to those of every faith. People cram in every corner, singing softly along with the singers, or absorbed in meditation. Nowhere in India have I witnessed such interior devotion in a public place. Upstairs a priest recites the holy book in front of an ancient copy some three feet square. People sit along the open gallery and watch the procession of people downstairs, or gaze out over the water which holds the entire scene in reflection. Around the Temple is a marble deck where more people sit, lulled by the water, the music and the moon. At its far end, the golden square narrows to a prow; there, pilgrims make use of a sunken step to soak their feet in the Pool of Bliss.

The Golden Temple is indeed a blessed place. No-one, of any race or religion, can fail to be moved by its astonishing beauty. The persecution of the Sikhs, like that of the Jews, has undoubtedly added to the fervour and devotion with which they regard their most holy shrine. It is as much a symbol of their communal identity, and their continuing survival in the face of all odds, as it is a monument to the glory of God. The two, the human community and the Divine, are for the Sikhs one and the same.

DILWARA: A JAIN TEMPLE

From midday until evening the shoe-rack at the entrance to the Jain Dilwara temple on Mount Abu is stacked to overflowing with every conceivable kind of footwear. The gatekeeper has in his charge all manner of leather objects that visitors have had to leave with him for the duration of their visit, in deference to a Jain injunction forbidding animal materials inside the temple.

The owners of the shoes have come from all over India and from around the world because they have read in their guide books of the unsurpassed beauty of the Dilwara temples, their delicate sculptures of white marble, the crystalline ceilings, like translucent snowflakes, the extraordinary counterpoise of simplicity and infinite detail, the scale which manages to be both human and divine at the same time. They cannot possibly be disappointed; unless, that is, they come hoping to find a living temple of worship.

'What can we do?' The manager of the temple sighed across the desk in his office. 'The government requires us to fulfil the needs of the tourists in the afternoons. It is understandable. Architecturally, this is a place of global significance. At least we have the morning to ourselves. Then only Jains are admitted. But come in the morning, as my guest. Then you will see a Jain temple instead of a tourist attraction.'

Sacred places all over the world are facing the same quandary. Tourism encourages a culture of observers, instamatic snappers, consumers of culture, sights, information, places of 'interest'. None of us, least of all me, an author of a book such as this, are untainted by it. We want to visit Stonehenge, Chartres Cathedral, Assisi, the Dilwara temples, and our motivation may well be that of a genuine pilgrim. We might even baulk at being described as a tourist. Yet however we like to think of ourselves, we must know that our visit can only add to the pressures on the place and steer it that little bit further towards being a secular monument instead of a source of awe and veneration.

The other places mentioned in this book are not subject to the same pressures as Dilwara because they are Hindu, and there are some 800 million Hindus who share a living faith. India has less than 5 million tourists a year who spread themselves across a vast country. The great Hindu temples of the south are deeply rooted in and sustained by their local culture, and the impact of tourists, both Indian and non-Indian, is still minimal. The Jains, however, number only 2 million in the whole of India. Their forebears happen to have constructed some of the most inspired temple architecture of all time. It is hardly surprising that the Jains are outnumbered in their own temple, at least in the afternoons.

The Jains have always had an influence in India far out of proportion to their insignificant numbers. Their religion ceased to attract many followers as long as two millennia ago, when the devotionalist movements of Hinduism began to gather momentum. Perhaps, like Buddhism, it was always too austere for the Hindu temperament. It also, again like Buddhism, refused to acknowledge either the caste system or the authority of the Vedas. The two rivals to Hinduism are so similar in many respects that until the turn of the century, Western scholars actually believed Jainism to be a Buddhist sect. In a convoluted way, one of the main reasons for their disproportionate influence in business affairs is the rigour with which the Jain community has always upheld its tenet of non-violence. For the Jains, everything, even the four elements, contains a living essence, or soul. Practically anything a human being does, then, is likely to result in the death of some living creature. Jain monks used to walk on stilts so as to minimize the number of insects they killed. They still wear masks over their mouths to prevent them inhaling some living being. Not only are hunting, military occupations and animal slaughter prohibited, but farming of any kind, since to plough the land will result in millions of tiny deaths. With such an extreme concern for the sanctity of life, there is little left for the Jain to turn to other than business. They have always been moneylenders, jewellers, and merchants. Today they run most of the country's banking services, as well as much of the cotton industry.

The Jains are not only rich, they are pious. The three hall-marks of their religion are non-violence, self-control and penance. Both monks and the lay community follow a strict moral code by which they undertake to avoid lying, accumulating surplus possessions and stealing; to eat only pure food; to tolerate a list of 22 sufferings (including insect bites, thorns, dirt, hunger and thirst); and to worship regularly three times a day. The monks follow one of the strictest rules of any ascetic tradition. One of the two sects, the Digambars, wear no clothes, while members of the other, the Suetambar, are allowed only two white robes. They can only stay in one place for a maximum of three days, they must walk barefoot, and never touch money.

The purpose of all this penance is to untangle the soul from the gross perceptions of the body. The Jains believe in a strictly dualistic universe, in which there is only dead matter and living soul. Their religion is in the same lineage as Persian Zoroastrianism and the Christian Cathars and gnostics who oppose spirit to matter. For the Jains, though, there is no redeeming god who can come to the rescue with the doctrine of grace. The soul pervades the human body, but is entrapped in the density of material perception by its own actions. The only way it can free itself of the materialist darkness is to engage in positive actions that will gain it merit. So Jains are generous with their charity, they build temples, they observe their vows and maintain a stoic acceptance of this world's contingencies.

Jainism is the supreme religion of self-reliance – the word itself comes from 'jina', meaning conqueror. Through one's own actions and merit, one can become God himself, greater than all the gods. The point of a temple is not to worship a god that does not exist, but to serve as an inspiration by upholding the examples of those great souls, the founders and teachers of the Jains, who have already shown liberation to be possible. While Mahavira, who was a contemporary of the Buddha in the 6th century BC, is normally thought to be the founder of the Jain religion, the Jains themselves contend that he was only the 24th in a line of *tirthankaras* – 'those who have crossed the ocean of becoming' – stretching back to the first great teacher, Adinatha, who lived in remotest history. The daily prayer of the Jains, then, is not directed to any version of god, but is an act of reverence and honour to these great souls and those like them.

I went to Dilwara the next morning, as instructed, and was surprised to find the shoe rack almost as full as the day before. A party of 150 Jains had arrived from Bombay, while 200 more were there from Ahmedabad, six hours away in Rajasthan. All the men were clothed in white robes, while the women were in saris that had clearly been brought for the occasion. At a level below the main courtyard I could hear people splashing water, laughing and talking. The manager's assistant told me there were baths there, which everyone had to visit before entering the temple. The white robes were obligatory too, as were the fresh clothes.

We followed the stream of devotees into the main complex, known as the Vimala Shah temple, after the King of Gujarat's chief minister, who commissioned the building in 1031. Vimala Shah is still there, seated on his horse facing the entrance to the temple, eternally proud of his magnificent accomplishment. It is not its size which is impressive – unlike a southern temple, the whole of Dilwara, like any Northern Hindu temple, covers no more than a couple of acres – but the sheer genius of its workmanship. The hardest sculpting material in the world has been carved as if it were lace into pillars and ceilings of the utmost delicacy. The entire structure is in white marble, which was dragged from 300 miles away by a team of 400 elephants. The elephants are immortalized in the elephant hall outside the entrance to the rectangular court-yard which protects the inner sanctum.

Inside the rectangle, facing the sanctum, is a ceiling which is an inverted step pyramid of 7 tiers, tapering down to a bud at the end. It was carved from one solid block of marble, and the craftsman worked with such attention that in places the material is almost transparent. Around the ceiling are statues of the goddesses, Saraswati with her peacock, Lakshmi and her lotus, Shakti with her cobra, Parvati and her cow. Standing in that hall beneath such a monument to human genius, my only thought was for the nobility of mind and hand that had conceived such a work. The vision of it filled me, a tourist passing by a thousand years later, with gratitude for the gifts of our ancestors, and for the impulse in the human spirit that has always aspired to the sublime.

In front of the sanctum a Brahmin priest was completing a puja to a small statue of Santinath, the 16th Tirthankara. The statue was seated in the middle of a five-tiered silver construction which resembled a portable wedding cake on wheels. The priest had just performed abishekam of milk and water over the statue, and he was now applying sandalpaste to its third eye, its heart, shoulders and navel, as if he were clothing it with magical armour. Another priest was performing the same ritual for the main idol in the inner sanctum, which is of Adinath, the religion's founder. Adinath is a larger-than-life figure just visible through the gloom of the sanctum. As with a Hindu image, the eyes stand out starkly, though the eyes of the Jain images are not looking at the devotee. There is no darshan: Adinath is gazing into the middle distance, deep in his own contemplation. His heart, for the Jains the seat of the soul, is marked out in the centre of his chest with a jewel. His body, of clear marble, is in the lotus pose, with erect back and an almost military tautness of concentration.

The priest had barely finished his work when the crowd that had been milling around the courtyard came pushing into the sanctum, all of them wearing protective gauzes or cloths in front of their mouths. 'Those who have made the largest offering to the front!' the peon cried. The priest went off to the side, his work over. The Jains have no priests of their own, but they employ Brahmins to perform the temple pujas to the images. A Jain is his or her own priest. They came in turns before Adinath, presented him with a plate of flowers and sandalpaste, daubed him in the same spots the Brahmin had already covered, and then sat on the floor in front of the image. The women drew swastika designs on the floor in rice grains, and placed a coin in the middle. The swastika has been a symbol in India for at least 4,000 years, and signifies the emergence of the phenomenal world from the still point at the centre. Over their swastikas the women traced a half moon with a dot above it, which traditionally represented the open lotus of liberation, surmounting the cycle of rebirth. Here, though, they placed another coin over the dot, so perhaps they had another kind of freedom in mind.

I wandered away from the sanctum, where the women were now chanting the namaskar mantra, to look at the other statues that lined the courtyard. They were all much the same, a stern Tirthankara, each in his own cell, gazing out of the half light into the middle distance. At the far corner of the court, though, was an open room. Inside was an image unlike any other in the temple. It was not just that it was of black marble, and that it was clearly much older than the others, but it exuded a deep peace that seemed to emanate from the whole of its time-smoothed body. The huge, impassive eyes added to the sensation.

I stood there for half an hour or more, and whoever came in did so silently, in contrast to the noise and the bustle in the main sanctum. I recalled the answer of a Jain saint who, when questioned about the Jain's need for images, since they do not believe in God or grace, replied that the point of an image was to instil its mood in whoever was in its presence. The Jain image is imbued with the attitude of the *tirthankara*, the impassive silence of one who has gone beyond the realm of form. In the presence of the black Adinath, I understood the saint's meaning.

SUFI INDIA

14

Islam is the second religion of India after Hinduism, and India has the third largest Muslim population anywhere in the world, some 120 million. It is not surprising then, that many schools of Sufism, representing the mystical dimension of Islam, should be found all over India today.

The seeds of the sufi movement were present from very early on in Islam. Even as early as the second generation of Mohammed's followers, a significant reaction grew in response to the worldly power of the ruling Umayadds, with many Muslims taking to an ascetic life. In the centuries following the death of Mohammed, Islam gradually evolved a legalistic orthodoxy which frowned on personal experiences of the Divine and the folk expressions of religious devotion through music, dance and ecstatic trance. In counterpart to this, some began to proclaim the supremacy of love over the law, and by the 8th century, many great personalities who stressed inner practices above formalistic worship had attracted followings in various parts of the Muslim world. One of the greatest exponents of love in the 8th century was Rabiah. She would often be seen wandering about carrying fire in one hand and water in the other. When asked what she was doing, she would reply that she was going to burn Heaven and extinguish Hell, so that people would worship God for His own sake alone.

The purpose of Sufism is to generate a personal experience of what is already the central mystery of Islam – Tauhid – a unity with God in which nothing can be adored except God Himself. Far from distancing themselves from the Shariat, the Muslim law, the sufis see themselves related to it in the way a walnut is related to its shell. The law protects them, as it does every Muslim, from harmful influences, both external and internal. The oil of the nut, even though it is invisible, is present everywhere, including the shell. The sufis liken the oil to the Haqiqat, the Ultimate Reality. The sufi's desire is to die to himself and to come truly alive through complete surrender to Allah. 'Surrender' is the meaning of the word 'Islam'.

The sufis have often had to meet strong opposition from the Muslim orthodoxy, and in 922 the master Al Hallaj was martyred for daring to proclaim that he and God were one and the same. Some countries today, notably Saudi Arabia, still condemn sufi practices. In India, however, the sufis have always met with a warm response, and have been a powerful harmonizing influence between Hindus and Muslims. India is home to many mystical streams, and of all countries, is the one which most encourages tolerance and a universal spiritual perspective. Sufism in India has taken on much of the Indian character, and has often intertwined with the indigenous bhakti movements, with which it has many similarities. As such, its tone is quite distinct to sufism elsewhere.

The three main sufi schools in India are the Naqshbandi, the Qadiriyah, and the Chishti Orders. The Naqshbandis first arrived in India in the 17th century, having already developed a strong political influence all over Central Asia. They are the champions of orthodoxy, tolerating no music in their worship, and upholding the Sharia in the strictest detail. The Qadiriyah Order, founded in Baghdad by Abdul Qadir al Gilani, who died in 1166, is widespread all over the country, especially in the Hyderabad area. Introduced into India in the 14th century, the Order's ideal of unity is rooted in the pain of separation, just as the Gaudiya Vaishnava's love of Krishna is intensified by viraha, the sense of distance from Him. One of their members, Waris Shah, a prominent poet from the Punjab in the 16th century, even re-worked the Krishna story for his own people, calling it Heer Ranjha. For the Qadiriyah, the primacy of love is absolute, and has its expression as much in the horizontal domain of daily life, cutting across Muslim-Hindu divides, as it does in the vertical relationship with Allah.

Mu'inuddin Chishti, who was from Persia, brought his Order of sufis to India in 1292. The Chishtis declaim the primacy of love in relation to all life: to God, to the Sheikh – the head of a particular Chishti lineage – and to all fellow human beings. Poetry, the sama – a gathering for devotional music – and hospitality and service to followers of all faiths are their hallmarks. Much of the Islamization of India is attributed to the broad popularity of the Chishtis, who also enjoyed long periods of royal patronage.

Though the sama is a practice common to many sufi schools, it is the Chishtis who have elevated it to an art form whose music, known as qawwali, has become popular among Hindus and Muslims alike. Instead of the call and response form commonly used in bhajans, the qawwali is sung by qawwals, professional musicians who perform in groups, with one or two solo singers. They sing mystical poetry in Persian, Hindi, or Urdu, with frequent repetition and improvization. The aim is to transport the listener as well as themselves into a state of unity with the Divine. At the Partition, most qawwal migrated to Pakistan, and the best groups are in great demand by the Indian sufis, who say their music transmits an ethereal current into the qalb, the inner heart, purifying the whole being. Hand-clapping, drums and harmonium help raise the atmosphere to an ecstatic pitch. When someone falls into ecstasy, the singers repeat the couplet he swooned on until he returns to normal consciousness. More than one Sheikh has been known to die from the ecstasy raised by qawwali, and in the case of Hazrat Khwaja Qutubbudin of Delhi, the qawwal had to continue singing the same couplet for three days until the Sheikh was buried! The couplet that transported the

Sheikh to the Other World was:

> For the victims of the sword of Divine Love,
> There is a new life every moment
> From the 'unseen'.

The other practice common among most sufi Orders is the zikhr, the repetition of God's Name in a group, accompanied sometimes with tabla and harmonium, and always with some form of bodily movement, usually swaying from side to side in unison, with rhythmic movements of the head symbolizing the descent into the Heart and the casting off of the ego. One zikhr I attended in Madras went on for hours, continually rising to a pitch and then subsiding again, with the men becoming progressively transported by the collective intensity. The only females in the room were the two young daughters of the Sheikh's son. Our heads moved in unison from right to left, down to the heart, over and over again, faster and faster, then slower, then faster again. The chant, alternating between 'la ilah illah Allah' – There is no God but God – and 'Allah Hu!' was now pushed out of our mouths with the outbreath, now murmured softly like words to a lover.

The zikhr was led by the Sheikh's eldest son, a man in his 30s with a genuine tenderness. He sat in front of the rest of us in an inconspicuous room down a side street somewhere in the Muslim district of Royapettah. The Sheikh himself, Sayed Mohammed Omar Amir Kaleemi Shah, is an acknowledged master in both the Chishti and the Qadiriyah Orders. He is elderly now, and was ill when I came. He is currently grooming his eldest son to take his place.

The members of the Order take an oath from the Sheikh, called the Bayed, to follow his guidance. The son told me that their group meet every 100 days for a 24-hour zikhr, and that in everyday life, each sufi recites the name of God internally on the breath. Though his group is independent of any other, it was apparent as he talked that they were part of a network of Sheikhs and Orders that spans the whole country. His father's own Sheikh was Noori Shah of Hyderabad, whose own son, Noorullah Shah, is now a respected Sheikh in that city. The day before I came, they had had an official visit from the Chishti Sheikh of Ajmer, who I was soon to meet on his own territory.

THE CHISHTI TOMB IN AJMER

The sufis generally practise their devotions in private. The only public evidence of their existence are the shrines of sufi saints, which are venerated in India as much as any Hindu shrine. Even though it is frowned upon by the orthodoxy – because in Islam, no-one other than God is worthy of veneration – pilgrimage to shrines has always been popular throughout Islam, and in India it is one of the practices that unites Hindus and Muslims. These shrines are everywhere. The tomb of Hamid Aoulia in Kanchi is a haven of quiet where locals come in a small but continuous stream to strew rose petals over the shrine. The tourists flock to the Hindu temples, usually unaware of the existence of the tomb. In Delhi the famous shrine of Nizamuddin Aulia draws thousands of pilgrims every day. Nizamuddin, who died in 1325, was a Sheikh of the Chishti Order, and is one of the most revered figures of Muslim India. A few streets away from his tomb is the shrine of Hazrat Inayat Khan, the Chishti musician and Sheikh who brought his lineage to the West in the 1920s.

The most celebrated shrine of all is that of Chishti himself, who died in Ajmer in the early-13th century. Chishti embodied all the virtues of the Faith. His mission was nearness to God through absolute self-abnegation and renunciation. In his lifetime he was considered to be Allah's evangelist to Hindustan. He had authority over the Mughal emperors and worked countless miracles, which is one of the main reasons for his shrine's popularity.

It first began to attract large numbers of pilgrims in the 14th century, but its fame spread across the country in the 16th century, when the Emperor Akbar visited it 16 times. He made a vow to go every year at the Urs celebration, the anniversary of the saint's death, in December. He also went after every victorious battle. When he had a son, he fulfilled a vow to walk from Agra to Ajmer, and there are miniatures in the Victoria and Albert Museum in London showing Akbar on his journey. Akbar organized the management of the shrine, the accommodation for the pilgrims, and built a mosque next to the tomb in 1571. The Emperor Jehangir lived in Ajmer for three years, and bored holes in his ears (plugging them with pearls) to show he was Chishti's slave. Jehangir was convinced he owed his very existence and throne to the saint.

The shrine's popularity continued down through the centuries. In 1911 Queen Mary of England paid her respects there, and Indira Ghandi visited in 1976. Since the saint is believed to intercede for those buried close by, many tombs of the rich and famous are within the precincts. In 1879, 20,000 pilgrims were present for the Urs. In 1976, there were 100,000, another indication of how improved transport has vastly increased pilgrim traffic all over India.

The tomb today is in a domed marble building which itself is in the middle of a courtyard. Akbar's mosque takes up one side of the court, while columned walkways full of flower sellers make up the rest of the enclosure. Striped canvas sheets attached to gnarled old trees provide shade from the desert sun. Arid hills with the remains of the city walls surround the dargah, the shrine compound. As I came in, a vast cauldron at the entrance was simmering on the roof of a small dome which housed a raging fire. The cauldron was swimming with soup which was about to be distributed to the poor. At one of the gateways to the tomb, a group of qawwals were singing. I sat by them with other pilgrims for an hour or so, in turns lulled and inspired by their songs of love, whose sentiments were easy to fathom, even without a knowledge of the language. Part of the court is a covered arcade. Men sat there on blankets talking, praying; women sat alongside, knitting, watching the children who were blowing balloons. The atmosphere was quiet; there was a tangible respect for the place and the music. I went there for a while to write notes. A man came up to me and asked what I was writing about.

'About the qawwal,' I replied.

'Then please,' he asked in a deferential tone, 'Take your book off your foot.'

Later, I followed the pilgrims into the shrine. At the entrance one of the administrative staff – the khuddam, whose families have managed the shrine for centuries – tried to extract an exorbitant donation, pointing to a book with the sums given by other pilgrims. I had been forewarned of these predators, and handing over the normal token offering, I covered my head with a shawl and went in. The tomb, surrounded by a low silver railing, was piled high with flowers and cloths, offerings of the pilgrims. Some threw their flowers directly onto the tomb, others handed them to the attendant, who placed them on the tomb and then returned them to the pilgrim, like the prasad of a Hindu temple. The devout followed the narrow walkway which circled the tomb, whispering their prayers and petitions under their breath, and occasionally sitting on the floor to recite some verses of the Koran or just to absorb the atmosphere. Nobody spoke in the shrine, and despite the continual stream of people, the place still manages to retain a charged feeling of sanctity.

Pilgrims come to Ajmer for the same reasons they go to any holy shrine in India, be it Muslim or Hindu – and people of all faiths come to the shrine of Chishti. Most of them want something from the saint – the sick come to be cured, the poor come to be fed, the childless pray for a boy, the possessed come to be freed of the evil spirit. Some make the journey solely for the sake of devotion. They arrive, bow low and make their prayers and petitions. Strings are tied to the marble screens of the mausoleum to remind the saint of their plea. When their wish is fulfilled, they return to remove the string.

The celebration of Urs – a term for marriage festivities, used in this context to mean the union of the saint with God – draws pilgrims from all over the world. The culmination of the festival, the musical sama, is only attended by men. It starts in the early evening and continues throughout the night until the next morning. The Diwan – the head of the sufi brethren there and the spiritual representative of the saint – sits under a silken canopy supported by silver posts. The musicians sit opposite him, faced by the most distinguished guests. As the qawwali music reaches a crescendo, someone in the assembly may roll in ecstasy on the floor, spin like a whirling dervish, or rock to and fro. When the state of wajd, ecstasy, is achieved, the Diwan and the whole audience rise in honour, and the couplet is repeated until the ecstatic returns to waking consciousness. At 3am tea with cardamon and saffron is brought in by attendants in long velvet gowns. After another hour of song, rose water which has been used to wash the tomb is brought in and passed round in bowls, signifying the end of the occasion.

The present Diwan lives up a narrow flight of stairs on the first floor of a house overlooking the street leading to the Dargah. Looking distinctly ordinary out of his official regalia, Syed Zainul Abedin Ali Khan was sprawled on one of the mattresses which were spread on the floor, with his head out of the window, watching the life of the town go by. He has held his position for 20 years, having taken it over when he was 23, on his father's death. The walls were lined with tattered books. I would never have suspected that I was in the presence of one of the most influential Sheikhs in India – although his influence is more temporal than spiritual, deriving as it does from his hereditary position. As the representative of the most widely revered saint in Muslim India, he enjoys a substantial income and an official residence, known as the haveli. However, he was quick to tell me, as soon as I was settled at the other corner of the window, rival claimants to his position occupy parts of the haveli, and the building is in bad repair because no-one will accept responsibility for its maintenance. He has had to let out much of it to shops in order to maintain his income, because the kuddam do not give him the percentage of the shrine's offerings that they should. The kuddam and the Diwan have continued an ongoing struggle for power and revenue for much of this century, and even longer. I was reminded of the stories of corruption I had heard in temples all over the subcontinent, and began to realize that, Muslim or Hindu, some of the most sacred places in India, being the source of enviable revenues for those who have them in their charge, are all too often the very places where ethics and ordinary human dignity are most lacking.

It happened to be a Thursday, the day of the week when the Sheikh presides over a formal session of qawwali, but since for some reason he was unable to go, his younger brother was to take his place. Glad of the opportunity, I accompanied the brother to the haveli, a building much like any other bordering the Dargah. With an unusual composure and degree of attentiveness, the man went into a small room off a courtyard and changed from his ordinary clothes into an orange turban and robe. He knelt on the ground and said some silent prayers, then signalled me to follow him and his attendant into the Dargah. He moved swiftly, without speaking. Leaving his white slippers at the main gate and going straight to the shrine, he circulated the tomb and threw rose petals over it. As we came out, men came forward to kiss his hand or to give a polite greeting. He responded formally, with a dignity that bore no trace of superiority.

We walked the same fast pace to the open court that serves as the entrance to the mosque. There, two attendants with silver staffs were waiting, with three qawwals. The representative of the Sheikh sat cross-legged on the floor between the attendants, opposite the singers. Another attendant placed two silver pots before him, which were a gift to the Diwan of his time from Akbar. The qawwals began to play, and people gathered round, while the 'Sheikh' continued to sit in noble composure, eyes closed, body swaying slightly to the rhythm of the music. As the music gathered pace, people got up one at a time as the inspiration moved them, and with a bow gave some money to the 'Sheikh'. He gave it to the attendants, and they passed it on to the qawwals.

233

After half an hour or so, the music quietened, and the 'Sheikh' reached into the silver pots to hand out the sweets they contained. Then he rose, signalling an end to the ritual, and strode off to the haveli to become an ordinary man again.

When I thanked him for showing me that corruption was not the only feature of Ajmer, he took a book from the shelf on the life of Mu'inuddin Chishti, offered it to me as a gift, and said, 'The spirit of Chishti lives here as it has always done.' Without another word, he walked swiftly off into the crowded street.

BUDDHISM IN INDIA

Mind precedes all phenomena
mind matters most, everything is mind-made.
If with an impure mind
you speak or act
then suffering follows you
as the cartwheel follows the foot of the draft animal.
If with a pure mind
you speak or act
then happiness follows you
as a shadow that never departs.
The Buddha

15

Long before they were centres of Hindu pilgrimage, places like
Ayodhya, Ellora and Badrinath were part of a network of
Buddhist holy places which spread throughout India and Pakistan as far west as Afghanistan. In the last few centuries
before Christ, with the support of the great Emperor Ashoka
in the 3rd century, the religion of the Buddha put the Brahminical tradition onto the defensive, and established itself as a
radical alternative to tired ritual and the caste hierarchy.

Buddha was born at Lumbini, in northern India, some
2,500 years ago. Instead of a religion based on belief in scriptural and priestly authority, he advocated personal verification of his teachings through sustained inner inquiry. His Four
Noble Truths assert that all sentient beings suffer, and that
they do so because of the clinging nature of the mind. There is
a way out of this suffering, and that is the practice of meditation. Through meditation, the individual comes to see how he

causes his own suffering through identification with the mind's processes. The path is one of gradual or sudden release of these identifications. The end result is genuine happiness, which everyone, affirms the Buddha, is secretly searching for, whatever distorted methods they may be applying. Buddhism points out the direction and provides the necessary means to find the happiness that passes understanding.

Though it enjoyed royal patronage and expansion for several centuries, the way of the Buddha eventually retreated from India in the wake of fresh revivals of the Brahminical tradition, and in the face of the continuing tenacity of the caste system. Buddha's assertion that everyone is subject to the same causes of suffering bestows an equality on all that directly contradicts the foundation of India's social structure as it still persists 2,500 years later. Practically all the great Buddhist sites in India are now 'places of historical interest' rather than living witnesses to the sacred. Today, barely two million people in India are Buddhists.

Yet the teachings are currently enjoying a revival that is worldwide. Buddhism in the West is gaining more support every year. While the population of Christian monasteries is aged and in steep decline, a new Buddhist monastery seems to open somewhere every week. The three-year waiting list to enter Amaravati, the Theravadin Monastery in Britain, is not unusual. The rational science of mind that Buddhism offers, based on experiential inquiry rather than received belief and dogma, fits well with the contemporary climate.

Buddhism is also attracting renewed interest of a special kind in its country of origin. As long ago as 1956, Dr B. R. Ambedkar, along with hundreds of thousands of Mahars, a backward caste, converted to Buddhism in symbolic protest to the oppressions of caste inequality. While Ambedkar's decision was a carefully considered intellectual one, more recent conversions have been overtly political. In 1995, Phoolan Devi, the Bandit Queen, was also on the point of conversion. Phoolan Devi achieved notoriety and a vast following among the underprivileged because of her armed resistance to repressive landlords. On her release from prison, she confirmed her intention to enter politics. She considered converting to Buddhism solely in the hope of furthering her popularity among the masses, but in the event, she decided against it, having been advised it would not serve her cause – though her husband converted instead.

The great majority of Indian conversions to Buddhism – which still remain relatively small – are a vehement protest against the iniquities of the caste system.

In the May 1995 edition of an India publication entitled *Sunday Magazine*, Professor H. C. Joshi, President of the Buddhist Society of India, was quoted as saying, 'I am an untouchable ... Brahmins will not accept water from us. We have taken on Buddhism as a means to a great social revolution, as part of our fight against Hinduism. Revenge will take place ... We are not peace lovers. We will use all our might, arms and every means at our disposal, to fight oppression.'

It would be difficult to find a quote less Buddhist in character anywhere. Buddhism does not proselytize, never seeks to convert, and is categorically against violence of any kind. It is less a religion than a body of knowledge to be applied for personal realization. There are those among the educated in India who see Buddhism in this light, and who take meditation courses for the same reasons as their counterparts in the West. In 1994, over 25,000 people took courses at the Goenka Vipassana centres alone, and the same centres taught meditation to 6,000 children in the same year. They are currently seeing a 25 per cent year-by-year increase of students, and these figures compare with those of other meditation centres in India.

The people who take courses of this kind rarely call themselves Buddhists – they are there for the meditation techniques, which are purely practical, without any religious overlay. As for those in India who do convert for social reasons, they rarely experience any change in attitude towards them by Hindus, since everyone in their community knows their origins. Buddhism has done little to change the lot of the lower castes. What conversion does sometimes do is to give the individual a new self-respect in their own eyes, and a pride in having made a gesture on behalf of their own humanity.

Conversion as a phenomenon has no bearing on the spiritual vitality of Buddhism in India. Buddhism – like any religion – survives first and foremost through individuals who embody the teachings in their daily lives. These are the genuine representatives of the Buddha nature. 'The Three Jewels' of Buddhism are The Buddha-nature, the teaching, known as the Dharma, and the Sangha, the community of spiritual practitioners. These 'Three Jewels' together ensure the living continuity of the tradition.

As the generous host to The Dalai Lama and the Tibetan community in exile, India is home to the most revered example of 'Buddha nature' alive today. Other Buddhist traditions like Zen, and the Theravada school of south-east Asia, also have teachers in India with outstanding reputations. The Buddha himself walked this land, so India remains a place of pilgrimage for Buddhists the world over. The two Buddhist holy places that most retain a living sense of the sacred are Bodh Gaya, where the Buddha attained enlightenment at the foot of the Bodhi tree, and Sarnath, near Banaras, where he gave his first discourse in The Deer Park. The local populations in these places, though, count no Buddhists among them. On the other hand, Buddhists come to these villages from all over the world to retrace the steps of one of mankind's greatest teachers, and to visit the temples of the different Buddhist traditions there.

Peter Matthiessen, in his book, *The Snow Leopard* (Viking, 1978) describes his own visit to the bodhi tree like this:

Here, in a warm dawn, 10 days ago, with 3 Tibetan monks in maroon robes, I watched the rising of the Morning Star and came away no wiser than before. But later I wandered if the Tibetans were aware that the bodhi tree was murmuring with gusts of birds, while another large pipal, so close by that it touched the holy tree with many branches, was without life. I make no claims for this event: I simply declare what I saw there at Bodh Gaya.

TIBETAN BUDDHISM IN INDIA

> We are born without a need for religion, but not without
> a need for human affection.
>
> *H. H. The Dalai Lama*

Tibetan Buddhism is the religion of Ladakh which, although
politically part of India, belongs culturally and geographically
to the Tibetan plateau. As such, it will be introduced in a later
book in this series. Apart from Ladakh, Tibetan Buddhism has
at least 500 monastic and educational centres around the
world. By far the largest number of these are in India, where
over 100,000 Tibetan refugees are now settled. Two monasteries in Mysore have over 2,000 monks, and two more near
Hubli, in Karnataka, have 2,000 monks each. The Sakya Order
has a college and monastery near Dehra Dun, the Nyingma
sect have small monasteries in Darjeeling, Mysore, and in
many other places. The Institute for Tibetan Studies in Sarnath
offers an education in Tibetan and Buddhist Studies up to Doc-
torate level, and also houses the main body of Tibetan manu-
scripts. The Dalai Lama and the Government in Exile, along
with monasteries, cultural institutes, the State Oracle and a
School of Dialectics, are in Dharamsala, popularly known as
'Little Tibet'. Anyone can attend the daily lectures in English at
the Tibetan Library there on aspects of Buddhist teaching.
Since 1987, at least 7,000 monks and nuns have escaped from
Tibet to come to the monasteries in India, which are now far
more well endowed with teachers and students than those in
Tibet itself. In Dharamsala, a group of 100 nuns have recently
arrived, and are beginning the task of building themselves a
nunnery. In 'Little Tibet', 'The Three Jewels' of Buddhism are
alive and well.

This is above all due to the presence there of Tenzing Gyatso, The 14th Dalai Lama. His infectious laugh, his exuberant
joy and vitality, his uncontrived simplicity and humility, have
touched the hearts of people the world over. He is the greatest living Tibetan teacher alive today, and one of the most

important Buddhist thinkers of the century. His knowledge and learning are formidable, yet his essential message is one that everyone can grasp: inner disarmament. Tenzing Gyatso's unswerving attitude of non-violence towards those who have brutally occupied his country since 1959 earned him the Nobel Peace Prize in 1989. He applies the same fundamental attitude to spirituality and its daily practice.

For him, as a Buddhist, happiness is everyone's ultimate concern. One's own happiness ultimately arises from the development of love and compassion. These in their turn come from the realization of the profound interdependence of every living being. This is why, perhaps alone among all the religious leaders of the world, he can place the need for affection above the need for religion itself. Over and again, he tells audiences around the world that evil is not intrinsic – that its causes can be found in one's own mind, and can be uprooted. The compassion he speaks of, far from being an emotional response, is one based on reason and self-observation. While Christianity bears the same message of love, Buddhism stresses the importance of wisdom as the foundation for love. Wisdom is acquired not through the intellect, but through the practice of meditation. Once one begins to see in meditation that all are equal in their wish for happiness and their right to obtain it, a sense of responsibility begins to form in relation to others. The head and the heart, the Dalai Lama says, must work together, rather than our being subject on the one hand to intellectual distance, and on the other, to emotional identification.

Though he talks in a far more specialized way to those who are seriously engaged in the teachings, the Dalai Lama has the rare gift of being able to couch his wisdom in terms that speak to people in the everyday world as well as to those who are monks. Every year, in March, he holds public teachings in Dharamsala for an international audience. Though he is a monk himself, and practises a minimum of four hours meditation a day, his life is utterly given over to the role he was born for. He is a world statesman and politician as well as a spiritual leader, and his schedule would daunt the hardiest of business

240

travellers. When asked what he would do if Tibet gained its freedom in his lifetime, he says he would like to revert to being 'a simple monk'. This, he says, would allow him to deepen his wisdom with more meditation practice. Tenzing Gyatso is a rare statesman indeed.

GOENKA AND VIPASSANA MEDITATION

S. N. Goenka, a disciple of the Burmese teacher U Ba Khin, who died in 1971, is the teacher who has done most in India to establish the Theravadin tradition of Vipassana meditation. A former industrialist and leader of the Indian community in Burma, his life took an entirely new turn when he met U Ba Khin in 1955. His teacher assured him there was no need to be a Buddhist to practise Vipassana (which means 'insight'), and Goenka began to devote every spare moment he had to the practice. In 1969 U Ba Khin declared him a teacher in his own right, and Goenka returned to India to open a centre.

His headquarters, in Igatpuri, north of Bombay, has been running meditation retreats ever since. There are now Vipassana Institute branches all over the country which offer classes lasting from an evening to ten days. Unlike Tibetan Buddhism, with its strong emphasis on philosophy and dialectics as well as meditation, the Theravadin school is almost entirely practice-based. Although he gives 'dharma talks' every evening in his courses, Goenka stresses that 'liberation can only be gained by practice, never by mere discussion.'

The heart of the practice is awareness of the breath. Respiration, Goenka teaches, is the bridge from the known to the unknown, from the conscious to the unconscious. The words we use for God and for spiritual religious experience vary from culture to culture; but everyone breathes, everyone knows suffering. A retreat with Goenka begins and ends with these factors common to us all. There are no symbols, Buddhist or otherwise, on the plain white walls of his centres. There are no sectarian, even religious teachings, of any kind. What you do is sit for hours at a time and watch your breath. You begin with intentional breathing, then settle into an awareness of the natural breath. The breath and the mind, the practitioner soon discovers, are intimately connected. As one watches the breath entering and leaving the nostrils, one begins to notice that thoughts have no logical sequence, and that they have as their object something either pleasant or unpleasant. The mind is normally filled with either indifference, craving or aversion. While the attention is firmly on the breath, these three cannot arise, and then the mind is free. These moments of purity act on the impurities stored in the unconscious, encouraging them to rise to the surface. The task is to sit through these negative upsurges without reacting to them. If the practitioner succeeds in this, he will know the joy of seeing his negativities rise up and float away.

The two main aims of the technique are to break the barrier between the conscious and the unconscious – which is to free oneself of ignorance – and to generate equanimity in the place of reaction. One learns to act instead of reacting. Over the period of ten days, the practitioner comes to see that his suffering comes through attachment to his desires, to his views and beliefs, to the concept of 'I and mine'. Goenka also suggests that attachment to religious rites and rituals is a cause of suffering. The enemies one meets on the way, he says, are doubt, agitation and laziness. Beyond mind and matter is *nirvana* – that state in which nothing arises or passes away.

Goenka's courses are not for the half-hearted. They begin at 4am with two hours meditation, and continue from 8–11am with just two five-minute breaks. Another $4^{1}/_{2}$ hours of sitting awaits in the afternoon. Practitioners see the teacher three times a day in small groups, and eat three very light meals in the time that is left. All medicines are to be given in at the start of the course. If this regime doesn't help you to see your own suffering and its causes, it is difficult to imagine what will. The suffering, however, is not for its own sake: as the Buddha himself taught, the awareness of its causes brings the birth of compassion, for oneself and for all living beings.

242

A JESUIT ZEN MASTER

Though Indian by birth, Amo Samy is an unusual blend of different cultures and religious traditions – the kind of synthesis that has always flowered so happily in the environment of India. He was born in Burma, and lived there until he was ten, surrounded by a culture that was deeply Buddhist. Then his parents returned to India, where he was sent to a Jesuit school. In 1972 he was ordained as a Jesuit priest, but he became progressively disenchanted with the Jesuit context, which did not seem able to help him to a direct experience of God. He visited Hindu ashrams, met great saints, did Vipassana meditation with Goenka, became a sannyasin for a while, and eventually settled down to a solitary life at the shrine of Saint Paul the Hermit for some years.

Then he met Fr Lasalle, the Jesuit who had trained in Zen in Japan, and whose books Amo Samy was familiar with. It was one of those meetings of destiny that determine the course of a life. What he had read of Zen, and what the person of Lasalle conveyed, inspired Amo Samy to go to Japan to train in Zen practice himself. *Advaita* and the teaching of Ramana Maharshi had long served as Amo Samy's philosophical framework, but Zen, he felt, was a means to put the philosophy of the non-dual into practice. With the help of Fr Lasalle, he went to Japan and lived in a Jesuit's house while training with his Zen master, Yamada Ko-Un Roshi, who was a layman, and consequently had no monastery. He went between the Jesuit's house and the *zendo* for four years, from 1978 to 1982. On his return to India, he continued to visit his master annually.

Yamada Ko-Un Roshi confirmed Amo Samy as a teacher, and for the next ten years Amo Samy lived as a Jesuit in one of their retreat centres in Madras, running his own zendo there with the support of his Provincial and the Bishop. He now has his own Bodhi Zendo retreat centre near Kodaikanal, in the south of Tamil Nadu, where he runs week-long retreats, primarily for Westerners.

243

'What we practise is not Christian Zen,' he told me. 'I do not try to blend the two traditions. Rather, we are Christians practising Zen. The only concession to Christianity is that the Eucharist is available to those who want it. What is the Eucharist, after all, if not the great Bodhisattva vow of infinite compassion enacted and realised? It is optional in my retreats, but many attend it and find it meaningful. Some get annoyed, though, and say that the Christian thing should have no place in Zen. For the rest, we sit in practice just like in any other zendo.'

Amo Samy is concerned that the popular image of Zen is all too often fixated on the heroic image of absolute egolessness, clarity of consciousness, and passionless indifference to emotions. This, for him, represents a flight into the narcissistic personality pattern. The real point of Zen practice, he feels, is to take the individual to the limits of his world, where he cannot avoid the fact of his own utter powerlessness, his impotency and self-centredness. In the face of his own abyss, the practice invites him to take one further step – to let go, to die, to surrender into emptiness and nothingness. In that act of letting go, Amo Samy says, one realizes the Emptiness as the Mystery of being. Only then can you awaken to the Self that you truly are, 'The Man or the Woman of No Rank', as the Zen tradition describes it. This is the beginning of the Zen path. The end, far more difficult and long term, is the inner freedom to move at will between duality and non-duality – in short, to live one's knowing in the world in daily relationship with others.

CHRISTIAN INDIA

16

There are ten times more Christians in India than there are Buddhists, some 21 million people. Christianity reached India through the Apostalate of Saint Thomas, who travelled both in the north and the south of India less than 50 years after Christ's crucifixion. India was home to thriving Christian communities long before it was even heard of in most regions of Europe. Among many others, a 2nd-century Syriac text mentions the Apostalate of Thomas in India, and several English records refer to an envoy sent by King Alfred to India with the mission of giving alms to the communities descended from the converts of Thomas. Thomas was an exponent of the Syrian rite, and in Kerala the Syriac Church continues to have a strong presence. To this day, these communities, who still call themselves 'Thomas Christians', are almost exclusively from the high caste Brahmin sect whose members Thomas originally converted.

Thomas was murdered outside present-day Madras, so India has its own tomb of the martyr and Apostle in the Cathedral of Saint Thomas in Mylapore, now a district of the city itself. In a despatch of 1293, Marco Polo mentions the strong devotion of all, Hindus, Moslems, and Christians, to the tomb. In the 16th century, the Catholic saint, Francis Xavier, stayed there for four months, praying for guidance in his own mission. The name 'Madras' is a reminder of the 'Madrasa', the Syriac for monastery, that once flourished in the area.

When the Portuguese excavated the tomb in 1523, they discovered the spear head which ended the apostle's life while, an unbroken tradition says, he was praying before a stone cross fashioned by his own hands. They also found parts of the apostle's skull and remnants of the spine. The tomb, with the relics, is now in the crypt of the cathedral. The ardent devotion offered to it by adherents of all religions is due to the miracles said to have occurred by the apostle's grace. The cross reputedly made by Thomas, also discovered by the Portuguese, drew thousands of pilgrims for more than 150 years, because of its annual 'sweating' on December 18, the Feast of the Expectation of Our Lady. A journal of the time reports that on that day, in 1558,

> When the singing of the Mass started, the stone of the cross began to turn black in colour and to distil water in such large quantity, that those who so willed, soaked their linen and rosaries in it.[1]

The phenomenon continued until 1704, when it stopped as suddenly as it had started. Today the Cathedral, now Anglican, is a 19th-century neo-Gothic building with a wooden roof and a kitsch set of Victorian Stations of the Cross around the walls. A larger than life figure of Christ, dressed as both priest and king, stands over the altar with outstretched arms, flanked by peacocks on either side. Though the Cathedral is still a major place of pilgrimage for Indian Christians, those who want miracles now have to go elsewhere. Fortunately, India has her own version of Lourdes a few hundred miles down the Coromandel coast, at the tiny fishing village of Velankani, near Nagapattinam. Pilgrims of all religions flock there to receive the healing grace of Our Lady, to be granted children, or to receive Her assistance in some venture. The frequent 'success stories' guarantee the continuing popularity of the shrine.

The Bishop of Madras: A Voice for the Oppressed

Unlike Saint Thomas, Saint Francis Xavier converted southern fisherfolk to the Catholic faith, and the Catholic church in India still draws most of its congregation from the lowest classes. The same is true for the Protestants who, while their presence was evident long before, spread their faith out from the English-dominated cities of Bombay and Calcutta in the 19th century. Like Buddhism, Christianity, as a caste-free religion, represents an opportunity for the underprivileged to recover a sense of self-worth and equality with others. Ordination into the priesthood, especially, is a way of combining a respectable career with a sense of mission, and the numbers seeking to enter the ministry – above all from the lowest castes – is greatly on the increase. The bishops, however, are mostly Brahmins, and the authorities are currently under pressure to address the balance in favour of the lower castes.

M. Azariah, who was made the Anglican Bishop of Madras in 1990, is one of the few *dalits*, or untouchables, to have risen to such an elevated position in the Church. Azariah has a burning mission to relieve the suffering of the oppressed (the literal meaning of *dalit*) in his country. The dalits are the *Panchamas*, 'the fifth people', comprising the so-called Scheduled Castes and Tribes. They are beyond the pale of the Brahmin system of the four castes, and have been so for 2,500 years, ever since the Hindu Law of Manu (ch.19 v.43) decreed that 'the untouchables are born slaves'. In 1950 the Constitution included a law which abolished untouchability, but like so many other laws in India, it remains true only on the paper it was written on.

Attitudes remain much the same as ever, especially in rural India, which continues to sustain the most ignored yet glaring example of apartheid the world has ever known. A dalit cannot drink from the same well as the other castes, cannot touch food to be eaten by them, and risks assault if he dares even to look at a Brahmin in the street. He rarely owns property, and usually relies for his living on the caprice of the local landowner. Many are bonded labourers, which means they are in debt to the landowner, who gives them a subsistence meal in return for twelve or more hours work a day. They may have borrowed 50 rupees (£1) to begin with, which they pay back at 5 rupees a month on compound interest. The interest ensures the debt is never repaid, and the landowner receives free labour for the dalit's lifetime. Bonded labourers are little more than slaves; if they try to escape, they are hunted down and often killed or tortured. When they become too old to work, they are thrown out on the street, where they can only survive through begging.

Azariah awakened the world community to the reality of the dalits' plight in his speech to the Assembly of the World Community of Churches in Vancouver, in 1983. Few of those present were aware that 200 million untouchables are the subjects of discrimination and oppression in India. He took the same message to the World Conference on Human Rights in Vienna, in 1993. A study he organized of the homeless in the vicinity of Madras station showed that all were convinced that fate was the cause of their plight. For Azariah, this is the fundamental attitude that needs to change. The poor themselves need to feel their own value, and that they can take charge of their own destiny – inspired, though, by a spiritual, rather than a humanist vision. Like the Liberation Theologians of South America, he believes that peace will only come through struggle; but their empowerment must come, he says, not through guns but through the descent of the Holy Spirit.

'I am not for soul salvation,' he said to me, eyes gleaming, hand gesticulating across a desk piled high with papers and files and notes to himself. 'I am for *whole* salvation – social, economic, cultural, and spiritual.'

The empowerment of the people to determine their own destiny is for Azariah the essence of Christian mission. Education is the key. In four years he has built 70 churches-cum-schools in rural areas, and training centres in Kanchi and Guindy which teach self-employment skills. His diocese has organized a scheme through which 30,000 urban dwellers have donated a bicycle, a bible and shoes to 30,000 rurals. The bicycle symbolizes self-reliance, the bible, self-realization, and the shoes – dalits are not allowed to wear shoes in a caste village – represent self-respect. Instead of funding schemes from the top down, Azariah works as a catalyst and inspiration to develop this sense of mission within the wider congregation, and to encourage them to address the issues of the poor in their area. Congregations meet regularly to discuss the needs of the community in which they live and to agree on appropriate action.

The Bishop's path is not an easy one. On the announcement of his impending ordination, the *sudras* in his diocese – the lowest of the four Hindu castes – tried to take his nomination to court. The court hearing was due on a Monday, but Azariah managed to get his ordination rescheduled to the previous Saturday. When he went by invitation to address the devotees of Bangaru Adigala, the guru at Malmeathur who becomes possessed by Adi Parashakti (the guru also denounces the caste system), the same Christian sudras greeted him on his return with a flower garland, meaning that he had forsaken the faith to become a Hindu. Azariah's assistant, Fr Agostini, regularly receives anonymous phone threats from the caste members of the church of which he is pastor. Azariah's courage, though, is firm in a conviction deeper than any fear for his personal safety. I first met him in a Jesuit retreat house in Madras where, I discovered, he regularly comes for a day of silence, however pressing his engagements. It is clear to anyone who meets him that Azariah is a man of action; but his deeds, far from riding on the zeal of a missionary, spring from a genuine source of compassion.

The Bishop is only one of the more prominent spokesmen in a pan-India Dalit Liberation Movement, which was originally inspired by the Jesuits. The 32nd General Congregation of the Jesuits stipulated that whatever work a Jesuit may be involved in should be informed by a liberative attitude towards the poor. In Tamil Nadu, and in the area of Ranchi, the movement is particularly confrontational. In 1994 thousands of dalits attended a non-violent sit-in in front of Chengleput police station. Tension mounted, and a crowd eventually attacked the police station. Some dalits were killed, and a Jesuit was taken to prison.

Sharing and Caring

Another way of helping the underprivileged to help themselves is illustrated by the work of Steven and Sheila Arokiasamy, who are quietly transforming the life of some villages to the north of Madras. Some years ago, they became aware of the plight of the bonded labourers in the village of Katchur. The landowners were buying the milk from the labourers' buffalo at the pittance of 3 rupees (6 pence) a litre. The labourers had to sell them the milk at the price dictated by the landowners to help pay off their debts. The Arokiasamys paid off the labourers' debts, bought them some more buffalo, and began to buy the milk at 6 rupees a litre. They went to meet the landowners, and assured them their only interest was to assist other human beings in need. They expressed nothing but goodwill towards them, instead of the hostility the landowners expected. Now the landowners buy the milk from Arokiasamy at 6 rupees a litre, and out of their increased income, the labourers have repaid the price of the buffalo to the Arokiasamys. The couple's simple but difficult creed is that unsentimental, non-discriminating love is the only answer.

They are successful because they are a living example of what they believe in. Their ethos, like that of the dalit movement, is to help people to help themselves. They have started small savings schemes in six villages, with groups in each village supporting each other. The savings also help the members get loans during emergencies. They have started tailoring and shoe making units that the villagers run themselves, and orphanage-schools for street children. The elderly poor often suffer most among the dalits. The family has no extra food to feed them, since the landowner only feeds those who are working. The couple has set up a day centre in Katchur which now gives free food and medical care to 100 people over 60. Yet this couple live in a Madras apartment with their family and work in a mental hospital there during the week! Their office takes up one of their rooms, and their only source of revenue is from a few well-wishers abroad, along with a small grant from Help The Aged. Their aim is to 'adopt' 25 dalit villages for a programme of non-formal education and self-reliance. Of all the thousands of aid organizations in India crying out for funds, this is one of the very few where the donor can be sure that his money goes to the people he intends it for, instead of funding cumbersome administrations, or lining the pockets of a whole chain of people along the way.[2]

Mother Teresa of Calcutta

The best known example of Christian 'love in action' in India is the work of Mother Teresa. Hindus and Christians alike regard her as a saint, and treat her with the awe and reverence they extend to any holy personage. As soon as she came out to meet me from a door in her Mother House in Calcutta, streams of people emerged from nowhere to touch her feet. She was ready for them: she delved into her pocket and gave each one a tiny alloy medallion of the Virgin, a pat on the head, and a few words of greeting. Yet this was no mechanical blessing: she gave her attention unstintingly. Though she spent no more than a few seconds with each person, it was as if she had all the time in the world. When the crowd had thinned, she turned to me, gave me a medallion, and told me about her work.

Volunteers come to the Mother House from all over the world and are allocated tasks on a daily basis from there. Anyone who wishes to help can just turn up at 6am.[3] The Sisters of Charity, as her order is known, have projects in every town and city in India, as well in a hundred other countries. In Calcutta, they run a Home for the Dying, a leprosy clinic, a TB clinic, dispensaries, homes for abandoned children, nursery classes, homes for the mentally retarded, for unmarried mothers, and more.

The 250 nuns and novices in Calcutta start their day at 5am with meditation, and mass at 6am. By 8am they are fanning out all over the city in pairs – either on foot or by public transport. With over 4,000 nuns and novices around the world, the order has one of the largest novitiates in the world; yet they do no fundraising, nor do they receive any assistance from the government or the Church. Everything is paid for through private donations. Mother Teresa sells all her awards to add to the funds.

The Sisters have changed the attitude of Calcutta towards those who are dying on the streets. Nowadays, instead of being ignored by the public authorities, they are either taken to hospital or to the Sisters' Home for the Dying.

Not many seemed to be dying when I visited the Home. There were perhaps 30 men, all in blue, on beds with blue sheets, with another room for women. Many were rickshaw wallahs, who had contracted TB from pulling fat clients around the muggy city streets. Others had chronic diarrhoea. There were almost as many volunteers as there were inmates.

'We are mainly here to share a prayer and love,' said Doug, from Australia. 'The Indians are very keen to have prayers said for them. When they get a little better, they are sent on. The beds are needed for a constant flow of serious cases.'

Mother Teresa has her critics, among them Tariq Ali, the producer of a recent television documentary screened on Channel 4 in Britain. He and others, have pointed out that the people in the Home for the Dying do not get proper medical treatment and are sent away before they are cured. What her critics fail to see is that she and her sisters do not set out to provide an alternative to hospital or to available medical treatment. Their only real medicine is love. They are not so much social workers as workers of the spirit. On the wall of the men's ward there is a quote from the French Catholic writer, Paul Claudel, which points to the essence of Mother Teresa's mission:

Jesus did not come to explain suffering or to take it away: He came to fill it with His Presence.

CHRISTIAN ASHRAMS

While Christian charity and liberation theology have long since been established throughout the world, the Christian ashram is a development unique to India. Pioneers in the 1950s like Abishiktananda, and later, Father Bede Griffiths, established communities which were founded on the practice of contemplation rather than on the sacramental rites of the established church. They sought an expression for Christianity which reflected the depth of spiritual interiority that was so evident in the Hindu culture around them – a Christianity which could truly be called Indian, instead of one which perpetuated Western values regardless of the soil it lived on. Since then, the Indianization of Christianity, known as 'inculturation', has become one of the central themes of the Church in India.

The Christian ashram is not only a synthesis of East and West: it represents a step beyond the Church hierarchy altogether. It is open to the lay community and to people of all faiths. It looks to a more universal ideal of God rather than one which is exclusively Christian. It encourages solitude and meditation rather than good works, community activity, and a reliance on the sacraments. Though the sacraments have a place in ashram life, they include Hindu elements like the waving of the arati flame, the singing of bhajans, and the placing of the tilak dot on the forehead. In its simplicity, its loose-knit community of individuals, and its emphasis on prayer life, the ashram resembles the ideal of the early Desert Fathers, whose spirituality bore little relation to the later institution of the Western Church.

The many 'born-again' Christians in India, along with the majority of parish priests – especially the Protestants – naturally regard the ashrams with great suspicion. Sister Brigitta, an Anglican sister who has lived 18 years in Christa Prema Seva Ashram, in Poona, told me that the Catholics are generally far more receptive, and practically all Indian ashrams are Catholic. The Jesuits, especially, take Hinduism very seriously, and have contributed much to the comparative study of Hinduism and Christianity. Yet all ashrams find it difficult to attract new members. Christians in India are generally better educated than average, and their sights are on Western values and goals, rather than on a return to the traditional Hindu life of simplicity that an ashram represents.

Ironically, it is just this simplicity that draws so many Western visitors to the Christian ashrams. Many who come are disaffected with institutional Christianity, and find great relief in the open and reflective ashram atmosphere. It is common to hear of individuals who arrive with feelings of negativity towards Christianity in general, and who leave with a rediscovered faith in their own spiritual heritage. The return to grass roots, to spirituality rather than religion, to the wellspring of silence rather than the excitement of action, may well point to the only option for a living Christianity of the future. The ashram is India's contribution to this new, yet ancient Christian spirit.

Aanmodhaya Ashram

Aanmodhaya Ashram – the name means 'Self-Awakening' – was started just three years ago outside Kanchipuram in Tamil Nadu by Fathers Amalraj and Samarakone. It follows the usual ashram pattern of a number of huts clustered around a meditation hall and a chapel. Flower borders trace the paths between the huts, and recently planted trees give shade to the entrance. Already, it is a rare oasis of serenity and beauty in India.

Amalraj has done much in his 40-something years. He has practised Zen meditation in Japan, Astanga Yoga in India, and received his PhD for a comparative study of Nataraja, The Dancing Lord, and Christ, The Lord of Resurrection. It was during a 40-day solitary retreat in a mountain cave that he realized his vocation as a priest-mediator. He had been a priest since his early 20s, but the retreat pointed him towards becoming a spiritual guide. He had been including talks on Zen and yoga in his classes at the Bangalore seminary for some years when his order, The Oblates of Mary Immaculate, finally agreed with him that an ashram would be a more suitable context for his interests, and provided him with the necessary means to establish one.

He was soon joined by his former Superior at the seminary, Father Sam, as he is affectionately known. Bede Griffiths and Vandana Mataji had long been important influences on his thinking, and Sam had strongly encouraged the attitudes of inculturation in his seminary. For him, the whole stream of humanity, with all its different religions, is proceeding towards a universal kingdom of communion, beyond all names and forms. He sees the ashram as a place where this universality can flow into the Indian soil and flower in its own unique way.

Jains, Buddhists and Hindus regularly come to Aanmodhaya, where the liturgy includes texts from the different religions. Ashramites practise Zen meditation, mantra, yoga and Christian contemplation. There is a morning discourse, and 'Mother Earth Meditation', when everyone works in the garden. The evenings are silent from 6pm.

Jeevan Dhara Ashram

Vandana Mataji was one of the original members of the ecumenical CPS Ashram in Poona, which started in 1972 and still continues today. Along with other ashramites, she spent six months of the year for five years living in Hindu ashrams, absorbing the traditional way of life there, studying Hindu texts and practices, and absorbing the teachings of her guru, Swami Chidananda of Sivananda Ashram in Rishikesh. Jeevan Dhara Ashram grew organically around her and another sister, an Englishwoman called Eeshpriya Mataji. It sits on a spectacular ridge in the Himalayas, some four hours from Rishikesh.

An American known as Krishna, who has been to more ashrams than most people, had this to say about his stay at Jeevan Dhara:

Services were held three times a day in a beautiful chapel-temple, with prayers from the Bible and Hindu scriptures. The arati flame would be waved before the sacrament, the Bible, the symbols of the world's religions set around the room, to the mountains and the village and to the light in us. Mornings were silent, and the time when we all shared in community tasks. At sunset on Thursdays I was always deeply moved by a ceremony known as the pada puja, in which the two Matajis would wash the feet of everyone present.

On some mornings, Eeshpriya Mataji would give talks on yoga philosophy which were as incisive as any I have heard. She is one of those rare scholars who have leavened their studies with personal experience. For the ashramites here, the seeking is over, Christ is Risen and the personal drama has been completed. I have rarely felt such a sense of family and community in an ashram. When a visitor left, the entire community would accompany them to the gate and see them off. Even though the two Matajis are withdrawing in 1996 for indefinite personal retreats, this ashram will continue to be a beacon for Westerners and Indians alike.

Saccidananda Ashram

Saccidananda Ashram, at Shantivanam, is the Christian community in India best known to Westerners due to its founder, Father Bede Griffiths, who died in 1993. Though the ashram was technically begun in 1950 by Abishiktananda and another French father, Jules Monchanin, it only became a community when Father Bede took it over in the 1960s. Bede, originally an English Benedictine, was an inspired voice for a mystical spirituality that transcended all religious divisions, and his books have carried his vision around the world. He is widely regarded as a modern-day saint.

The ashram he left behind continues to be a place of meeting and prayer for people of all creeds or none. Ashramites wear the saffron robe of the Hindu sannyasi, walk barefoot, sit on the floor, and eat with the hand. Visitors and ashramites eat together in silence while someone reads aloud from a chosen text. Individuals live in their own thatched hut, and meet for common prayer three times a day.

The exterior of the chapel-temple is a flamboyant mix of Christian imagery and Hindu style. Inside, the court where the congregation sits on the floor is simple and bare, open to the light and air of the day. The inner sanctuary, or garba griha, is dark, like the 'cave of the heart', and contains a bare stone altar. During the services, sandalpaste, kum-kum, and vibhuti are placed on the forehead.

Saccidananda Ashram is now under the spiritual direction of Brother Martin, who spent several years in close living contact with Bede, who was his spiritual father. Yet Brother Martin has had his own realizations and profound inner experiences; anyone who hears his radical talks on advaita in Christianity can be forgiven for thinking that in Martin, the ashram may well have a leader who will take it even further along the mystical path than Bede himself was able to do.

1   D'Souza, Herman, Rt. Rev. *In The Steps of St. Thomas*. Diocesan Press, Madras 1983.
2   For details of how to help the Arokiasamy's work, see the Christian section in the appendix, Gurus, Ashrams and Retreat Centres.
3   See entry for Mother Teresa in the Christian section of the appendix, Gurus, Ashrams and Retreat Centres.

GAZETTEER
OF SACRED PLACES IN INDIA

Compiled by Dr. Rana P. B. Singh, lecturer in Geography at Banaras Hinhu University, and Executive Editor of the *National Geographical Journal of India.*

JAMMU AND KASHMIR

Amarnath

This cave is situated 120km from Srinagar. Pilgrims first stop at Pahalgam (96km), then pass through Chandanwari, Shesh-nag and Panchtarni where they halt for a night, and then further proceed to the Amarnath cave (4,300m) where Lord Shiva is worshipped in the form of a lingam-shaped ice block. There are other ice formation faces of Ganesh, Parvati and Bhairava. July-August is the main season for pilgrimage.

Jammu

This is the second largest city in the State and the last railway stop linked by direct trains from Delhi. Important temples are Raghunath Temple and Rambireshvar Temple.

Leh

Connected by road from Srinagar (434km) and Jammu (739km) and also by regular air services from Chandigarh, Leh is famous for a 15th-century Gompa and the Palace. From here one can also visit several other Buddhist holy sites and Gompas like Alchi (70km), Lekir (13km) and Hemis (45km).

Martand

Near Srinagar in the lower Lidder Valley lies the 8th-century temple. Although major portions are ruined, it still attracts large numbers of people. There are also idols of Vishnu and the Ganga.

Vaishno Devi

North of Jammu, in a cave there are three images of the goddess: Kali, Lakshmi and Sarasvati. Pilgrims walk about 13km from Jammu road to reach the cave, where they pass through ankle-deep cold water to get a glimpse of the deity. March-July is the main season.

HIMACHAL PADESH

Chamba

One can reach Chamba (134km) from Pathankot by bus, passing through Dalhousie. The 10th-century Lakshmi Narayan temple is opposite the palace and contains several shrines. Another famous temple is the Hariraya temple.

Dharmasala

Well connected by the bus route from Simla (317km), this township was founded in 1855 as a British hill station. Since October 1959, His Holiness the Dalai Lama has lived here. The famous Centre of Tibetan Studies and the Dalai Lama's residence attract many visitors and Buddhist pilgrims.

Jvalamukhi

South of Kangra, a famous goddess temple is set against a cliff and forms a fissure from which comes a natural inflammable gas which accounts for the 'Eternal Flame'. This icon symbolizes the tongue of the goddess.

Kangra

South of Dharmasala, Kangra is famous for the fort and the temple of Bajesvari Devi. Both were damaged in the earthquake of 1905. The main Devi is also called Kangra Devi. About 14km away there is a temple of Chaumunda Devi at the bank of Banaganga.

Kullu

Connected by direct buses from Simla (235km), the town is famous for the Dasahara festival (September/October), honouring the goddess Durga. The notable temples in the city are Raghunathji, Bhekhli and Bijili Shiva.

HARYANA

Kurukshetra

North of Delhi a famous battlefield of the Mahabharata War is now well known for Brahmasar, a sacred pond (about 1km long), surrounded by temples and ghats. This site is famous for ancestral rituals and sacred bathing in the pond.

PUNJAB

Amritsar

Well connected by rail and bus from Delhi (447km) and Chandigarh (230km), this site is known for the Golden Temple, the Hari Mandir, the centre of the Sikh universe.

Chintapurni

A lump-shaped symbol of the goddess lies on the hills at the top of 160 steps. Pilgrims get here by bus from Hoshiarpur.

RAJASTHAN

Amber

North of Jaipur, Amber is famous for a 13th-century palace and Jagatsiromani temple.

Eklingji

South of Nathdvara, there is an 8th-century Ekling Shiva temple which was rebuilt by Raimal in the 15th-century.

Mount Abu

West of Udaipur, the hill is famous for the Dilwara Jain temples among which Adinath (the First Jain Tirthankara), Vimala Shah and Ambika (goddess) are notables. Other Jain temples include Risah Deo and Keminath. In the south-east, 3km from Dilwara, is the famous Durga Temple. Adhar Devi lies on a hill approached by 200 steep steps.

Nathdvara

North of Udaipur, Nathdvara is famous for its Srinathji temple (Vishnu), the patron deity of Vallabha Sampradaya. There are several Vaishnavite temples. There is also a group of seven small temples collectively known as *Sath Svarupa*.

Pushkar

Near Jodhpur and Ajmer, the famous Pushkar lake is surrounded by temples of Brahma, Badrinarayan, Varahaji, Atmeshvara, Shiva and Savitri. The only Brahma temple in the country is believed to have sprung from a lotus flower dropped by Brahma. On the occasion of Kartikai Purnima (full moon, October/November), India's greatest cattle and camel fair takes place and is attended by over 200,000 visitors and pilgrims.

GUJARAT

Chandod

Near Vadodara on the Narmada river, Chandod contains seven temples one each being dedicated to the Sun, Chandaditya, Chandika, Narayana, Kapileshvara Shiva, Pingaleshvara Shiva and Devi. An old temple of Somnath is also here.

Dakor

Near Nadida, Dakor is a non-sectarian Vaishnavite compound of temples like Vallabha, Swaminarayana and other forms of Vishnu. The image of Sri Ranchhodraiji is similar to the image at Dvaraka. Every full-moon day it attracts a large number of devotees.

Dvaraka

Reached by rail or bus from Jamnagar, Dvaraka is famous for being one of Hinduism's four Holy Abodes of Vishnu. The 12th-century Rukmini and the 16th-century Dvarakanath temples are most attractive places for pilgrims. From Okha, Beyt Dvaraka island can be visited by boat, where there is a Krishna palace and temples of Rhadyumna, Ranachnodji and Tikamji. There are many sacred ponds and shrines.

Girnar

The sacred hill of Girnar with several Hindu and Jain temples and Buddhist caves is 16km east of Junagadh city. The five peaks of the hill are dedicated to the deities Amba Mata, Gorakhnath, Oghad Shikara, Dattatreya and Kalika. There are also three sacred ponds and a fortress.

Modherea

About 35km north of Mehsana, Modhera is known for its 11th-century Sun temples, two centuries older than Konark. A rectangular pool with several subsidiary shrines faces the east front of the temple. This is specially visited on the occasion of solar equinoxes.

Nageshvara

On the way from Dvaraka to Beyt Dvaraka, there is the well-known jyoti lingam of Shiva, one among the twelve.

Patan

Connected by rail and road at a distance of 25km north-west from Mehsana, lying on the south bank of Sabarmati, Patan is famous for 100 10th–11th century Jain temples, a tank and a compound of 1,000 Shiva lingas. This is a famous Jain Tirtha.

Pavagadh

Near Vadodara, and Godhra, Pavagadh fort dominates the skyline and is itself dominated by Hindu and Jain temples. The Maha Kali (Dakshina Kali) temple attracts many pilgrims. This was the seat where the sage Vishvamitra performed his austerity.

Satrunjaya

South-west from Palinana, Satrunjaya hill (a 600m climb) is the largest temple city of its kind in India, consisting of 863 Jain temples in its compound. Tradition says that the First Tirthankara Adinath (Rishabhadeva) visited this hill several times. There are over 11,000 images.

Sidhpur

South from Abu road, Sidhpur is a famous cremation site for mothers in the way that Gaya is for fathers. This was also an ashram of Kardama, and his son Kapil was born here. In the nearby small town there is a temple of Sarasvati. Here Shiva takes the form of Brahmadesvara. About 1.5km away is the Vindu Sarovar.

Somnath

East of Veraval, Somnath is one of the 12 jyoti lingas of Shiva and a major Hindu pilgrimage place. The original temple was destroyed in 1024 by Mahmud of Ghazni, but it was rebuilt several times. Finally in May 1951 a new temple was constructed and since then several additions have been made. Nearby is the ruined Rudreshvara temple.

Vadanagar

North-east of Mehsana, connected by rail and road, this is the site of Hatkeshvara Shiva – one among the three popular ones in the south. Mythology tells how the first step of the Vamana ('dwarf') form of Vishnu can be found here. Another famous shrine is that of Amther Mata.

MADHYA PRADESH

Amarkantak (1050m)
By road From Jabalpur via Mandla one can reach Amarkantak Hill which is the source of the three rivers, Narmada, Son and Mahanadi. On the hill there are temples of Amarntah, Narmada Devi and several Shiva- and Vishnu-related temples, and a holy pond.

Chanderi
Near Lalitpur, Chanderi has many Jain images (10th-century) carved in the Khander Hill, and also ruined palaces, mosques and tombs.

Chitrakut
West of Allahabad (UP), the holy town of Chitrakut is in Uttar Pradesh and Madhya Pradesh. Lord Rama with Sita and Lakshamana stayed here during the period of exile, on the top of the hill, Kamadagiri. Pilgrims perform circumambulation of this hill while visiting 56 shrines along the route. Bharatakup, Valmiki Ashram and Gupta Godavari make together a cosmogonic triangle. Atri Ashram, Janaki Kunda, Sphatika Shila are the other holy spots.

Khajuraho
Well connected by road and air routes, Khajuraho is wellknown for its 10- and 11th-century erotic temple sculptures built under later Chandela kings. Temples of fantastic architectural beauty are Lakshmana, Varaha, Vishvanath, Matangeshvara, Chausathi, Yogini, Duladeo and Chaturbhja. There are three Jain temples of Parsvanath, Adinath and Santinath which attract Jain pilgrims.

Kaheshvara

About 58km from Mandhu on the north bank of Narmada, the temple of Maheshvara records its antiquity to the Ramayana and the Mahabharata periods. Other temples are Kaleshvara, Rajarajeshvara, Vithaleshvara and Ahileshvara. Rani Ahilyabai of Indore (*d.* 1795) was responsible for revitalizing the city by building temples and a fort complex.

Mahoba

North of Khajuraho, Mahoba is known for its 8th-century architectural antiquities of the Chandela. There are many Buddhist and Jain sculptures, images of dancing Ganesh, the Sun god and a Shiva temple on an island in Madan Sagar.

Mandu

By road from Indore, Mandu is famous for its 10th-century fort. The Royal Enclave consists of many monuments and gates. Hoshang Shah's Tomb (*c.* 1440) in Mandu Bazaar is India's first marble monument.

Omkareshvara (Mandhata)

East of Maheshvara, on an island at the confluence of the Narmada and the Kaveri, lies the image of Omkareshvara Shiva, one among the 12 jyoti lingas. Other temples are Siddhnath and Gauri Somnath. There is a gigantic Nandi bull. Near to it are the 24 avatars and a cluster of Hindu and Jain temples.

Sanchi

Near Bhopal, Sanchi is famous for the Great Stupa, the largest one in India, plus Gupta temples and monasteries. This is an architectural and archaeological site with several Buddhist monuments.

UTTAR PRADESH

Allahabad (Prayaga)
Famous for its situation at the confluence of the Ganges, the Yamuna and invisible Sarasvati, Allahabad is the most sacred site for a holy dip. Bhardwaj Ashram and the temple of Naga Vasuki are the popular holy spots for pilgrims. The world famous bath festival, Kumbh Mela, takes place here every 12 years – the last happened in 1989 when about 13 million bathed in the Ganges. This sacred city is known as the 'King of all the Sacred Places', Tirtharaja.

Ayodhya
East of Lucknow is the birthplace of Lord Rama. Ayodhya is one of the seven sacred cities. Archaeological evidence supports its dating to the 4th/3rd century BC. The town is full of monasteries and ashrams. The legend of the Fish incarnation of Vishnu is related to this site. Hanumangarhi, Kanak Bhavan, Janaki Bhavan, Agni Tirtha and Rama Ghat are the important holy spots. On 6 December 1992, the Babari mosque was demolished by militant Hindus.

Badrinath (3,150m)
Badrinath is near Kedarnath. No pilgrimage would be complete without a visit to Badrinath, one among the four abodes of Vishnu. Images and temples of Nara-Narayana, Shri Devi, Bhu Devi, Lakshmi and Shankaracharya are the famous sacred spots. Important sacred ponds are of Brahma, Trikona, Soma and Urvashi.

Banaras (see Varanasi)

Devaprayaga
From Rishikesh towards Yamunotri the road passes by Devaprayaga which is situated at the confluence of the two main streams, the Bhagirathi and the Alakananda, which together at this site take the form of the Ganges river.

Devi Patan

From Gonda by road, passing through Balrampur, one can reach Devi Patan, a famous Shakti pitha, at the border with Nepal. There are some ancient remains and an old temple of Shiva.

Gangotri (3,140m) and Gomukh (3,970m)

Near Rishikesh, the Ganges river originates at Gomukh, but the real drain starts at Gangotri (27km down) where the 18th-century granite temple of the Ganga lies. There are many ashrams and shrines at Gangotri.

Gorakhpur

North of Varanasi, Gorakhpur is a pilgrimage centre of a renunciate Hindu sect, Nath, whose chief seat is the temple of Gorakhnath.

Kedarnath (3,584m)

Kedarnath temple is one of the 12 jyoti lingas of Shiva. There is a huge triangular shaped piece of rock in the place of the image. There are statues of Five Pandavas and many sacred ponds and springs. Pilgrims carry waters from the sources of the Ganges and the Yamuna rivers to offer to Kedarnath.

Haridwar

Haridwar was the hermitage seat of the sage Kapila. The Ganges enters the plains at this site. Vishnu's footprint is the most sacred spot here. Brahma Kunda and Narayana Bali temples are the other pilgrimage spots. Every 12 years the Kumbha Mela is held here.

Kushinagar/Kasia

East of Gorakhpur, kushinagar is where the Buddha died. There are many monasteries. The Buddha's relics after cremation are preserved in the Muktabandhana Stupa.

Mathura

Celebrated as the birth place of Lord Krishna, Mathura is one of the seven sacred cities. Pilgrims take baths at Vishram Ghat in the Yamuna river and visit temples of Keshava, Gopi Nath, Jugul Kishor and Radha.

Nainital

Nainital is a hill resort and famous for many lakes like Sat Tal, Bhim Tal and Naukuchiya Tal. The most famous is the jade green Garud Tal named after Vishnu's vehicle, followed by olive green Rama Tal and Sita Tal. The temples of Naina Devi and Pashani Devi and, at a distance of 20km at the bank of Bhima Tal, Bhimeshvara temple are the important pilgrimage sites.

Rishikesh

North of Haridwar, along the right bank of the Ganges, Rishikesh is famous for various ashrams and the Lakshman temple. Aarati (offering oil lamps) to the Ganges at Triveni Ghat each evening is the most attractive scene.

Sarnath

About 10km north-east of Varanasi, Sarnath is one among the four Buddhist pilgrimage sites, where the Buddha gave the first sermon, 'Turning the Wheel of Law', after attaining enlightenment at Bodh Gaya (Bihar). Pilgrims from Burma, Thailand, China and Japan regularly visit this site. There are many archaeological monuments, and temples constructed by societies from Burma, Thailand, China, Japan and Sri Lanka. There is also a Jain temple dedicated to Shreyanshanath.

Varanasi (Banaras/Kashi)

Varansi is well known as the Cultural Capital of India and the most sacred place for Hindus. Along the left bank of the Ganges river there are 84 Ghats (steps to the water) and also over 3,000 Hindu temples and images, and some Buddhist, Jain and Sikh shrines. Sacred bathing in the Ganges and visits to Vishvanath (Golden) temple, Annapurna, Kalan Bhairava, Bad Ganesh, Snakatmochan and Durga temples are common among pilgrims.

Vindhyachal

East of Allahabad and 78km east of Varanasi, at the right bank of the Ganges, Vindhyachal is the seat of three forms of goddess – Kali, Sarasvati and Lakshmi. Their temples together identify the sacred territory to which pilgrims perform the journey. During Navaratri (March/April; October/November) there are many pilgrims here. There are many natural springs and shrines.

Vrindavana

North of Mathura, Vrindavana is famous for many temples related to Krishna like Govind Deo, Sri Ranga, Madan Mohan and many ashrams. The Madan Mohan temple stands above a ghat on an arm of the river. There is a pavilion decorated with cobra carvings. Shiva is believed to have struck Devi here and made it a place for curing snake bites. Close to Mathura and Vrindavana there are many holy spots related to Krishna's life like Gokul (2km, Vishnu incarnated as Krishna), Govardhan (26km, Krishna raised this hill to escape people), Barsana (8km, the home of Krishna's wife, Radha) Baldeo (8km, home of Krishna's elder brother Baladeva), etc.

Yamunotri (3,251m)

About 165km from Devaprayaga, the source of the Yamuna river is Yamunotri. Sacred bathing, visits to Yamunotri temple and the Someshvara temple are the most common activities.

BIHAR

Bodh Gaya

South of Gaya lies the small town of Bodh Gaya. The Bodhi tree under which the Buddha enlightenment, and the sandstone slab Vajrasila on which he sat in meditation, are the sacred spots for Buddhist pilgrims. Mahabodhi temple, Animeshlochana, a Japanese temple, a giant Buddha statue and a Tibetan temple are the spots visited by pilgrims.

Deoghar (Deogarh)
Deoghar is the site of Vaidyanath Shiva, one of the 12 jyoti lingas. Pilgrims take baths in the Sivaganaga Lake and worship Lord Shiva. Every year a million pilgrims gather here to attend Shravani Mela (July/August). This place also marks the spot where the heart of Sati, the corpse-form of Parvati, fell down. Pilgrims collect the Ganges water from Sultanganj, 100km away, and offer this to Vaidyanath.

Gaya
Gaya together with Varanasi and Allahabad, makes the cosmic bridge through which a soul passes to heaven. The Vishnupad temple has Vishnu's footprints on a rock inside set in a silver basin. Gaya is famous as a site for cremation and funeral rituals at the bank of the Phalgu river.

Nalanda
North-east of Gaya are the ruins of the world's oldest university founded in the 5th century AD. There are sixteen monuments and monasteries and several mounds. At this site Buddha passed 14 rainy seasons. Recently developed Nava Nalanda Mahavihar and a Thai temple are the new attractions. Only 15km from here is Rajgir, another famous Buddhist and Jain spot.

Patna
The capital city of Patna was founded by Ajatasatru in the 6th century BC. Har Mandir is the temple honouring the birthplace of the 10th Sikh Guru Govind Singh.

Sonepur

Across the Ganges from Patna, at the confluence of the Ganges and the Gandak, Sonepur is famous for the temple of Harihar Nath. This town is also witness to Asia's biggest cattle fair, which begins on Kartikai Purnima, the first full moon during September/October, and continues for a month. This is also the main season for pilgrims, who take sacred baths and pay visits to the Harihar Nath temple.

WEST BENGAL

Calcutta

Calcutta is famous for Kalighat where there is a celebrated shrine of Kali marking the spot where the goddess' little toe is said to have fallen when Shiva carried her charred corpse. Dakshineshvar Kali temple was built in 1847 by Rani Rashmoni and was associated with Ramakrishna. Daily goat sacrifice is offered to Kali. For Bengali pilgrims this is the most important site.

Gangasagara

South of Calcutta on the Sagar Island exists the Kapil Muni temple and ashram. This place identifies the mouth of the Ganges and attracts a million Hindu pilgrims each year who come to bathe on the occasion of Makar Samkranti (winter solstice). Most of the pilgrims stay there for three days. Ferry services are available to reach Kochuberia Ghat (30 minutes).

Navadvipa

North of Caluctta on the western bank of the Hoogly (Bhagirathi) river, Navadvipa is the most sacred place for the Gaudiya Vaishnava sect. At this site Chaitanaya, an incarnation of Vishnu, appeared and started the Gaudiya Krishna cult. Radha, Krishna and Chaitanya are the associated deities. There are many temples and monasteries here.

271

Tarakeshvar

Tarakeshvar is well connected by train and bus services from Calcutta (95km north-east). This is the most visited place of pilgrimage in West Bengal, both by Shakta and Vaishnavite pilgrims. The image of Shiva as Tarakanath gives relief from transmigration of the soul, and also helps to settle the soul into heaven.

ASSAM

Kamaksha/Kamakhya

North-west of Guwahati, on the Nilachal Hill, Kamakhya is dedicated to the goddess Kamakhya, famous for Tantric Hinduism. The genital organ of the goddess Sati fell here. This is the most famous of the 51 goddess pithas. The original temple was built in the 10th century, but after destruction it was rebuilt in 1665. 12km from Guwahati the Vashishtha Ashram is a natural beauty spot with three mountain streams flowing nearby. On Peacock Island, north of Guwahati Town, in the Brahmaputra river, there is a temple of Umanada built in 1594 and dedicated to Shiva's wife.

TRIPURA

Agartala/Udaipur

The tiny state of Tripura is almost entirely surrounded by Bangladesh. About 57km from Agartala, the capital town, is Iripurasundari Temple. Built in the mid 16th-century, it is claimed to be one of the 51 Shakti pithas.

ORRISA

Bhubaneshwar

In the capital city of Bhubaneshwar, 480km south-west of Calcutta, there are temples of Parasurameshvara, Nukteshvara, Siddheshvara, Gauri, Rajrani, Brahmeshvara, Lingaraja and Vaital Deul – related to Vishnu, the goddess, Rama and Shiva.

Konark

South of Puri, Konark represents one of the most vivid architectural treasures of Hindu India. The temple ruins belong to the 9th–13th-centuries among which the temple of the Sun god is the most famous. This is mostly a tourist site and pilgrims rarely visit here.

Puri

South of Bhubaneshwar, the town of Puri is famous for the Jagannath temple, where pilgrims stay for 3 days and nights and worship Jagannath, Balbhadra and Subhadra. The famous chariot festival, Rathayatra, is held every year for a fortnight in the bright half of Ashadha (June/July).

MAHARASHTRA

Bhovargiri

About 60km west of Poona in a small town of Bhovargiri the temple of Bhimashankar is one of the 12 jyoti lingas. It marks the source of the Bhima river where Shiva killed the demon Tripurasura and took rest. The icon is of five-headed Shiva. On every 13th dark fortnight there is a big festival.

Ghushmeshvara

North-west of Aurangabad is Ellora, famous for the Hindu, Buddhist and Jain caves. Nearby is the temple of Ghushmeshvara, one of the jyoti lingas of Shiva. The present temple was built by Rani Ahilyabai of Indore in the mid-18th century.

Kolhapur

Connected by road and rail from Poona, Kolhapur is situated at the south bank of Panchaganga, a tributary of the Krishna river. In the Marthi region this is famous as a resort of Maha Lakshmi (the great 'wealth' goddess), locally known as Amba Bai. There are about 250 shrines and temples. The sacred procession of taking the goddess to the temple of Tamblai, 5km east of the city, is an important occasion for pilgrimage.

Nasik

Nasik is famous for the greatest bathing festival, Kumbha Mela, every 12 years which attracts a million pilgrims. About 30km south of this town the Godavari river originates where the sacred temple of Trayambakeshvara, one of the 12 jyoti lingas, exists. Sage Gautam ashram and a sacred pond are also there. The Gangasagar Tank is on the hill, approached by 690 steps. Important temples are of Ganga, Krishna, Rama, Parasurama, Kedareshvara and Gayatri. 40km north of Nasik is the Saptashringi Devi temple approached by 750 steps; very few pilgrims reach this place.

Pandharpur

South-east of Poona along the bank of Bhima river, a 13th-century temple of Vithoba, an incarnation of Vishnu, exists at Pandharpur. This is the most sacred and popular place of pilgrimage in the state. Great saint-poets like Jnaneshvara, Namdeo and Tukaram of the medieval period were associated with it. There are a dozen bathing ghats on the river banks, and during the main pilgrimage season of July (the Ekadashi fair) tens of thousands of people come.

ANDHRA PRADESH

Amaravati

About 40km west of Vijaivada, the medieval capital of Reddi, king of Andhra, Amaravati is famous as a Mahayana Buddhist centre where the Buddha is revered as Amreshvara. The Great Stupa (Chaitya) is supposed to be bigger than the one at Sanchi and it originates back to the 3rd/2nd centuries BC.

Pithapuram

Near Annavaram, Pithapuram is one among the five sites for ancestral rituals. South Indian pilgrims frequently visit Pithapuram for this purpose. The Kukuteshvara Shiva and Madhu Svami temple are famous. On every 13th day of dark fortnight a festival takes place and attracts many pilgrims from the region.

Simhachalam

North of the city port of Vishakhapatnam, on a hill of about 800 metres, there is a Boar-form statue of Vishnu, called Narsimha. Throughout the year the icon is covered by sandal-paste. The 16 pillared mandapam possesses a stone chariot. There are many images nearby.

Srishailam

200km south of Hyderabad and 170km east of Kurnool on the route to Doranala, Srishailam is one of the 12 jyoti lingas. On the hill, the main temple of Mallikarjuna belongs to the 14th century. This site is described as Kailash of the South, and the river Krishna is known as Patala Ganga (the Ganga of the netherworlds). The image of Mallikarjuna is an old metal image of Shiva Nataraja. Srishailam is the principal seat of Shaivism and has one of the five principal monasteries of the Vira Shaivas. It is also a well-known Shakti pith of Brahmar-Ambika.

Tirupathi

Standing 247km north-east of Bangalore, and 162km north of Madras, lying on the Tirumalai hills, Tirupathi is the most famous holy site in South India. The surrounding seven hills are compared to the 7-hooded serpent God Shesha who protects Vishnu. North of Tirupathi in Tirumalai, the temple of Venkateshvara is known as Balaji or Srinivas Perumalai. The temple is originally 10th-century with several later additions. Of all India's temples, this draws the largest number of pilgrims. An estimate records that on average about 50,000 pilgrims visit this place every day.

Tiruttani

North from Arkonam railway station, Tiruttani represents one of the six Karttikeya pithas. The famous temple of Subrahmanyam (Karttikeya/Murugan/Skanda) is here which attracts many pilgrims.

KARNATAKA

Belur

North-west of Hassan, on the bank of Yagachi river, is the 12th-century Chennakesava temple of Belur. Dedicated to Krishna it stands in a courtyard surrounded by a rectangular wall. The winged figure of Garuda, Vishnu's carrier, guards the entrance. To the west is Viranarayan temple.

Gokarn

Close to Ankola on the NH17 highway, Gokarn is famous for a lingam in the form of 'Shiva's Soul', also known as Mahabaleshvara. Siddha Ganesh, the Great Nandi, Saptakotishvara Shiva, Bhairava and a half-Vishnu/half-Shiva image are the famous sites and images. There are many sacred ponds too. About 0.5km closer to the coast in a temple complex there are images of Rama, Lakshamana and Sita.

Sringeri

In the Kadur District, 112km from Hassan, the hills of Sringa were the birthplace of sage Rishyasringa. The Adi Sankaracharya had established a monastery here in the 8th-century AD. There is a mother Sharda image and a Sri Chakra. There are ruby figures of Venugopal and Srinivas, and the Nandi of a large single pearl.

Srirangapatnam

North of Mysore, this place is known for the 10th-century temple of the Vishnu Sri Rangam. The great Vaishnavite philosopher Ramanuja took shelter here. The famous fort here was built under the Vijayanagar kings in 1454.

Udipi

North of Mangalore on the NH17 highway, Udipi is a famous pilgrimage spot as the birthplace of the 12th-century saint Madhava, and the Krishna temple established by him. The idol of Krishna is made of Saligram stone.

Vijayanagar (Hampi)

Hampi is the seat of Pampavati (Pampa Sarovar) and Virupaksha Shiva, on the bank of Tungabhadra river. There are images of Bhuvaneshvari Devi, Parvati, Ganesh and many caves and images in the hills. Mythology tells how the caves were made by Hanuman and his monkey soldiers. 8km north-east from Hampi are Malyavan Hills where Rama and Lakshmana passed four rainy months; their idols are there.

KERALA

Guruvayur

West of Trichur on the coast is Guruvayur Tirtha, representing the original idol of Krishna. Closeby, Mammipurappan Shiva lingam was established by Dharmaraja, the elder brother of the Pandavas of the Mahabharata.

Kaladi

North of Kochi, on the bank of the Periyar river, Kaladi is the birthplace of India's greatest philosopher Sankaracharya (8th century). There are now two shrines in his memory, one is Dakshinamurti and the other to the goddess Sharada.

Sabarimalai

In the forest clad hills 191km north from Tiruvantapuram, and 63km east from Kottayam, lies Sabarimalai (914m), the most famous Hindu pilgrimage site for the Ayyappan sect. The route from Kottayam goes through Erumeli, Chalakkayam and Pampa (5km from the temple). There is then about two hours steep walking and climbing to the shrine. The pilgrims are readily visible in many parts of south India as they wear *black dhotis* as a symbol of the penance they must undergo for 41 days before they make the pilgrimage.

Trichur

North of Ernakulam, Trichur is built round a hill on which stands the Vadakkunnatha temple, a multi-shrined complex with three principal shrines dedicated to Vadakkunatha, Sankaracharya and Rama. There are also Ayyappa and Krishna temples decorated with fine wood carvings.

TAMIL NADU

Chidambaram

South of Cuddalore, 241km south of Madras, the city is famous for its temple dedicated to Shiva Nataraj. There are also shrines dedicated to Vishnu and Ganesh. East of Sivaganga tank is the Hall of 1,000 Pillars.

Kanchipuram

West of Madras, Kanchipuram is known as 'The Golden city of a Thousand Temples', established in the 2nd century. The largest one is Ekambareshvara Siva temple (9ha) which has 5 enclosures and a Thousand-Pillared Hall. 1.6km west of the city, is the Kailashnatha Shiva temple. 1km south-west is the Vaikuntha Perumal temple dedicated to Vishnu, built in 8th century. Kamakshi Amman (Parvati) is another temple popular among pilgrims.

Kanyakumari

South-east of Tiruvantapuram (Trivendrum), this is the sacred resort of the goddess Kumari, the virgin incarnation of Parvati whose image is in the Kanyakumari temple. The Bay of Bengal, the Indian Ocean and the Arabian Sea meet here. On a rock island, about 500m from the shoreline, is the Vivekanand Memorial built in 1970. Many pilgrims also pay visits here.

Kumbakonam

At 244km south of Madras, and 32km from Mayruam, the town is famous for the Nageshvara Svami temple and a monastery of Kumbakonam Sankaracharya. Sarangapani, Kumbeshvara and Ramasvami temples are famous. Mahamagham tank is visited for bathing by huge numbers of pilgrims every 12 years when Jupiter passes over the sign of Leo, and on that occasion the Ganges is believed flow in it.

Madurai

On the bank of the Vaigai river, in the famous town of Madurai, are the temples of the goddess Minakshi, and of Sundareshvara, a form of Shiva. The temple's nine towering gopurams stand out with their colourful stucco images of various deities and animals. A kilometre from Minakshi temple is the temple of Sundararaja Perummal, a form of Four-headed Vishnu, where there are also images of the Sun god, Narsimha, and Lakshmi called Madhuballi. Nearby in the south-east is a great sacred tank named Vandiyur Mariammam Teppakulam, which has a small shrine in the centre.

Rameshwaram

About 160km south of Madurai, Rameshwaram is the site where Rama, Lakshmana and Hanuman worshipped Shiva before crossing the strait to reach Sri Lanka. The famous temple is of Ramalingeshvara, one of the 12 jyoti lingas of Shiva. The patron deity Ramalingasvami (Rameshvara) is seated with his consort Parvatvardini, and Visvanathasvami with his consort Visalakshi Amman. Nearby there is the gold plated Garuda pillar.

Srirangam

On an island west of Trichy, between the two branches of the river Kaveri, there is the celebrated Vishnu temple of Lord Ranganatha. The temple is surrounded by seven concentric walled courtyards. Of the eight most sacred images of Vishnu, this is the most famous one. Nearby are the images of Nathamuni, Yamunacharya and Ramanujacharya.

Tiruvanaikkaval

East of Srirangam is Jambukeshvara Shiva temple with its five walls and seven gopuram. The unusual lingam is under a *jambuka* (blackberry, *Syzgium jambolana*) tree and always remains underwater. This temple is considered to be the best representative of Dravidian style. There are many idols and statues of deities, including Parvati and Ganesh.

Tiruvannamalai (Arunachala)

North-west of Villupuram, on the holy fire hill of Arunachala, the city is thought of as the home of Shiva and Parvati. As such it is a major pilgrimage centre. There are over 100 temples of which Arunachala temple is the largest one. The ashram of Ramana Maharshi is also here and attracts many pilgrims both from India and abroad.

Thanjavur (Tanjor)

East of Trichy (Tiruchirappali) this is famous for the Brihadish-var Shiva temple, founded by the Chola king in the 10th century. The town is also known as Dakshina Meru. By the side of the main temple there are shrines of Subrahmanyam or Kart-tikeya, the goddess Brihannayaki, Ganapati and the great Nandi (4m high). The temple complex is in the compound of a fort. This is the highest temple in India, at 66m.

THE PAN-INDIA GROUPS OF SACRED PLACES

(according to the puranas)

Four sacred abodes of Vishnu, *Dhams*	Badrinath (north, UP), Puri (east, Orissa), Dwarka (west, Gujarat), and Rameshwarem (south, Tamil Nadu).
Five Kashi (regional symbols/ microcosoms of Banaras) manifested at	Gupt Kashi, Uttarkashi (north); Dakshina Kashi, Ten Kashi, and Shiva Kashi (south).
Seven sacred cities bestowing salvation (*Puris*)	Kanchipuram (Tamil Nadu), Dwarka (Gujarat), Mathura (UP), Haridwar (UP), Ayodhya (UP), Varanasi (UP), and Ujjain (Madhya Pradesh).
Twelve jyoti lingas of Shiva	Kedarnath (UP), Vishveshvara (Varanasi, UP), Vaidyanath (Deoghar, Bihar), Mahakala (Ujjain, Madhya Pradesh), Omkara (Mandhata, MP), Nageshvara (Dwaraka, Gujarat), Somnath (Gujarat), Triyambaka (Maharashtra), Ghushmeshvara (Ellora, Maharashtra), Bhimashankar (Maharashtra), Mallikarjuna (Srishailam, AP), and Rameshvaram (Tamil Nadu).

| Four Buddhist sites related to the Buddha's life | Lumbini (birth, Nepal), Bodh Gaya (enlightment, Bihar), Sarnath (first sermon, Varanasi, UP), and Kushinagar (nirvana, Deoria, UP). |

Four Buddhist sites related to the Buddha's life

Lumbini (birth, Nepal),
Bodh Gaya (enlightment, Bihar),
Sarnath (first sermon, Varanasi, UP),
and Kushinagar (nirvana, Deoria, UP).

Five sacred Ponds, *Sarovaras*

Vindu (Sidhapur, Gujarat),
Narayana (Kutch, Gujarat),
Pampa (Vijayanagar, Karnataka),
Pushkar (Rajasthan), and
Mansarovarar (Tibet).

Seven most sacred rivers

The Ganga,
Yamuna,
Godaveri,
Saraswati (now vanished),
Cauvery,
Narmada, and
Sindhu (Indus).

Nine sacred forest areas, *Aranyas*

Dandaka (eastern MP),
Saindhava (between the Indus and
    Satluj rivers, Pakistan),
Pushkar (central Rajasthan),
Naimisha (central-east UP),
Kuru (northern UP),
Utpalavarta (south of Vaigai river,
    Tamil Nadu),
Jambu (north-west Rajasthan),
Himavada (between Indus and
    Satluj, Tibet), and
Arbuda (south-east Rajasthan).

FIFTY-ONE SHAKTI PITHAS OF THE GODDESS:
THE PLACES WHERE SOME PART OF SATI'S BODY FELL TO EARTH

	Place	Fallen Object	Goddess's Form	Shiva's Form	Location, State
1	Kirit	crown (tiara)	Vimala	Samvarta	24 Parganas, WB, near Batnagar
2	Vrindavan	hair (head)	Uma	Bhutesha	Bhuteshvara temple, near Vrindavan, UP
3	Karvir (Kolhapur)	third eye	Mahishamardini	Krodhisha	Amba Bai, Kolhapur, MR
4	Sriparvat	right temple	Sri Sandari	Sundarananda	along the Indus in Ladakh, JK
5	Varanasi (Kashi)	ear ring/eyes	Vishalakshi	Kala Bhairava	Varanasi, Vishalakshi temple, UP
6	Koti Tirth	left temple	Vishveshi	Dandapani	along the Godaveri river (Rly St.), AP
7	Suchindram	upper teeth	Narayani	Samhara	13km west from Kanyakumari, TN
8	Panchasagar	lower teeth	Varahi	Maharudra	Not yet known
9	Jvalamukhi	tongue	Siddhida	Unmatta	34km south-east from Kangra, HP
10	Bhairavaparvat	upper lip	Avanti	Lambakarna	12km west of Ujjain, MP
11	Attahas	lower lip	Phullara	Vishvesha	93km from Bardwan, near Labpur, WB
12	Janasthan	chin	Bhramari	Vikritaksha	Bhadrakali temple, near Nasik, MR
13	Amarnath	throat	Mahamaya	Trisandheshvara	ice-form image in the cave, JK
14	Nandipur	necklace	Nandini	Nandikeshvara	33km from Bolpur under a fig tree, WB
15	Srishailam	neck	Mahalakshmi	Sambarananda	Mallikarjuna temple, AP
16	Nalhatti (Naihatti)	intestine	Kalika	Yogisha	75km from Bolpur, 3km from naihatti, WB
17	Uchhaith (Mithila)	left shoulder	Uma	Mahodara	51km east of Janakpur, Nepal
18	Ratnavali	right shoulder	Kumari	Shiva	Madras City, Tamil Nadu

	Place	Fallen Object	Goddess's Form	Shiva's Form	Location, State
19	Prabhas	stomach	Chandrabhaga	Vakratunda	Ambaji temple, north Gujarat
20	Jalandhar	left breast	Tripuramalini	Bhishana	Jalandhar City, Punjab
21	Ramagiri (Chitrakut)	right breast	Shivani	Chanda	Banda Dt, UP
22	Deoghar	heart	Jai Durga	Vaidyanath	famous in Bihar
23	Vaktreshvar	mind	Mahishamardini	Vaktranatha	between Naihatti and Mandipur, WB
24	Kanyakumari	back	Sharvani	Nimisha	southernmost spot, TN
25	Bahula	left hand	Bahula	Bhiruka	144km west of Calcutta, in Brahmagram, WB
26	Ujjain	elbow	Mangalyachandika	Kapilambara	Harsiddhi temple, Ujjain MP
27	Manivedika	both wrists	Gayatri	Sarvananda	near Pushkar, Rajasthan
28	Prayaga	fingers	Lalita	Bhava	Alopi, Dvi, Allahabad, UP
29	Puri	navel	Vimala	Jagata	Jagannath temple, Orissa
30	Kanchipuram	skeleton	Devagarbha	Ruru	south of Madras, TN
31	Kalmadhav	left nipple	Kali	Asitanga	
32	Sona	right nipple	Sonakshi	Bhadrasena	Sararam district, Bihar
33	Kamakhya	genital organs	Kamkhya	Umananda	west of Guwahati, Assam
34	Jayantia (Baurgram)	left thigh	Jayanti	Kramadishvara	53km east from Shillong, Meghalaya
35	Patna	right thigh	Sarvanandakari	Vyomakesha	Patneshvari Devi, Patna, Biahar
36	Trisrota (Shalbadi)	left leg	Bhramari	Ishvara	Kalpaiguri Dt, WB
37	Tripura	right leg	Tripurasundari	Tripuresha	57km west from Agartala, at Udaipur

38	Vibhasha	left ankle	Bhimarupa	Sarvananda	Tamluk, WB
39	Kurukshetra	right ankle	Savitri	Sthanu	Kurukshetra tank, Haryana
40	Ygadya	big toe (first)	Bhutadhatri	Kshirakantaka	32km from Burdwan, in Chhirgram, WB
41	Virat (Vairat)	right toes	Ambika	Amrita	64km north of Jaipur, Rajasthan
42	Kalipitha (Calcutta)	other toes,	Kalika	Nakulisha	Kali temple, Calutta, WB
43	Manasa	right palm	Dakshayani	Amara	Mansrovarar lake, Tibet
44	Nellore	anklet	Indrakshi	Rakshasheshvara	Nellore, Sri Lanka
45	Gandaki	right cheek	Gandaki	Chakrapani	source area of Gandaki river, Muktinath, Nepal
46	Pashupatinath, Nepal	both knees	Mahamaya	Kapala	Guhyeshvari temple, at the bank of Bagamati
47	Hingula	brain	Bhairavi	Bhimalochana	250km west of Karachi, along the Hingol river, 30km up from sea coast, Pakistan
48	Sugandha	nose	Sunanda	Trayambaka	21km from Barisala, Bangladesh
49	Kartoya	left sole	Aparna	Vamana	32km from Bogada in Bhavanipur, Bangladesh
50	Chatthal	right arm	Bhavani	Chandrashekhar	38km from Chittagong at Sitakund, Bangladesh
51	Yashor	left palm	Yashoshesvari	Chanda	Jessore town, south-west Bangladesh

Sources: *Sivacaritra, Dakshayani Tantra, Yogini Tantra* and *Tantracunamani*

Compiled and © Rana P. B. Singh

GURUS, ASHRAMS
AND RETREAT CENTRES

FEES

Most ashrams accept donations for room and board, a typical offering being around 100 rupees daily. The Krishnamurti centres have set fees, which differ little from the normal donation. Aurobindo Ashram guest houses have set fees for room only, as do the Auroville communities. Osho International Commune has no accommodation. They charge a daily entrance plus aids test fee, and a scale of Western prices for their different courses.

Ananda Ashram

P.O. Anandasram, Kanhangad Dt, Kasaragod, North Kerala 670531. The ashram of the late Papa Ram Dass, who was never separate from the Holy Name of Ram. Chanting of the Name continues there today. Accommodation available. Guests may follow their own rhythm and spiritual discipline.

Aurobindo Ashram

Pondichery, Tamil Nadu. The ashram's different cultural and educational activities are spread throughout the town, with the main point of interest being the mahasamadhi shrine of Aurobindo and his successor, The Mother. A variety of guest houses accommodate visitors. The best are Park Guest House (telephone 024 412) and The International Guest House (telephone 026 699).

Auroville

The 'experiment in international living' founded and inspired by The Mother, a few kilometres north of Pondichery. A few thousand people live there now in different small communities, many of them subsisting through alternative technology enterprises. The spiritual and physical centre of Auroville is the Matri Mandir, an unfinished meditation hall in the form of a huge dodecahedron, twelve-sided sphere. The main place to stay is Centrefield Guest House, telephone 2155. Most of the communities also have guest rooms. Further details from the Matri Mandir Information Centre.

Avatar Meher Baba Trust

King's Rd, Post Bag 31, Ahmednagar, Maharashtra 414 001. Meher Baba was the guru who observed silence for most of his life, and who was made popular in the West in the late 1960s by celebrity disciples like Pete Townsend of The Who. Foreigners are welcome to the centre only between June 15 and March 15. The Meher Baba Pilgrim Centre can accommodate 58 people, with men and women sleeping separately. Three meals a day are provided. Pilgrims can reserve in advance for up to one week's stay, though no bookings are taken more than six weeks before arrival. Modest clothing is essential. Meher Baba's tomb, at Meherbad, is open for darshan daily from 6.30am to 8pm.

Silence is essential. The Master's home is at Meherazad, nearby. The nearest main town is Ahmednagar, north of Bombay.

Chandra Swami

Sadhana Kendra, Domet Village, P.O. Ashok Ashram, Dt Dehra Dun 248125 U.P. Visitors must be willing to meditate four hours daily.

Ma Amritanadamayi

M. A. Math, Kuzhithura P.O. (Via Athinand), Quilon Dt, Kerala 690542. Guests are invited to participate in the daily ashram routine, which begins at 5am with chanting, and

288

includes three group meditations and a hour of work. When she is there, Ammachi sits for darshan daily. From Quilon get a bus/taxi to Vallickavu Jetty and take the ferry across to the ashram.

Ma Ananda Mayi Ma
Ashrams in the memory of this great saint exist in many towns throughout India. Her mahasamadhi shrine is in the ashram at Khankal, near Haridwar, Uttar Pradesh. No accommodation available, though there is a dharmsala in the village.

Nanagaru
C/o Andhra Ashram, Ramanashram P.O., Tiruvannamalai, Tamil Nadu. Nanagaru is always on the move, though he is likely to be found at this address in the summer and rainy season, and letters there will reach him. No accommodation available.

Osho Commune International
17 Koregaon Park, Poona, 411011 Mahashtra. Telephone 0091 212 628562, Fax 0091 212 624181.

The Osho Commune offers a wide variety of courses in personal therapy, body work, and meditation. No accommodation is available. Visitors must pay up to 200 rupees for an Aids test before being admitted. Maroon robes must be worn at all times on the property. The Commune has excellent restaurants, and various sports and recreation facilities.

H. W. L. Poonja (Poonjaji)
20/144A Indira Nagar, Lucknow, Uttar Pradesh 226016. Anyone in Lucknow will tell you where the district of Indira Nagar is, and anyone there can direct you to Poonjaji. Poonjaji holds satsangs for two hours most weekday mornings in his own house. Visitors can turn up and enquire there about places to stay, which are often rented out by long-term disciples. There is no ashram.

Ramakrishna Mission:
The Institute of Culture, Gol Park, Calcutta 700029. Telephone
033 741 303/4/5. A cultural and educational centre with a
fine library, daily lectures and other events. Accommodation
available.

Satya Sai Baba:
The best known of all gurus in India has his main ashram in
Shanti Nilayam, at Puttaparthi, five hours by bus from Bangalore. There is no need to book; accommodation is in dormito-
ries and in 'flats' which house three or four people. What you
get depends on availability. The main feature of the day is darshan in the early morning with Sai Baba. There is a canteen
serving Western food as well as an Indian canteen. At least
several thousand devotees are in the ashram at any one time.
Sai Baba usually goes to his smaller ashram at Kodaikanal, in
the Nilgiri Hills, southern Tamil Nadu, during the hot season of
April/May. He also visits Whitefields, his ashram in Bangalore,
at various times. To know where he is, and for information on
the other ashrams, contact Puttaparthi by telephoning 08555
7375/7236, or faxing 08555 7390.

Shirdi Sai Baba:
The shrine of Shirdi Sai Baba in the village of Shirdi, in Maharashtra, is one of India's most popular pilgrimages. Shirdi is a
six-hour bus ride from Poona. Also in Shirdi is Sarath Babuji, a
devotee of Shirdi Sai Baba who is likely to become widely
known as a guru in his own right in the next decade. He is at
Saipatham Ashram, Pimpalwadi Road, Shirdi, Dt. Ahmednagar,
Maharashtra. Accommodation not available at the ashram, but
there are plenty of dharmsalas in the village.

Shivananda Ashram:
Shivananda P.O., Rishikesh, U.P. This ashram holds regular
programmes in yoga and in studies of classic texts like the
Upanishads and the Bhagavad Gita. It has a large number of
guest rooms in apartment blocks, but these are often full with

long-term students. Swamis Krishnananda, Brahmananda, and Chidananda, all of whom were close disciples of Shivananda, are in residence at the ashram. If you wish to stay, it is essential to write and explain your interests and reasons. Casual visitors to Rishikesh are better off staying at Ved Niketan – see below.

Sri Ramanasramam:
Tiruvannamalai 606 603, Tamil Nadu. Telephone 23292/22491. The ashram of Ramana Maharshi on the slopes of Arunachala. Essential to write beforehand for accommodation, which even then cannot be guaranteed.

Ved Niketan:
On the other side of the Ganges river from Shivananda Ashram, this is where most travellers stay. The enterprising old Swami there collected funds to start building more than 20 years ago, and now has a property with more than 100 rooms around a large open courtyard, which are let out almost exclusively to foreigners at approximately 50 rupees a day. There is no food available, and the place is uncared for, since he won't employ people to do even the routine tasks of cleaning the rooms; nevertheless, it is a mellow place right on the river, with a good atmosphere. In the winter months he has someone teach yoga classes, which is practically the only detail that distinguishes Ved Niketan from any other cheap hotel.

Krishnamurti Centres
These are all set in beautiful surroundings, offering a haven for the serious retreatant. While information and material is available on Krishnamurti's teaching, there is no formal pattern that needs to be followed, and guests are expected to conduct their own retreat. Reservation is essential.

Bangalore
Bangalore Education Centre, 'Haridvanam', Bangalore 560062. Telephone 080 8435.

Banaras
Krishnamurti Study Centre: Rajghat Fort, Banaras.
Telephone 330218.

Uttarkashi
C/o Vijendra Ramola, Bagirathi Valley School, Dunda P.O. Dt
Uttarkashi, Uttar Pradesh. Telephone 01374 81206/81217.

BUDDHISM

Bodhi Zendo
Amo Samy, Bodhi Zendo, Perumal Malai, Kodaikanal Hills,
Tamil Nadu 624108. Amo Samy teaches in Germany and Hol-
land during the summer. The Bodhi Zendo zen Buddhism
centre runs retreats from October to April.

Christopher Titmus and Friends
Annual winter Vipassana retreat at Bodhgaya. Information: c/o
Thomas Jost, Bodhgaya P.O., Bodhgaya, Bihar. Fills quickly, so
book early.

Tushita Retreat Centre
McLeod Ganj, 176219 Dharamsala, H.P. Telephone 01892
24966, Fax. 01892 23374 (mark f.a.o. Tushita). Tushita holds
regular introductory courses in Tibetan Buddhism. Accommodation available only for those on a course.

Goenka Centres

Vipassana Centre:
Dhamma Thali, P.O. Box 208, Jaipur 302001, Rajasthan. Telephone 0141 49520.

Vipassana International Academy:
Dhamma Giri, Igatpuri, 422 403, Maharashtra. Telephone
02533 4076, Fax. 02533 4176.

Vipassana International Meditation Centre:
Dharma Khetta, Nagarjun Sagar Rd, Kusum Nagar, Hyderabad 500661. Telephone 040530 290.

CHRISTIAN ASHRAMS AND CHARITABLE TRUSTS

Aanmodhaya Ashram:
De Maznod Nagar, Enathur Village, Vedal P.O., Tamil Nadu 631552. Accommodation available.

Christa Prema Seva Ashram:
Shivajinagar, Poona 411 005. The ashram is a courtyard round a luxuriant garden. Run by Sister Brigitta, an Anglican, and a Catholic, Sister Sarah Grant. Accommodation available throughout the year.

Jeevan Dhara Ashram:
Jaiharikhal, Garwhal Hills 246139, Uttar Pradesh. Accommodation available in the summer months for serious retreatants, but early booking is essential. You will be disappointed if you just turn up on the offchance.

Mother Teresa and the Sisters of Charity:
53 Lower Circular Road, Calcutta. Though the Sisters have houses in every town in India, Calcutta is where Mother Teresa is based, and where most volunteers come to work. To help at any of the numerous centres in Calcutta, arrive at the Mother House in Lower Circular Road by 6am, and you will be allocated a task.

Saccidananda Ashram:
Shantivanam, Tannirpalli P.O., 639107 Kulittalai, Tiruchi Dt, Tamil Nadu. Telephone 04323 3060. Accommodation available, but reservation is needed in the winter months.

Sadhana Institute:

Lonavala, Maharashtra. Founded by the late Anthony de Mello. This Jesuit centre runs courses combining spiritual practices with psychotherapeutic models and techniques. Accommodation available by prior arrangement. Lonavala is halfway between Poona and Bombay.

Share and Care Children's Welfare Society:

28 Arumugan Street, Perambur, Madras 11. This is the umbrella organisation for the work of Arokiasamy and his wife, described in the chapter on Christian India. Undoubtedly a worthy cause whose donors can be sure their money is wholly used for the purposes they send it for – a rare case in India.

HINDU FESTIVALS AND CALENDAR

Caitra (March/April):
 Nava Pratipada (New Year)
 Holi (colour festival of Krishna)
 Navaratri (nights of the goddess: Durga and Gauri)
 Ramanavami (Ram's birthday – last day of Navaratri)

Vaisakha (April/May):
 Narasimha Jayanti (birth of Vishnu's lion incarnation)

Jyestha (May/June):
 Ganga Dasahara (Ganga's birthday)

Asadha (June/July):
 Rathayatra (Vishnu in form of Lord Jagannatha)
 Guru Purnima (full moon day of the teacher)

Sravana (July/August):
 Nava Gauri (nine 'bright' goddesses)

Bhadrapada (August/September):
 Ganesh Cathurti (Ganesh's birthday)
 Krishna Janmastami (Krishna's birthday)
 Mahalakshmi Yatra (pilgrimage to Lakshmi)

Asvina (September/October):
 Pitrpaksa (in honour of ancestors)
 Navaratri (homage to the nine forms of Durga)
 Dasahara (last day of Navaratri – celebrates Ram's victory
 over the demon Ravana)

Kartikai (October/November):
   Hanuman Jayanti (Hanuman's birthday)
   Dipavali ('row of lights' in honour of Lakshmi)
   Annakuta (Krishna as cowherd)

Margasirsa (November/December):
   Bhairavastami (pilgrimage to Bhairava)

Pausa (December/January):

Magha (January/February):

Phalguna (February/March):
   Mahashivaratri (great night of Shiva)
   Holika (fire ritual)

GLOSSARY

Abishekam	Ritual bathing, ablution of the deity image with substances prescribed by Agamic scripture.
Acarya	Teacher, master.
Advaita	'Not two' – non-dualism.
Agamas	Sacred texts of Shaivites which prescribe temple ritual.
Ahamkar	The egoic principle
Ahimsa	Non-violence
Akash	Space, or ether; the fifth of the traditional five elements.
Amrta	'Non death'. The nectar of immortality.
Ananda	Divine joy, bliss
Arati/arti	The offering of light to a deity
Ashtanga yoga	'Eight-limbed union'. The classical raja yoga system of eight progressive stages or steps, described by Patanjali in his Yoga Sutras. The eight limbs are: restraints (yama); observances (niyama); postures (asana); breath control (pranayama); sense withdrawal (pratyahara); concentration (dharana); meditation (dhyana), and absorption (samadhi).
Astral	'Of the stars'. Belonging to the subtle, non-physical world.
Asura	Demon

Atman	The eternal self, identical with Brahman, The Absolute.
Aum	The original sound from which all creation emanates.
Avatar	A descent, incarnation of a god.
Barakat	Blessing. The spiritual power of a sufi saint.
Bayed	Oath of allegiance from a sufi disciple to his Sheikh.
Bhajan	Individual or group singing of devotional songs.
Bhakta	A devotee.
Bhakti	The way of devotion.
Bhramacharya	'Godly conduct'. One of the ethical restraints known as the yamas, it means sexual purity. Also the first asrama, stage of traditional Hindu life.
Bilva	Bael; species of tree sacred to Shiva.
Brahmin	Member of the highest, priestly caste.
Buddhi	Intellect, intuitive intelligence.
Chakra	'Wheel'. Any of the many centres of energy and consciousness in the human body. The seven principal chakras are situated along the spine.
Chillum	The pipe that sadhus use to smoke types of marijuana.
Cit	Consciousness.
Dana	Gift, charity.
Danda	Ascetic's staff, emblem of spiritual power.
Dargah	'Court'. Tomb of a muslim saint.
Darshan	'Auspicious sight'. Vision of the divine.
Dharma	Divine law; the law of being. Defined broadly as the way of righteousness, or 'that which holds one's true nature'.

	The fulfilment of an inherent nature or destiny. To follow dharma means to act in accordance with Divine Law.
Dhikr	Recitation of the name of God.
Dhyana	Contemplation, meditation.
Diksa	Initiation
Ganesh	'Chief of the ganas'. The first son of Shiva, the elephant-faced patron of art and science, Remover of Obstacles and Lord of Beginnings. A great god created by Shiva to assist souls in their evolution.
Garbagriha	The innermost chamber, or sanctum sanctorum, of a Hindu temple, in which the primary deity is installed.
Ghat	Step to the river: a bathing place
Ghee	Purified butter
Gopi	Wife of cowherd in Krishna myth.
Gopuram	Gateway of South Indian temple.
Guru	'Remover of darkness'. Spiritual guide – though it can be used for a teacher of any subject.
Hrdaya	The inner heart, or heart of hearts.
Jagat	The world.
Japa	Repetition of God's name or mantra.
Jnana	Wisdom.
Jnani	A sage who has attained perfect knowledge.
Jyoti	'Light'. Refers to a type of lingam, of which there are twelve in India, that materialised out of light.
Kali Yuga	The fourth age of the four-fold cycle of the universe. The 'dark age' we live in now.
Kama	Lord of Desire and Love.

Kapala	Skull (of Bhairava, which stuck to Shiva's hand).
Karma	'Deed or act'. Karma more broadly describes the principle of cause and effect, as well as the totality of one's actions.
Kirtan	A religious discourse accompanied with bhajans.
Krpa	Grace.
Ksatriya	'Warrior'. The military caste.
Kum-kum	Literally, 'red-red'. The powder used by Hindus for the dot in the centre of the forehead. Symbolizes the wisdom of the goddess.
Kundalini	The life energy stored at the base of the spine, which rises to the crown of the head through the various chakras due to spiritual practices, notably raja, or kundalini yoga.
Lila	'Play' of the gods; spontaneous, unpremeditated activity.
Mahant	Head of a monastery or religious foundation.
Mahasamadhi	The 'great death' of a saint.
Manas	Mind.
Mandala	Schematic map of the sacred universe.
Mandapam	A hall in a temple.
Mantra	Sacred sound, chanted with a rosary, or internally. Usually given at initiation by a guru.
Mati	Clay, mother, flesh.
Maya	In the Shankara school of Vedanta, maya means the manifest world itself – since everything arises and eventually passes away, nothing is permanent, or therefore substantially real. In Kashmir Shaivism,

	maya is the light, the divine radiance of the Godhead. It is no less real than sunlight, which derives from the sun, but is not the sun itself. Its light brings all forms into being.
Moksha/Mukti	Two terms which mean liberation from the round of births and death.
Mudra	'Seal'. Symbolic gesture of hands or fingers.
Murthi	'Image'. Sculpted, carved or painted image of God, or a god used in worship.
Murugan	'Beautiful one'. The brother of Ganesh, who instructs aspirants in the secrets of yoga.
Naga	Snake deity. Also name of one of the sadhu sects.
Namarupa	'Name and form'. The body-mind complex.
Namasivaya	'Adoration to Shiva'. The supreme mantra of Shaivism.
Namaskaram	Traditional Hindu greeting. Hands are raised, palms together in front of the chest, to honour the Divine in others, or in a temple deity.
Nataraja	Shiva as Lord of the Dance.
Navagraha	Temple shrine to the planets.
Nayanmars	Sixty-three canonised saints of South India. All but a few were householders, recognised as outstanding devotees of Shiva. Many were poets whose works are still sung in south Indian temples today.
Neem	The margosa tree, sacred to Shiva.
Nirguna	Without qualities or attributes.
Omkara	The sign, representation, of the sound Om.

Pandit	One who is learned in the scriptures.
Panth	'Road', or 'way'. A religious group
Pathi	Lord.
Pipal	Ficus religiosa. Most sacred of all trees in India. Dwelling place of Hindu trinity.
Pir	'Elder'. Title for muslim saint.
Pitha	Seat of the goddess – where one of the pieces of Sati's body fell to earth.
Pradakshina	'Right facing'. Act of worshipful circumambulation, walking clockwise round a temple sanctum or other holy place. Same as Parikrama, term used in North India.
Prakasa	Light.
Prakrti	The female principle of active energy in the Samkhya system of philosophy. Nature.
Prana	Vital energy or life principle. Literally, 'vital air'.
Pranayama	Breathing exercise.
Prasad	Food or other offerings that are presented to the deity during puja, or to a guru. Blessed by the deity or guru, the offerings are distributed to devotees.
Prema	Pure love.
Puja	Rite of worship performed to the deity to invoke a psychic connection with the god.
Puranas	Mythical histories of gods and kings, mostly composed in the first millennium of our era.
Purnima	Full moon day.
Purusha	Spirit. The first form of Vishnu. Also the male principle of eternal Being in Samkhya philosophy.
Qawwali	Sufi music recital intended to generate ecstasy.

Rasa	Taste, aesthetic sensibility. Originally a term used in the appreciation of dramatic performance, it came to mean the 'taste' of Lord Krishna.
Rishi	A seer, wise man.
Rudraksha	'Eye of Shiva'. Marble-sized, multi-faced, reddish-brown seeds from the species commonly called the Blue Marble tree. Sacred to Shiva, they are worn as a rosary around the neck or wrist. Used for japa, or mantra meditation.
Sabda	Sound; word; scriptural authority.
Sadguru	'Good, or true, teacher'. The supreme teacher.
Sadhaka	'Accomplished one'. Serious aspirant who practises spiritual disciplines.
Sadhana	'Effective, leading straight to the goal.' The practice of spiritual disciplines.
Sadhu	An ascetic, usually a wandering mendicant.
Saguna	With qualities, attributes.
Sakta	A follower of the cult of the goddess.
Sakti	The principle of female power. Divine energy.
Sama	Musical devotional sessions held by the sufis.
Samadhi	A state of union, undifferentiated bliss, with the Divine.
Sampradaya	'Tradition'. It refers both to an oral tradition of teaching passed on by a guru, and also to a historical lineage, a living theology within Hinduism.
Samsara	The ceaseless round of birth and death. Ignorance.
Samskara	'Impression'. The imprint or traces left in the mind after an experience, whether in this or previous lives.
Sanatana Dharma	The eternal way; perennial wisdom.

Sangam	The confluence of two rivers, which is revered as a sacred place.
Sannyasin	One who lives the ascetic life.
Santi	Peace.
Sat	The true, the real.
Satguru	One who has realized the ultimate truth and is able to lead others along the spiritual path.
Sati	The ancient Earth Mother, wife of Shiva. When she died, Shiva was so stricken with grief that he wandered over the world with her over his shoulder. Vishnu, out of compassion for Shiva, lightened his load by cutting pieces off Sati's body – a variation on the world-wide myth of the dismemberment of the goddess. Sati also refers to truth.
Sati Mata	A woman who follows her husband onto the funeral pyre when he dies. Burnt alive, she is thereafter regarded as a saint.
Sattva	Goodness, virtue.
Seva	Service.
Shakti	'Power, energy'. The active, feminine power of Shiva or other deities. The Goddess in her various forms. The divine energy experienced in meditation or with a guru is called shakti (lower case.)
Shariat	The Law of God. The canonised body of Islamic law.
Shastra	A Hindu text or treatise considered to be of divine origin.
Shikara	The tower of the temple that is built over the sanctum.
Siddha	One who has attained extraordinary powers through ascetic discipline.
Siddhanta	'Final attainments, or conclusions'. The ultimate understanding arrived at

in a given field. Also refers specifically to Shaiva Siddhanta, the major school of Shaivism in the south.

Siddhi   Occult power or attainment.

Shishya   'To be taught'. A pupil or disciple of a guru.

Smrti   What has been committed to memory – that class of scriptures which has been recorded by man, as distinct to direct divine revelation.

Sruti   A class of scriptures which are considered to originate directly from God.

Sudra   A member of the fourth and lowest caste.

Sutra   'Thread'; a scripture in the form of a collection of aphorisms.

Swami   'He who knows himself'. Title for a Hindu holy man.

Tapas   'Heat' generated by spiritual practices.

Tat   That; a pointer to the Divine Being.

Tirtha   Crossing place; place of pilgrimage.

Tirthankara   'One who has crossed over'. Jain term for their gurus, of whom there are twenty-four.

Tirukural   'Holy couplets'. The ethical and moral scripture written by Saint Tiruvalluvar on dried palm leaves over 2,000 years ago near Madras.

Tiruvalluvar   Tamil weaver and householder saint who wrote the major Shaivite ethical scripture, Tirukural.

Tulsi   Ocymum sanctum (basil). Wood sacred to Vishnu. Vaishnavites wear malas made of tulsi wood.

Upadesa   Teaching, religious instruction.

Urs   'Marriage with God'. The festival commemorating the death of a sufi saint.

Vac	Goddess of speech; sacred word.
Vaisya	The third caste; the merchant class.
Vanaprastha	Forest dweller; the third stage in a brahmin's life.
Vasanas	The unconscious impressions in the mind.
Vedanta	'The end of the Vedas'. The philosophical systems based on the Upanishads.
Vedas	The four Vedas are the earliest literature of the Indo-European peoples, dating to c. 1200–1000 bc.
Vibhuti	Sacred ash.
Vicara	Inquiry, investigation.
Vidya	Knowledge.
Viveka	Discriminative power, intelligence.
Yajna	Vedic sacrifice.
Yantra	'Vessel, container'. A mystic diagram composed of geometric and alphabetic figures – often etched in gold, silver or copper – which focusses spiritual energies. A yantra is generally installed with each temple deity.
Yatra	A pilgrimage to a holy place or person.
Yoga	'To yoke, or unite'. The process of uniting individual consciousness with the Divine, and the method to achieve this goal.
Yogi	One who practises yoga, especially kundalini or raja yoga.
Yuga	'Period, age'. One of four ages which chart the duration of the world according to Hindu thought. They are Sat, Treta, Dvapara, and Kali Yuga. In the first period dharma reigns supreme, but as time progresses virtue diminishes and wickedness increases. At the end of the Kali Yuga, the darkest period – which we are in now – the cycle begins with a new Sat Yuga.

BIBLIOGRAPHY

Fiction
The two books below vividly evoke 'Old India'.
Mehta, Gita, *A River Sutra*. Viking Penguin, London 1993.
Narayan, R. K., *The Guide*. Penguin, London 1988.

Travel
Grewal, Rowena, *Sacred Virgin*. Penguin, New Delhi 1994.
Lewis, Norman, *The Goddess in the Stone*. Macmillan, London 1992.
Moorhouse, Geoffrey. *Om*. Hodder and Stoughton, London 1993.

The Popular Tradition
Bhardwaj, S. M., *Hindu Places of Pilgrimage in India*. University of California, Berkelely 1973.
Fuller, C. J., *The Camphor Flame*. Penguin, New Delhi 1992.
Meyer, Adrian, *Caste and Kinship in Central India*. University of California Press 1960.
L. Nathan and C. Seely, trans., *Grace and Mercy in Her Wild Hair: Selected Poems to the Mother Goddess*. Gt. Eastern, Boulder 1992.
Singh, Rana, P. B., ed., *The Spirit and Power of Place: Human Environment and Sacrality*. The National Geographic Society of India, Banaras 1994.
Swami Nikhilananda, trans., *Gospel of Sri Ramakrishna*. Ramakrishna Vivekenananda Centre, New York 1942.

Classical Sources
Deshpande, P. Y., *The Authentic Yoga: Patanjali's Yoga Sutras*. Rider, London 1978.
Easwaran, Eknath, *The Upanishads*. Arkana, London 1988.
Narayan, R. K., *The Ramayana*. Penguin, London 1993.

Pannikar Raimundo, *The Vedic Experience: An Anthology of the Vedas for Modern Man*. Motilal Banarsidas, Delhi 1994.

Rhadakrishnan, S., *The Bhagavad Gita*. Allen & Unwin, London 1967.

The Classical Tradition

Alper, Harvey, P., ed., *Mantra*. University of New York Press, 1989.

Blurton, T. Richard, *Hindu Art*. British Museum Press, London 1992.

Dimock, Edward, C. Jr., *The Place of the Hidden Moon*. University of Chicago Press 1966.

Eck, Diana, *Banaras: City of Light*. Penguin, New Delhi 1993.

Eck, Diana, *Darsan: Seeing the Divine Image in India*. Anima Books, Chambersburg, Pa. 1985.

Eliade, Mircea, *Cosmos and History: The Myth of the Eternal Return*. Harper and Row, New York 1959.

Eliade, Mircea, *The Sacred and the Profane*. Harcourt Brace, New York 1959.

Fuller, C. J., *Servants of the Goddess*. Oxford University Press, 1991.

Gonda, J., *Visnuism and Shaivism: A Comparison*. University of London, 1980.

Hawley, John Stratton and Wulff, Donna Maria, eds., *The Divine Consort: Radha and the Goddesses of India*. Berkeley Religious Studies, Berkeley, Ca. 1982.

Kamalabaskaran, Iswari, *The Light of Arunachaleswarar: The Temple in Tiruvannamalai*. Affiliated East West Press, New Delhi 1994.

Kinsley, David, *Hindu Goddesses*, Motilal Banarsidas, Delhi 1987.

Kramrisch, Stella, *The Presence of Shiva*. Princeton University, N.J. 1981, repr. 1992.

Kramrisch, Stella, *The Hindu Temple*, 2 vols. University of Calcutta 1946, repr. 1994.

Lannoy, Richard, *The Speaking Tree*. Oxford University Press 1974.

Mukerjee, Ajit, *Kali: The Feminine Force*. Thames and Hudson, London 1988, repr. 1991.

Padoux, Andre, *Vac: The Concept of the Word in Selected Hindu Tantras*. Sri Satguru Publications, New Delhi and State University of New York Press 1990.

Punja, Shobita, *Divine Ecstasy: The Story of Khajuraho*. Viking Penguin, Delhi 1992.

Rawson, Philip, *The Art of Tantra*. Thames and Hudson, London 1973, repr. 1993.

Rosen, S. ed., *Vaisnavism*. Folk, New York 1992.

Singh, Rana, P. B. ed., *Banaras: Cosmic Order, Sacred City, Hindu Traditions*. Tara Book Agency, Banaras 1993.

The Inner Tradition

Amritaswarupananda, *Mata Amritanandamayi: A Biography*. Mata Amritanandamayi Mission Press, Vellickavu, Kerala 1988.

Aurobindo, Sri, *Letters on Yoga*, Sri Aurobindo Ashram, Pondichery 1971.

Aurobindo, Sri, *The Synthesis of Yoga*. Sri Aurobindo Library, Madras 1948.

Balsekar, Ramesh S., *The Final Truth*. Advaita, Los Angeles 1989.

Bly, Robert, *44 Ecstatic Poems of Kabir*. Beacon Press, Boston 1977.

Cornelssen, Lucy, *Hunting The I*. Sri Ramanasram 1979, repr. 1991.

Eliade, Mircea, *Yoga, Immortality and Freedom*. Bollingen Series, Princeton University Press, N. J. 1973.

Evola, Julius, *The Yoga of Power: Tantra, Shakti and The Secret Way*. Inner Traditions Int., Rochester, Vermont 1992.

Frydman, Maurice, *I Am That: The Teachings of Nisargadatta Maharaj*. Chetana, Bombay 1973.

Ghurye, G. S., *Indian Sadhus*. Popular Prakashan, Bombay, repr. 1995.

Godman, David, *Be As You Are: The Life and Teaching of Sri Ramana Maharshi*. Penguin, London 1992.

Godman, David, *Living By the Words of Bhagavan: A Biography of Annamalai Swami*. Sri Annamalai Swami Ashram Trust, Tiruvannamalai 1994.

Godman, David, *Papaji: Interviews*. Avadhuta Foundation, Lucknow 1993.

Gross, R. Lewis, *The Sadhus of India*. Rawat Publications, New Delhi 1992.

Hartzuiker, Dolf, *Sadhus: Holy Men Of India*. Thames and Hudson, London 1993.

Hess, L. and Singh, S., trans., *The Bijak of Kabir*. Motilal Banarsidas, Delhi 1983.

Hixon, Les, *Great Swan: Meetings with Ramakrishna*. Shambala, Boston 1992.

Hughes, John, *Self Realization in Kashmir Shaivism: The Oral Teachings of Swami Lakshmanjoo*. Suny Press, Ithaca, N. Y. 1995.

Isherwood, Christopher, *Ramakrishna and His Disciples*. Advaita Ashrama, Calcutta 1964, repr. 1994.

Kasturi, N., *Loving God: Teachings of Sai Baba*. Sathya Sai Books, Prasanthi Nilayam (AP) 1965.

Rigopoulos, Antonio, *The Life and Teaching of Sai Baba of Shirdi*. Sri
Satguru Publications, Delhi 1993.

Roof, Jonathon, *Pathways to God: The Life and Teachings of Sathya Sai Baba*.
Leela Press, Faber, Va. 1991.

Westcott, G. H., *Kabir and the Kabir Panth*. Munshiram Manoharlal,
repr. 1986.

Buddhist India

Dalai Lama, H. H., *The World of Tibetan Buddhism: An Overview of its
Philosophy and Practice*. Wisdom Publications 1995.

Davids, T. W. Rhys, *Buddhist India*. Motilal Banarsidas, Delhi.

Dutt, Nalinaksha, *Buddhist Sects in India*, Motilal Banarsidas, Delhi.

Hart, W., *The Art of Living: Vipassana Meditation*. Vipassana Institute,
Igatpuri, Maharashtra.

Prasad, Sital, *A Comparative Study of Buddhism and Jainism*. Indian Books
Centre, Delhi 1995.

Christian India

Abrahams, E. W., *A Comparative Survey of Hindu, Christian, and Jewish
Mysticism*. Indian Books Centre 1995.

D'Souza, Herman, Rt. Rev., *In The Steps of Saint Thomas*. Diocesan Press,
Madras 1983.

Vandana Mataji, ed., *Christian Ashrams: A Movement with a Future?* ISPCK,
Delhi 1993.

Viyagappa, Ignatius, ed., *In Spirit and in Truth: Essays of Christians in
Contemporary India*. Aikiya Alayam, Madras 1985.

Sufi India

Faruqi, Azad, *Sufism and Bhakti*. Abhinav Publications, New Delhi 1984.

Rizvi, S. A., *A History of Sufism in India*, 2 vols. Munshiram Manoharlal
New Delhi 1983.

Schimmel, Anne-Marie, *Islam in the Indian Subcontinent*. E. J. Brill,
Leiden 1980.

MEDITATIVE JOURNEYS TO SACRED INDIA
WITH ROGER HOUSDEN

If you would like to join a small party led by Roger Housden twice yearly to one of the sacred places of India, please phone 01225 428557 for details, or write to:

Open Gate Journeys
P.O. Box 1892
Bath BA1 9YY

INDEX